R U N D E L
L I B R A R Y
F O U N D A T I O N

IN HONOR
OF
Amy Colucci

Bloom's Major Literary Characters

King Arthur

George Babbitt

Elizabeth Bennet

Leopold Bloom

Sir John Falstaff

Jay Gatsby

Hamlet

Raskolnikov and Svidrigailov

Bloom's Major Literary Characters

Elizabeth Bennet

Edited and with an introduction by
Harold Bloom
Sterling Professor of the Humanities
Yale University

CHELSEA HOUSE
P U B L I S H E R S
A Haights Cross Communications Company
Philadelphia

1-3419

©2004 by Chelsea House Publishers, a subsidiary of
Haights Cross Communications.

A Haights Cross Communications ✦ Company

Introduction © 2004 by Harold Bloom.

Printed and bound in the United States of America.

10 9 8 7 6 5 4 3 2 1

Library of Congress Cataloging-in-Publication Data
applied for.

ISBN 0-7910-7672-5

Contributing editor: Pamela Loos

Cover design by Keith Trego

Cover: ©Archivo Iconografico, S.A./CORBIS

Layout by EJB Publishing Services

Chelsea House Publishers
1974 Sproul Road, Suite 400
Broomall, PA 19008-0914

www.chelseahouse.com

Contents

HAROLD BLOOM

The Analysis of Character

"Character," according to our dictionaries, still has as a primary meaning a graphic symbol, such as a letter of the alphabet. This meaning reflects the word's apparent origin in the ancient Greek character, a sharp stylus. *Charactēr* also meant the mark of the stylus' incisions. Recent fashions in literary criticism have reduced "character" in literature to a matter of marks upon a page. But our word "character" also has a very different meaning, matching that of the ancient Greek *ēthos*, "habitual way of life." Shall we say then that literary character is an imitation of human character, or is it just a grouping of marks? The issue is between a critic like Dr. Samuel Johnson, for whom words were as much like people as like things, and a critic like the late Roland Barthes, who told us that "the fact can only exist linguistically, as a term of discourse." Who is closer to our experience of reading literature, Johnson or Barthes? What difference does it make, if we side with one critic rather than the other?

Barthes is famous, like Foucault and other recent French theorists, for having added to Nietzsche's proclamation of the death of God a subsidiary demise, that of the literary author. If there are no authors, then there are no fictional personages, presumably because literature does not refer to a world outside language. Words indeed necessarily refer to other words in the first place, but the impact of words ultimately is drawn from a universe of fact. Stories, poems, and plays are recognizable as such because they are human utterances within traditions of utterances, and traditions, by achieving authority, become a kind of fact, or at least the sense of a fact. Our sense that literary characters, within the context of a fictive cosmos, indeed are fictional personages is also a kind of fact. The meaning and value of every character in a successful work of literary representation depend upon our ideas of persons in the factual reality of our lives.

Literary character is always an invention, and inventions generally are indebted to prior inventions. Shakespeare is the inventor of literary character as we know it; he reformed the universal human expectations for the verbal imitation of personality, and the reformation appears now to be permanent and uncannily inevitable. Remarkable as the Bible and Homer are at representing personages, their characters are relatively unchanging. They age within their stories, but their habitual modes of being do not develop. Jacob and Achilles unfold before us, but without metamorphoses. Lear and Macbeth, Hamlet and Othello severely modify themselves not only by their actions, but by their utterances, and most of all through *overhearing themselves*, whether they speak to themselves or to others. Pondering what they themselves have said, they will to change, and actually do change, sometimes extravagantly yet always persuasively. Or else they suffer change, without willing it, but in reaction not so much to their language as to their relation to that language.

I do not think it useful to say that Shakespeare successfully imitated elements in our characters. Rather, it could be argued that he compelled aspects of character to appear that previously were concealed, or not available to representation. This is not to say that Shakespeare is God, but to remind us that language is not God either. The mimesis of character in Shakespeare's dramas now seems to us normative, and indeed became the accepted mode almost immediately, as Ben Jonson shrewdly and somewhat grudgingly implied. And yet, Shakespearean representation has surprisingly little in common with the imitation of reality in Jonson or in Christopher Marlowe. The origins of Shakespeare's originality in the portrayal of men and women are to be found in the *Canterbury Tales* of Geoffrey Chaucer, insofar as they can be located anywhere before Shakespeare himself, Chaucer's savage and superb Pardoner overhears his own tale-telling, as well as his mocking rehearsal of his own spiel, and through this overhearing he is emboldened to forget himself, and enthusiastically urges all his fellow-pilgrims to come forward to be fleeced by him. His self-awareness, and apocalyptically rancid sense of spiritual fall, are preludes to the even grander abysses of the perverted will in Iago and in Edmund. What might be called the character trait of a negative charisma may be Chaucer's invention, but came to its perfection in Shakespearean mimesis.

The analysis of character is as much Shakespeare's invention as the representation of character is, since Iago and Edmund are adepts at analyzing both themselves and their victims. Hamlet, whose overwhelming charisma has many negative components, is certainly the most comprehensive of all literary characters, and so necessarily prophesies the labyrinthine complexities of the will in Iago and Edmund. Charisma, according to Max Weber, its first codifier, is primarily a natural endowment, and implies a primordial and idiosyncratic power over nature, and so finally over death. Hamlet's uncanniness is at its most suggestive in the scene of his long dying, where the audience, through the mediation of Horatio, itself is compelled to meditate upon suicide, if only because outliving the prince of Denmark scarcely seems an option.

Shakespearean representation has usurped not only our sense of literary character, but our sense of ourselves as characters, with Hamlet playing the part of the largest of these usurpations. Insofar as we have an idea of human disinterestedness, we tend to derive it from the Hamlet of Act V, whose quietism has about it a ghostly authority. Oscar Wilde, in his profound and profoundly witty dialogue, "The Decay of Lying," expressed a permanent insight when he insisted that art shaped every era, far more than any age formed art. Life imitates art, we imitate Shakespeare, because without Shakespeare we would perish for lack of images. Wilde's grandest audacity demystifies Shakespearean mimesis with a Shakespearean vivaciousness: "This unfortunate aphorism about art holding the mirror up to Nature is deliberately said by Hamlet in order to convince the bystanders of his absolute insanity in all art-matters." Of *Hamlet*'s influence upon the ages Wilde remarked that: "The world has grown sad because a puppet was once melancholy." "Puppet" is Wilde's own deconstruction, a brilliant reminder that Shakespeare's artistry of illusion has so mastered reality as to have changed reality, evidently forever.

The analysis of character, as a critical pursuit, seems to me as much a Shakespearean invention as literary character was, since much of what we know about how to analyze character necessarily follows Shakespearean procedures. His hero-villains, from Richard III through Iago, Edmund, and Macbeth, are shrewd and endless questers into their own self-motivations. If we could bear to see Hamlet, in his unwearied negations, as another hero-villain, then we would judge him the supreme analyst of the darker recalcitrances in the selfhood. Freud followed the pre-Socratic Empedocles, in arguing that character is fate, a frightening doctrine that maintains the fear that there are no accidents, that overdetermination rules us all of our lives. Hamlet assumes the same, yet adds to this argument the terrible passivity he manifests in Act V. Throughout Shakespeare's tragedies, the most interesting personages seem doom-eager, reminding us again that a Shakespearean reading of Freud would be more illuminating than a Freudian exegesis of Shakespeare. We learn more when we discover Hamlet in the Freudian Death Drive, than when we read *Beyond the Pleasure Principle* into *Hamlet*.

In Shakespearean comedy, character achieves its true literary apotheosis, which is the representation of the inner freedom that can be created by great wit alone. Rosalind and Falstaff, perhaps alone among Shakespeare's personages, match Hamlet in wit, though hardly in the metaphysics of consciousness. Whether in the comic or the modern mode, Shakespeare has set the standard of measurement in the balance between character and passion.

In Shakespeare the self is more dramatized than theatricalized, which is why a Shakespearean reading of Freud works out so well. Character-formation after the passing of the Oedipal stage takes the place of fetishistic fragmentings of the self. Critics who now call literary character into question, and who proclaim also the death of the author, invariably also regard all notions, literary and human, of a stable character as being mere reductions of deeper pre-Oedipal desires. It becomes clear that the fortunes of literary character rise and fall with the prestige of normative conceptions of the ego. Shakespeare's Iago, who wars against being, may be the first deconstructionist of the self, with his proclamation of "I am not what I am." This constitutes the necessary prologue to any view that would regard a fixed ego as a virtual abnormality. But deconstructions of the self are no more modern than Modernism is. Like literary modernism, the decentered ego came out of the Hellenistic culture of ancient Alexandria. The Gnostic heretics believed that the psyche, like the body, was a fallen entity, mechanically fashioned by the Demiurge or false creator. They held however that each of us possessed also a spark or pneuma, which was a fragment of the original Abyss or true, alien God. The soul or psyche within every one of us was thus at war with the self or pneuma, and only that sparklike self could be saved.

Shakespeare, following after Chaucer in this respect, was the first and remains still the greatest master of representing character both as a stable soul and a wavering self. There is a substance that endures in Shakespeare's figures, and there is also a quicksilver rendition of the unsettling sparks. Racine and Tolstoy, Balzac and Dickens, follow in Shakespeare's wake by giving us some sense of pre-Oedipal sparks or drives, and considerably more sense of post-Oedipal character and personality, stabilizations or sublimations of the fetish-seeking drives. Critics like Leo Bersani and René Girard argue eloquently against our taking this mimesis as the only proper work of literature. I would suggest that strong fictions of the self, from the

Bible through Samuel Beckett, necessarily participate in both modes, the sublimation of desire, and the persistence of a primordial desire. The mystery of Hamlet or of Lear is intimately invested in the tangled mixture of the two modes of representation.

Psychic mobility is proposed by Bersani as the ideal to which deconstructions of the literary self may yet guide us. The ideal has its pathos, but the realities of literary representation seem to me very different, perhaps destructively so. When a novelist like D. H. Lawrence sought to reduce his characters to Eros and the Death Drive, he still had to persuade us of his authority at mimesis by lavishing upon the figures of *The Rainbow* and *Women in Love* all of the vivid stigmata of normative personality. Birkin and Ursula may represent antithetical and uncanny drives, but they develop and change as characters pondering their own pronouncements and reactions to self and others. The cost of a non-Shakespearean representation is enormous. Pynchon, in *The Crying of Lot 49* and *Gravity's Rainbow*, evades the burden of the normative by resorting to something like Christopher Marlowe's art of caricature in *The Jew of Malta*. Marlowe's Barabas is a marvelous rhetorician, yet he is a cartoon alongside the troublingly equivocal Shylock. Pynchon's personages are deliberate cartoons also, as flat as comic strips. Marlowe's achievement, and Pynchon's, are beyond dispute, yet they are like the prelude and the postlude to Shakespearean reality. They do not wish to engage with our hunger for the empirical world and so they enter the problematic cosmos of literary fantasy.

No writer, not even Shakespeare or Proust, alters the available stock that we agree to call reality, but Shakespeare, more than any other, does show us how much of reality we could encounter if only we retained adequate desire. The strong literary representation of character is already an analysis of character, and is part of the healing work of a literary culture, which implicitly seeks to cure violence through a normative mimesis of ego, *as if it were stable*, whether in actuality it is or is not. I do not believe that this is a social quest taken on by literary culture, but rather that we confront here the aesthetic essence of what makes a culture *literary*, rather than metaphysical or ethical or religious. A culture becomes literary when its conceptual modes have failed it, which means when religion, philosophy, and science have begun to lose their authority. If they cannot heal violence, then literature attempts to do so, which may be only a turning inside out of the critical arguments of Girard and Bersani.

I conclude by offering a particular instance or special case as a paradigm for the healing enterprise that is at once the representation and the analysis of literary character. Let us call it the aesthetics of being outraged, or rather of successfully representing the state of being outraged. W. C. Fields was one modern master of such representation, and Nathanael West was another, as was Faulkner before him. Here also the greatest master remains Shakespeare, whose Macbeth, himself a bloody outrage, yet retains our imaginative sympathy precisely because he grows increasingly outraged as he experiences the equivocation of the fiend that lies like truth. The double-natured promises and the prophecies of the weird sisters finally induce in Macbeth an apocalyptic version of the stage actor's anxiety at missing cues, the horror of a phantasmagoric stage fright of missing one's time, of always reacting too late. Macbeth, a veritable monster of solipsistic inwardness but no intellectual, counters his dilemma by fresh murders, that prolong him in time yet provoke him only to a perpetually freshened sense of being outraged, as all his expectations become still worse confounded. We are moved by Macbeth, however estrangedly, because his terrible inwardness is a paradigm for our own solipsism, but also because none of us can resist a strong and successful representation of the human in a state of being outraged.

The ultimate outrage is the necessity of dying, an outrage concealed in a multitude of masks, including the tyrannical ambitions of Macbeth. I suspect that our outrage at being outraged is the most difficult of all our affects for us to represent to ourselves, which is why we are so inclined to imaginative sympathy for a character who strongly conveys that affect to us. The Shrike of West's *Miss Lonelyhearts* or Faulkner's Joe Christmas of *Light in August* are crucial modern instances, but such figures can be located in many other works, since the ability to represent this extreme emotion is one of the tests that strong writers are driven to set for themselves.

However a reader seeks to reduce literary character to a question of marks on a page, she will come at last to the impasse constituted by the thought of death, her death, and before that to all the stations of being outraged that memorialize her own drive towards death. In reading, she quests for evidences that are strong representations, whether of her desire or her despair. Such questings constitute the necessary basis for the analysis of literary character, an enterprise that always will survive every vagary of critical fashion.

Editor's Note

My Introduction traces Elizabeth Bennet's descent from Samuel Richardson's Clarissa Harlowe, foundress of the Protestant Will in its drive for autonomy and in the romantic exchanges of mutual esteem.

Marvin Mudrick inaugurates the study of Austenian irony as a defensive invention, while Andrew H. Wright sketches Elizabeth Bennet as a transmutation of irony into freedom.

C.S. Lewis, a skilled dogmatist, finds in Austen a daughter of Dr. Samuel Johnson, after which Henrietta Ten Harmsel uncovers in Elizabeth a triumph of perceptiveness, and not of mere morality.

Arguing against Mudrick, Howard S. Babb emphasizes mutual vitality as the link between Darcy and Elizabeth, while Stuart M. Tave, in a classic discussion, addresses aspects of reality that inspire the happy resolution between the lovers.

Susan Morgan, lucidly discussing intelligence in Elizabeth Bennet, associates it with the heroine's new freedom at the novel's close, after which Bernard J. Paris offers a rather dark view, asserting that Darcy and Elizabeth will prosper together "as long as each continues to feed the other's pride."

In a Feminist perspective, Susan Fraiman regards the union of Darcy and Elizabeth as "a marriage of two classes," while Donald A. Bloom amiably associates Elizabeth Bennet's wit with the romantic power of heroines in Shakespeare, Dryden, and Congreve.

The final essay in this volume is by Gloria Sybil Gross, who very usefully juxtaposes Dr. Johnson's superb romance, *Rasselas*, with *Pride and Prejudice*.

HAROLD BLOOM

Introduction

The oddest yet by no means inapt analogy to Jane Austen's art of representation is Shakespeare's—oddest, because she is so careful of limits, as classical as Ben Jonson in that regard, and Shakespeare transcends all limits. Austen's humor, her mode of rhetorical irony, is not particularly Shakespearean, and yet her precision and accuracy of representation is. Like Shakespeare, she gives us figures, major and minor, utterly consistent each in her or his own mode of speech and being, and utterly different from one another. Her heroines have firm selves, each molded with an individuality that continues to suggest Austen's reserve of power, her potential for creating an endless diversity. To recur to the metaphor of oddness, the highly deliberate limitation of social scale in Austen seems a paradoxical theater of mind in which so fecund a humanity could be fostered. Irony, the concern of most critics of Austen, seems more than a trope in her work, seems indeed to be the condition of her language, yet hardly accounts for the effect of moral and spiritual power that she so constantly conveys, however implicitly or obliquely.

Ian Watt, in his permanently useful *The Rise of the Novel*, portrays Austen as Fanny Burney's direct heir in the difficult art of combining the rival modes of Samuel Richardson and Henry Fielding. Like Burney, Austen is thus seen as following the Richardson of *Sir Charles Grandison*, in a "minute presentation of daily life," while emulating Fielding in "adopting a more detached attitude to her narrative material, and in evaluating it from a comic and objective point of view." Watt goes further when he points out that Austen tells her stories in a discreet variant of Fielding's manner "as a confessed author," though her ironical juxtapositions are made to appear not those of "an intrusive author but rather of some august and impersonal spirit of social and psychological understanding."

And yet, as Watt knows, Austen truly is the daughter of Richardson, and not of Fielding, just as she is the ancestor of George Eliot and Henry James, rather than of Dickens and Thackeray. Her inwardness is an ironic revision of Richardson's extraordinary conversion of English Protestant sensibility into the figure of Clarissa Harlowe, and her own moral and spiritual concerns fuse in the crucial need of her heroines to sustain their individual integrities, a need so intense that it compels them to fall into those errors about life that are necessary for life (to adopt a Nietzschean formulation). In this too they follow, though in a comic register, the pattern of their tragic precursor, the magnificent but sublimely flawed Clarissa Harlowe.

Richardson's *Clarissa*, perhaps still the longest novel in the language, seems to me also still the greatest, despite the achievements of Austen, Dickens, George Eliot, Henry James, and Joyce. Austen's Elizabeth Bennet and Emma Woodhouse, Eliot's Dorothea Brooke and Gwendolen Harleth, James's Isabel Archer and Milly Theale—though all these are Clarissa Harlowe's direct descendants, they are not proportioned to her more sublime scale. David Copperfield and Leopold Bloom have her completeness; indeed Joyce's Bloom may be the most complete representation of a human being in all of literature. But they belong to the secular age; Clarissa Harlowe is poised upon the threshold that leads from the Protestant religion to a purely secular sainthood.

C. S. Lewis, who read Milton as though that fiercest of Protestant temperaments had been an orthodox Anglican, also seems to have read Jane Austen by listening for her echoings of the New Testament. Quite explicitly, Lewis named Austen as the daughter of Dr. Samuel Johnson, greatest of literary critics, and rigorous Christian moralist:

> I feel ... sure that she is the daughter of Dr. Johnson: she inherits
> his commonsense, his morality, even much of his style.

The Johnson of *Rasselas* and of *The Rambler*, surely the essential Johnson, is something of a classical ironist, but we do not read Johnson for his ironies, or for his dramatic representations of fictive selves. Rather, we read him as we read Koheleth; he writes wisdom literature. That Jane Austen is a wise writer is indisputable, but we do not read *Pride and Prejudice* as though it were Ecclesiastes. Doubtless, Austen's religious ideas were as profound as Samuel Richardson's were shallow, but *Emma* and *Clarissa* are Protestant novels without being in any way religious. What is most original about the representation of Clarissa Harlowe is the magnificent intensity of her slowly described dying, which goes on for about the last third of Richardson's vast novel, in a Puritan ritual that celebrates the preternatural strength of her will. For that is Richardson's sublime concern: the self-reliant apotheosis of the Protestant will. What is tragedy in *Clarissa* becomes serious or moral comedy in *Pride and Prejudice* and *Emma*, and something just the other side of comedy in *Mansfield Park* and *Persuasion*.

II

Rereading *Pride and Prejudice* gives one a sense of Proustian ballet beautifully working itself through in the novel's formal centerpiece, the deferred but progressive mutual enlightenment of Elizabeth and Darcy in regard to the other's true nature. "Proper pride" is what they learn to recognize in one another; propriety scarcely needs definition in that phrase, but precisely what is the pride that allows amiability to flourish? Whatever it is in Darcy, to what extent is it an art of the will in Elizabeth Bennet? Consider the superb scene of Darcy's first and failed marriage proposal:

> While settling this point, she was suddenly roused by the sound of the doorbell, and her spirits were a little fluttered by the idea of its being Colonel Fitzwilliam himself, who had once before called late in the evening, and might now come to inquire particularly after her. But this idea was soon banished, and her spirits were very differently affected, when, to her utter amazement, she saw Mr. Darcy walk into the room. In an hurried manner he immediately began an inquiry after her health, imputing his visit to a wish of hearing that she were better. She answered him with cold civility. He sat down for a few moments, and then getting up, walked about the room. Elizabeth was surprised, but said not a word. After a silence of several minutes, he came towards her in an agitated manner, and thus began:
>
> "In vain have I struggled. It will not do. My feelings will not be repressed. You must allow me to tell you how ardently I admire and love you."
>
> Elizabeth's astonishment was beyond expression. She stared, coloured, doubted, and was silent. This he considered sufficient

encouragement; and the avowal of all that he felt, and had long felt for her, immediately followed. He spoke well; but there were feelings besides those of the heart to be detailed, and he was not more eloquent on the subject of tenderness than of pride. His sense of her inferiority—of its being a degradation—of the family obstacles which judgment had always opposed to inclination, were dwelt on with a warmth which seemed due to the consequence he was wounding, but was very unlikely to recommend his suit.

In spite of her deeply-rooted dislike, she could not be insensible to the compliment of such a man's affection, and though her intentions did not vary for an instant, she was at first sorry for the pain he was to receive; till, roused to resentment by his subsequent language, she lost all compassion in anger. She tried, however, to compose herself to answer him with patience, when he should have done. He concluded with representing to her the strength of that attachment which, in spite of all his endeavours, he had found impossible to conquer; and with expressing his hope that it would now be rewarded by her acceptance of his hand. As he said this, she could easily see that he had no doubt of a favourable answer. He *spoke* of apprehension and anxiety, but his countenance expressed real security. Such a circumstance could only exasperate farther, and, when he ceased, the colour rose into her cheeks, and she said:

"In such cases as this, it is, I believe, the established mode to express a sense of obligation for the sentiments avowed, however unequally they may be returned. It is natural that obligation should be felt, and if I could *feel* gratitude, I would now thank you. But I cannot—I have never desired your good opinion, and you have certainly bestowed it most unwillingly. I am sorry to have occasioned pain to anyone. It has been most unconsciously done, however, and I hope will be of short duration. The feelings which, you tell me, have long prevented the acknowledgment of your regard, can have little difficulty in overcoming it after this explanation."

Mr. Darcy, who was leaning against the mantelpiece with his eyes fixed on her face, seemed to catch her words with no less resentment than surprise. His complexion became pale with anger, and the disturbance of his mind was visible in every feature. He was struggling for the appearance of composure, and would not open his lips till he believed himself to have attained it.

The pause was to Elizabeth's feelings dreadful. At length, in a voice of forced calmness, he said:

"And this is all the reply which I am to have the honour of expecting! I might, perhaps, wish to be informed why, with so little *endeavour* at civility, I am thus rejected. But it is of small importance."

Stuart M. Tave believes that both Darcy and Elizabeth become so changed by one another that their "happiness is deserved by a process of mortification begun early and ended late," mortification here being the wounding of pride. Tave's learning and insight are impressive, but I favor the judgment that Elizabeth and Darcy scarcely change, and learn rather that they complement each other's not wholly illegitimate pride. They come to see that their wills are naturally allied, since they have no differences upon the will. The will to what? Their will, Austen's, is neither the will to live nor the will to power. They wish to be esteemed precisely where they estimate value to be high, and neither can afford to make a fundamental error, which is both the anxiety and the comedy of the first proposal scene. Why after all does Darcy allow himself to be eloquent on the subject of his pride, to the extraordinary extent of conveying "with a warmth" what Austen grimly names as "his sense of her inferiority"?

As readers, we have learned already that Elizabeth is inferior to no one, whoever he is. Indeed, I sense as the novel closes (though nearly all Austen critics, and doubtless Austen herself, would disagree with me) that Darcy is her inferior, amiable and properly prideful as he is. I do not mean by this that Elizabeth is a clearer representation of Austenian values than Darcy ever could be; that is made finely obvious by Austen, and her critics have developed her ironic apprehension, which is that Elizabeth incarnates the standard of measurement in her cosmos. There is also a transcendent strength to Elizabeth's will that raises her above that cosmos, in a mode that returns us to Clarissa Harlowe's transcendence of her society, of Lovelace, and even of everything in herself that is not the will to a self-esteem that has also made an accurate estimate of every other will to pride it ever has encountered.

I am suggesting that Ralph Waldo Emerson (who to me is sacred) was mistaken when he rejected Austen as a "sterile" upholder of social conformities and social ironies, as an author who could not celebrate the soul's freedom from societal conventions. Austen's ultimate irony is that Elizabeth Bennet is inwardly so free that convention performs for her the ideal function it cannot perform for us: it liberates her will without tending to stifle her high individuality. But we ought to be wary of even the most distinguished of Austen's moral celebrants, Lionel Trilling, who in effect defended her against Emerson by seeing *Pride and Prejudice* as a triumph "of morality as style." If Emerson wanted to see a touch more Margaret Fuller in Elizabeth Bennet (sublimely ghastly notion!), Trilling wanted to forget the Emersonian law of Compensation, which is that nothing is got for nothing:

> The relation of Elizabeth Bennet to Darcy is real, is intense, but it expresses itself as a conflict and reconciliation of styles: a formal rhetoric, traditional and rigorous, must find a way to accomodate a female vivacity, which in turn must recognize the principled demands of the strict male syntax. The high moral import of the novel lies in the fact that the union of styles is accomplished without injury to either lover.

Yes and no, I would say. Yes, because the wills of both lovers work by similar dialectics, but also no, because Elizabeth's will is more intense and purer, and inevitably must be dimmed by her dwindling into a wife, even though Darcy may well be the best man that society could offer to her. Her pride has playfulness in it, a touch even of the Quixotic. Uncannily, she is both her father's daughter and Samuel Richardson's daughter as well. Her wit is Mr. Bennet's, refined and elaborated, but her will, and her pride in her will, returns us to Clarissa's Puritan passion to maintain the power of the self to confer esteem, and to accept esteem only in response to its bestowal.

MARVIN MUDRICK

Irony As Discrimination:
Pride and Prejudice

In *Pride and Prejudice,* for the first time, Jane Austen allows her heroine to share her own characteristic response to the world. Elizabeth Bennet tells Darcy:

> "... Follies and nonsense, whims and inconsistencies *do* divert me,
> I own, and I laugh at them whenever I can...." (pp 57)

The response is not only characteristic of Elizabeth and her author, but consciously and articulately aimed at by both of them. Both choose diversion; and both, moreover, look for their diversion in the people about them. Elizabeth, despite her youth and the limitations of a rural society, is— like the author of "Lesley Castle" and "The Three Sisters"—a busy "studier of character," as Bingley leads her to affirm:

> "You begin to comprehend me, do you?" cried he, turning towards her.
> "Oh! yes—I understand you perfectly."
> "I wish I might take this for a compliment; but to be so easily seen through I am afraid is pitiful."
> "That is as it happens. It does not necessarily follow that a

From *Jane Austen: Irony as Defense and Discovery.* © 1952 by Princeton University Press.

deep, intricate character is more or less estimable than such a one as yours."

"Lizzy," cried her mother, "remember where you are, and do not run on in the wild manner that you are suffered to do at home."

"I did not know before," continued Bingley immediately, "that you were a studier of character. It must be an amazing study."

"Yes; but intricate characters are the most amusing. They have at least that advantage." (pp 42)

"Character" gains a general overtone: with Elizabeth's qualifying adjective, it becomes not only the summation of a single personality, but the summation of a type, the fixing of the individual into a category. So Elizabeth sets herself up as an ironic spectator, able and prepared to judge and classify, already making the first large division of the world into two sorts of people: the simple ones, those who give themselves away out of shallowness (as Bingley fears) or perhaps openness (as Elizabeth implies) or an excess of affectation (as Mr. Collins will demonstrate); and the intricate ones, those who cannot be judged and classified so easily, who are "the most amusing" to the ironic spectator because they offer the most formidable challenge to his powers of detection and analysis. Into one of these preliminary categories, Elizabeth fits everybody she observes.

Elizabeth shares her author's characteristic response of comic irony, defining incongruities without drawing them into a moral context; and, still more specifically, Elizabeth's vision of the world as divided between the simple and the intricate is, in *Pride and Prejudice* at any rate, Jane Austen's vision also. This identification between the author and her heroine establishes, in fact, the whole ground pattern of judgment in the novel. The first decision we must make about anyone, so Elizabeth suggests and the author confirms by her shaping commentary, is not moral but psychological, not whether he is good or bad, but whether he is simple or intricate: whether he may be disposed of as fixed and predictable or must be recognized as variable, perhaps torn between contradictory motives, intellectually or emotionally complex, unsusceptible to a quick judgment.

Once having placed the individual in his category, we must proceed to discriminate him from the others there; and, in the category of simplicity at least, Elizabeth judges as accurately as her author. Jane Austen allows the "simple" characters to have no surprises for Elizabeth, and, consequently, none for us. They perform, they amuse; but we never doubt that we know what they are, and why they act as they do.

We know Mrs. Bennet, for example, at once, in her first conversation with her husband, as she describes the newcomer at Netherfield Park:

"... A single man of large fortune; four or five thousand a year. What a fine thing for our girls." (pp 3f.)

And the author curtly sums her up at the end of the first chapter:

> She was a woman of mean understanding, little information, and uncertain temper. When she was discontented, she fancied herself nervous. The business of her life was to get her daughters married; its solace was visiting and news. (pp 5)

Two subjects dominate her life and conversation: the injustice of the entail by which Mr. Bennet's estate will descend to his closest male relative rather than to his immediate family, and the problem of getting her daughters married. Out of these fixed ideas, untempered by any altruism, circumspection, wit, or intellect, derive all of her appearances and her total function in the story. The matter of the entail serves mainly to introduce Mr. Collins and to complicate the second and stronger fixed idea; it also provides Mr. Bennet with opportunities to bait his wife:

> "About a month ago I received this letter ... from my cousin, Mr. Collins, who, when I am dead, may turn you all out of the house as soon as he pleases."
>
> "Oh! my dear," cried his wife, "I cannot bear to hear that mentioned. Pray do not talk of that odious man. I do think it is the hardest thing in the world, that your estate should be entailed away from your own children; and I am sure if I had been you, I should have tried long ago to do something or other about it." (pp 61f.)

The problem of getting her daughters married, however, involves her much more directly in the tensions and progress of the narrative. It is her irrepressible vulgarity in discussing Jane's prospective marriage to Bingley which convinces Darcy that any alliance with Mrs. Bennet's family—for his friend or for himself—would be imprudent and degrading:

> ... Mrs. Bennet seemed incapable of fatigue while enumerating the advantages of the match. His being such a charming young man, and so rich, and living but three miles from them, were the first points of self-gratulation.... It was, moreover, such a promising thing for her younger daughter, as Jane's marrying so greatly must throw them in the way of other rich men....
>
> In vain did Elizabeth endeavour to check the rapidity of her

mother's words, or persuade her to describe her felicity in a less audible whisper; for to her inexpressible vexation, she could perceive that the chief of it was overheard by Mr. Darcy, who sat opposite to them. Her mother only scolded her for being nonsensical!

"What is Mr. Darcy to me, pray, that I should be afraid of him? I am sure we owe him no such particular civility as to be obliged to say nothing *he* may not like to hear." (pp 99)

Having decided that Darcy is too haughty to pursue any of her daughters, she goes out of her way, in fact, to offend him. When Darcy and Elizabeth exchange opinions on the limits of a country life, Mrs. Bennet cannot forbear adding her own comment:

"The country," said Darcy, "can in general supply but few subjects for such a study. In a country neighbourhood you move in a very confined and unvarying society."

"But people themselves alter so much, that there is something new to be observed in them forever."

"Yes, indeed," cried Mrs. Bennet, offended by his manner of mentioning a country neighbourhood. "I assure you there is quite as much of *that* going on in the country as in town."

Every body was surprised; and Darcy, after looking at her for a moment, turned silently away. (pp 42f.)

Her feeling toward Mr. Collins swings between extremes of deference and indignation, according as she must consider him a profit or a loss: a suitor, or the holder of the entail. When he is quite unknown to her except as the latter, she detests him. When, in his letter, he barely hints at courting one of the Bennet girls during his coming visit, she thaws almost at once:

"There is some sense in what he says about the girls however; and if he is disposed to make them any amends, I shall not be the person to discourage him." (pp 83)

When, on appearing, he seems quite bent on marriage,

Mrs. Bennet ... trusted that she might soon have two daughters married; and the man whom she could not bear to speak of the day before, was now high in her good graces. (pp 71)

After Elizabeth, in spite of Mrs. Bennet's strenuous pleading, has turned him down and he marries Charlotte Lucas instead, she can see him only as she saw him at first, gloating—and with a wife now to help him gloat—over the entail:

> "... And so, I suppose, they often talk of having Longbourn when your father is dead. They look upon it as quite their own, I dare say, whenever that happens." (pp 228)

Her obsession with material security overrides every consideration of kindness or solicitude toward her husband and her daughters. She sends Jane on horseback to Netherfield on the chance that she may be caught in a rainstorm and obliged to stay overnight; and, when news comes next morning that Jane is ill, Mrs. Bennet is quite unperturbed, even by her husband's sharpest sarcasm:

> "Well, my dear," said Mr. Bennet ... "if your daughter should have a dangerous fit of illness, if she should die, it would be a comfort to know that it was all in pursuit of Mr. Bingley, and under your orders."
>
> "Oh! I am not at all afraid of her dying. People do not die of little trifling colds. She will be taken good care of. As long as she stays there, it is all very well. I would go and see her, if I could have the carriage." (pp 31f.)

Forced to surrender the hope that Bingley will return to Jane, Mrs. Bennet remarks:

> "... Well, my comfort is, I am sure Jane will die of a broken heart, and then he will be sorry for what he has done." (pp 228)

Yet, though she can regard Jane's death as a potential comfort, though she can speak of her husband's death as if it is imminent, and only as it means that she will be turned out of her house by Mr. Collins, she is not at all prepared to contemplate her own:

> "Indeed, Mr. Bennet," said she, "it is very hard to think that Charlotte Lucas shall ever be mistress of this house, that I shall be forced to make way for *her*, and live to see her take my place in it!"

"My dear, do not give way to such gloomy thoughts. Let us
hope for better things. Let us flatter ourselves that I may be the
survivor."

This was not very consoling to Mrs. Bennet, and, therefore,
instead of making any answer, she went on as before ... (pp 130)

She fears one thing finally: her own physical discomfort, of which death—
when her husband maliciously thrusts its image before her—must seem the
severest and most frightening variety. An inadequate mind to begin with,
marriage to a man who treats her with contempt only, preoccupation with
the insistent material concerns imposed by society upon a woman of her
class—they have all combined in Mrs. Bennet's single continuously
operating motive: to be herself secure and comfortable, and to fortify her
own security by getting her daughters settled in prudent marriage, that
condition symbolic of material well-being. For Mrs. Bennet, everything in
life reduces itself to the dimensions of this motive; everything except her
daughter Lydia.

Lydia, is, of course, Mrs. Bennet as she must remember herself at the
same age:

Lydia was a stout, well-grown girl of fifteen, with a fine
complexion and good-humoured countenance; a favourite with
her mother, whose affection had brought her into public at an
early age. She had high animal spirits, and a sort of natural self-
consequence, which the attentions of the officers, to whom her
uncle's good dinners and her own easy manners recommended
her, had increased into assurance. (pp 45)

The coming of a militia regiment to Meryton has determined the course of
her life, as far ahead as she cares to look. Her sister Kitty is a willing and
easily led ally. They can think of nothing but dancing and flirtation, the
excitement of a uniform, the sense of importance at hearing and repeating
officer gossip, the perspective of innumerable balls and dress parades into the
future. When the regiment is ordered to Brighton, their world seems ready
to collapse, and Mrs. Bennet is scarcely less despairing:

"Good Heaven! What is to become of us! What are we to do!"
would they often exclaim in the bitterness of woe. "How can you
be smiling so, Lizzy?"

Their affectionate mother shared all their grief; she remembered what she had herself endured on a similar occasion, five and twenty years ago.

"I am sure," said she, "I cried for two days together when Colonel Millar's regiment went away. I thought I should have broke my heart."

"I am sure I shall break *mine*," said Lydia. (pp 229)

But Lydia, at least, is spared by receiving an invitation from her good friend, the colonel's wife, to accompany the regiment to Brighton. Parting from Lydia, Mrs. Bennet

> ... was diffuse in her good wishes for the felicity of her daughter, and impressive in her injunctions that she would not miss the opportunity of enjoying herself as much as possible; advice, which there was every reason to believe would be attended to ... (pp 235)

One of Jane Austen's triumphs in *Pride and Prejudice* is her refusal to sentimentalize Lydia (as well as Mrs. Bennet) once she has fashioned her to a hard and simple consistency. Lydia is a self-assured, highly sexed, wholly amoral and unintellectual girl. When she runs off with Wickham, nothing can lower her spirits or drive her to shame—not all the disapproval of society, not the horror and shame of her family (though her mother, of course, is neither horrified nor ashamed). She has done what she wanted to do; and if her uncle or father or someone else must pay Wickham to persuade him to legalize the union, that is their worry, not hers. She is not defiantly, but simply, impenitent: she recognizes no authority to which penitence or concealment is due. If marriage is valued by some, so much the better; if, for no effort on her part, it gives her a social precedence and dignity, she will take these, though she did not ask for them and could have lived without them. And, again, her defender is her mother, who, when the married pair return to Longbourn,

> ... stepped forwards, embraced her, and welcomed her with rapture; gave her hand with an affectionate smile to Wickham, who followed his lady, and wished them both joy, with an alacrity which allowed no doubt of their happiness. (pp 315)

Elizabeth may be "disgusted, and even Miss Bennet ... shocked," but

Lydia was Lydia still; untamed, unabashed, wild, noisy, and fearless. (pp 315)

What Elizabeth designates as Lydia's "susceptibility to her feelings," (pp 317) what the author has called her "high animal spirits," (pp 45) is Lydia's only motive, as it must once have been Mrs. Bennet's also; but Lydia has not abandoned it out of prudence or fear, has even seen it assume the unanticipated respectability of marriage:

> "Well, mamma ... and what do you think of my husband? Is not he a charming man? I am sure my sisters must all envy me. I only hope they may have half my good luck. They must all go to Brighton. That is the place to get husbands. What a pity it is, mamma, we did not all go."
> "Very true; and if I had my will, we should...." (pp 317)

And Lydia never repents; neither mother nor daughter even recognizes that there is anything to repent.

Mr. Collins and Lady Catherine, though "simple" also, differ from Lydia and Mrs. Bennet at least to the extent that Elizabeth can observe them more freely, without the sense of shame and responsibility she must feel toward her mother and sister. Mr. Collins is, indeed, so remote from Elizabeth's personal concerns that she and the reader can enjoy him as a pure fool, unweighted by moral import. The fact that he is a clergyman underscores his foolishness and moral nullity:

> "... I have been so fortunate as to be distinguished by the patronage of the Right Honourable Lady Catherine de Bourgh, widow of Sir Lewis de Bourgh, whose bounty and beneficence has preferred me to the valuable rectory of this parish, where it shall be my earnest endeavour to demean myself with grateful respect towards her Ladyship, and be ever ready to perform those rites and ceremonies which are instituted by the Church of England. As a clergyman, moreover, I feel it my duty to promote and establish the blessing of peace in all families within the reach of my influence; and on these grounds I flatter myself that my present overtures of good-will are highly commendable, and that the circumstance of my being next in the entail of Longbourn estate, will be kindly overlooked on your side, and not lead you to reject the offered olive branch...."[1] (pp 62f.)

"'... Can he be a sensible man, sir?'" Elizabeth asks; and her father replies:

> "No, my dear; I think not. I have great hopes of finding him quite
> the reverse. There is a mixture of servility and self-importance in his
> letter, which promises well. I am impatient to see him." (pp 64)

Mr. Bennet's expectation of amusement is fulfilled many times over. "Mr. Collins was not a sensible man," (pp 70) as the author begins a superfluous descriptive paragraph; and his fatuity, sycophancy, conceit, and resolutely unprejudiced wife-hunting are given ample range. Wherever he goes, whatever he does, he remains unshakably foolish. Elizabeth's declining his proposal, once he can believe that it is not to be ascribed to the "usual practice of elegant females," (pp 108) clouds his jauntiness for a moment; but he recovers soon enough to propose as fervently to Charlotte Lucas three days later, and when he leaves Longbourn he wishes his "fair cousins ... health and happiness, not excepting my cousin Elizabeth." (pp 124) As he likes to be useful to Lady Catherine, so he is useful to the plot: he provides a place for Elizabeth to visit, where she can observe Lady Catherine and see Darcy again; he draws out his "affable and condescending" patroness for Elizabeth's edification; he serves as a medium through which Lady Catherine's opinions on events in the Bennet family are graciously transmitted to the Bennets. And always he remains firm in the conviction of his importance and dignity, of his place at the center—or a little off the matriarchal center—of the universe, whether he is almost walking on air in contemplation of the advantage of Rosings:

> Words were insufficient for the elevation of his feelings; and
> he was obliged to walk about the room, while Elizabeth tried to
> unite civility and truth in a few short sentences. (pp 216)

or warning Elizabeth against a "precipitate closure" (pp 363) with Darcy's suit, or offering his clerical opinion on Lydia and Wickham:

> "... I must not ... refrain from declaring my amazement, at
> hearing that you received the young couple into your house as
> soon as they were married. It was an encouragement of vice; and
> had I been the rector of Longbourn, I should very strenuously
> have opposed it. You ought certainly to forgive them as a
> christian, but never to admit them in your sight, or allow their
> names to be mentioned in your hearing." (pp 363f.)

Like Mr. Collins, Lady Catherine is chiefly amusing because of the incongruity between the importance she assumes to herself and the actual influence she exercises upon the story. At first glance, she is, of course, far more formidable than Mr. Collins:

> Her air was not conciliating, nor was her manner of receiving them, such as to make her visitors forget their inferior rank. (pp 162)

She has her worshipful courtier in Mr. Collins, who, dining at Rosings, "looked as if he felt that life could furnish nothing greater." (pp 163) And she is confident of having her judgments explicitly followed:

> ... delivering her opinion on every subject in so decisive a manner as proved that she was not used to have her judgement controverted.... Elizabeth found that nothing was beneath this great Lady's attention, which could furnish her with an occasion of dictating to others. (pp 163)

Yet, in the story at least, she never does what she thinks she is doing or wishes to do. It is true—as Elizabeth remarks—that "Lady Catherine has been of infinite use, which ought to make her happy, for she loves to be of use." (pp 381) She is useful to the story; but only in ways she is unaware of and would repudiate with outrage if she knew of them. By her insulting condescension toward Elizabeth, she helps Darcy to balance off his distaste of Mrs. Bennet's not dissimilar shortcomings. She provokes Elizabeth into asserting her own independence of spirit, even to the point of impertinence. In her arrogant effort to dissuade Elizabeth from accepting Darcy, she gives Elizabeth the opportunity to set her own proud value upon herself as an individual, and later, having angrily brought the news to Darcy, encourages him to believe that Elizabeth may not refuse him a second time. Lady Catherine is a purely comic figure, not because she is not potentially powerful and dangerous in the authority that rank and wealth confer upon her, but because she is easily known for what she is, and because the lovers are in a position—Darcy by his own rank and wealth, Elizabeth by her spirit and intelligence—to deny her power altogether.

This quality of powerlessness is, indeed, peculiar to Elizabeth's, and the author's, whole category of simplicity: not merely in Mrs. Bennet, Lydia, Mr. Collins, and Lady Catherine, but in the predictably malicious Miss Bingley, in single-postured simpletons like Sir William Lucas and Mary Bennet, down to an unrealized function like Georgiana Darcy. They are powerless, that is, at the center of the story. They cannot decisively divert Elizabeth's or Darcy's mind and purpose because they cannot cope with the adult personality that either of the lovers presents. They are powerless, ultimately, because they are not themselves adult: They convince us of their existence (except, perhaps, Georgiana and Mary), sometimes even brilliantly; but they are not sufficiently complex or self-aware to be taken at the highest level of seriousness. Elizabeth's judgment of them is, then, primarily psychological, not moral: they have not grown to a personal stature significantly measurable by moral law. However Elizabeth, may console Bingley that a "deep, intricate character" may be no more "estimable than such a one as yours," (pp 42) the fact is that though she finds simplicity comfortable or amusing, it is only intricacy, complexity of spirit, that she finds fascinating, deserving of pursuit and capture, susceptible to a grave moral judgment.

It may be objected that Jane Bennet belongs in the category of simplicity also, and that Elizabeth, nonetheless, loves and admires her sister above anyone else. Both statements are true; but the latter is true only in a very special sense. There is something maternal, something affectionately envious, something of the nature of a schoolgirl passion in Elizabeth's feeling for Jane. Jane is gentle, sweet, forbearing, incapable of vindictiveness, incapable almost of believing ill of anyone:

> "... You are a great deal too apt ... to like people in general. You never see a fault in any body. All the world are good and agreeable in your eyes. I never heard you speak ill of a human being in my life."
> "I would wish not to be hasty in censuring any one; but I always speak what I think." (pp 14)

Elizabeth may counter with a remark on her sister's "good sense":

> "I know you do; and it is *that* which makes the wonder. With *your* good sense, to be so honestly blind to the follies and nonsense of others! ..." (pp 14)

Yet it is this honest blindness, not the good sense, that we observe in operation. Jane believes good of everyone, not out of any rational or intuitive knowledge beyond Elizabeth's, but out of a total incapacity to accept the possibility of evil until it quite bluntly proclaims itself. She is a good person because she is by nature too easy and temperate to be otherwise. The difference between her natural, uncomplex, unintuitive, almost unseeing goodness and Elizabeth's conscious, reasoned, perpetual examination into motive—this is a difference not merely between individuals, but between altogether different orders of mind. Elizabeth loves Jane as Jane is a kind and loving sister, she envies Jane her facile solution—or her plain ignorance—of the problems of interpreting personality, she even plays the schoolgirl to her older sister as confidante; but Elizabeth never doubts that Jane's opinions of others have no objective value, and that Jane's response toward people and society is much too simple, even too simple-minded, to be hers. So Elizabeth, as Jane defends Bingley's sisters against her charge of snobbery,

> ... listened in silence, but was not convinced; their behaviour at the assembly had not been calculated to please in general; and with more quickness of observation and less pliancy of temper than her sister, and with a judgment too unassailed by any attention to herself, she was very little disposed to approve them. (pp 15)

The surest proof of Elizabeth's, and the author's, attitude toward Jane is the lover they are both delighted to supply her with. Bingley is a person of secondary order far more obviously than Jane. He is handsome, very amiable and courteous, lively, properly smitten by Jane almost at first glance. That, and his considerable wealth, make up the extent of his charms. It is significant that Elizabeth never has a twinge of feeling for him, except as he seems a fine catch for her sister. In his conversation with Elizabeth at Netherfield, he fears that he gives himself away out of shallowness (pp 42); and, despite Elizabeth's graceful denial, he does. There is nothing below the surface. His strong-willed friend, Darcy, leads him about by the nose. Though he is supposed to have fallen seriously in love with Jane, the merest trick of Darcy's and his sister's is enough to send and keep him away from her. As Darcy explains:

> "... Bingley is most unaffectedly modest. His diffidence had prevented his depending on his own judgment in so anxious a case, but his reliance on mine, made every thing easy...." (pp 371)

"Modest" is a charitable word here. Darcy has been equally successful, moreover, in turning about and persuading Bingley that Jane is in love with him; whereupon

> Elizabeth longed to observe that Mr. Bingley had been a most delightful friend; so easily guided that his worth was invaluable.... (pp 371)

It is true that Jane pines over Bingley for a long time. She is a sincere and faithful lover; but our admiration of this trait tends to diminish as we think about the object of her love. Jane and Bingley provide us, then, with one of the book's primary ironies: that love is simple, straightforward, and immediate only for very simple people. Jane and Bingley could, of course, have served very well as a pair of story-book lovers, tossed romantically on a sea of circumstances not only beyond their control but beyond their understanding. In the pattern of the novel, however, they have their adult guardians and counterparts—Jane in her sister, Bingley in his friend—to haul them in when the sea gets too rough; and though, like the standard lovers of romance, they will never have to worry about growing up, we are obliged, by the presence of Elizabeth at least, to admit that it is possible—perhaps even preferable—for lovers to be complex and mature.

To this point Elizabeth's judgment is as acute and ironic as her author's. Elizabeth, indeed, is far more aware of distinctions in personality than any of the author's previous heroines: Catherine Morland, Elinor or Marianne Dashwood. In *Northanger Abbey*, the author could not allow her heroine to be aware from the outset since her story developed precisely out of Catherine's unawareness of distinctions (a quality suggested, perhaps, by Jane Austen's early tendency to assert an arbitrary omniscience over the objects of her irony). In *Sense and Sensibility*, Jane Austen, yielding for the first time to the moral pressures inevitable upon a woman of her time and class, allowed Elinor only the solemn and easy discriminations of bourgeois morality, and finally smothered the threatening spark of Marianne's much livelier and more observing consciousness. In *Pride and Prejudice*, however, there is no compulsion—personal, thematic, or moral—toward denying the heroine her own powers of judgment. There is, on the contrary, a thematic need for the heroine to display a subtle, accurate, a perceiving mind. In *Pride and Prejudice*, as in the previous novels, Jane Austen deals with the distinction between false moral values and true; but she is also dealing here with a distinction antecedent to the moral judgment—the distinction between the simple personality, unequipped with that self-awareness which alone makes choice seem possible, and the complex personality, whose most crucial complexity is its awareness, of self and others. This distinction, which in her youthful defensive posture Jane Austen has tended to make only between her characters and herself, she here establishes internally, between two categories of personality within the novel. The distinction is, in fact, one that every character in *Pride and Prejudice* must make if he can; and the complex characters—Elizabeth and Darcy among them—justify their complexity by making it, and trying to live by its implications, through all their lapses of arrogance, prejudice, sensuality, and fear. Elizabeth is aware because, in the novel's climate of adult decision, she must be so to survive with our respect and interest.

Yet the distinction must be made in a social setting, by human beings fallible, if for no other reason, because of their own social involvement. The province of *Pride and Prejudice*—as always in Jane Austen's novels—is marriage in an acquisitive society. Elizabeth herself, being young and unmarried, is at the center of it; and it is this position that sets her off from such an external and imposed commentator as Henry Tilney. Her position of personal involvement subjects her, moreover, to a risk of error never run by the detached Mr. Tilney. She can tag and dismiss the blatantly simple persons very well; it is when she moves away from these toward ambiguity and self concealment, toward persons themselves aware enough to interest and engage her, that her youth and inexperience and emotional partiality begin to deceive her.

They deceive her first with Charlotte Lucas. The two girls have been good friends. Charlotte, according to the author, is a "sensible, intelligent young woman," (pp 18) and she shares Elizabeth's taste for raillery and social generalization. Even when Charlotte offers her altogether cynical views on courtship and marriage, Elizabeth refuses to take her at her word:

> "... Happiness in marriage is entirely a matter of chance. If the dispositions of the parties are ever so well known to each other, or ever so similar before-hand, it does not advance their felicity in the least. They always continue to grow sufficiently unlike afterwards to have their share of vexation; and it is better to know as little as possible of the defects of the person with whom you are to pass your life."
>
> "You make me laugh, Charlotte; but it is not sound. You know it is not sound, and that you would never act in this way yourself."
> (pp 23)

It is not that Elizabeth misjudges Charlotte's capabilities, but that she underestimates the strength of the pressures acting upon her. Charlotte is twenty-seven, unmarried, not pretty, not well-to-do, living in a society which treats a penniless old maid less as a joke than as an exasperating burden upon her family. But Elizabeth is inexperienced enough, at the beginning, to judge in terms of personality only. She recognizes Mr. Collins' total foolishness and Charlotte's intelligence, and would never have dreamed that any pressure could overcome so natural an opposition. Complex and simple, aware and unaware, do not belong together—except that in marriages made by economics they often unite, however obvious the mismatching. The trick, as

Charlotte decides upon accepting Mr. Collins' proposal, is to have as little as possible to do with the personal accessory to her material well-being:

> The stupidity with which he was favoured by nature, must guard his courtship from any charm that could make a woman wish for its continuance; and Miss Lucas, who accepted him solely from the pure and disinterested desire of an establishment, cared not how soon that establishment were gained. (pp 122)

Living under a pall of economic anxiety has, in fact, withered every desire in Charlotte except the desire for security:

> "... I am not romantic.... I never was. I ask only a comfortable home; and considering Mr. Collins's character, connections, and situation in life, I am convinced that my chance of happiness with him is as fair, as most people can boast on entering the marriage state." (pp 125)

What Charlotte has resolved, finally, is to grow progressively unaware, to reduce herself to simplicity; and, in the meantime, while that is not yet possible, to close her eyes and ears. Her decision is clear when Elizabeth visits Hunsford:

> When Mr. Collins said any thing of which his wife might reasonably be ashamed, which certainly was not unseldom, she involuntarily turned her eye on Charlotte. Once or twice she could discern a faint blush; but in general Charlotte wisely did not hear.... To work in his garden was one of his most respectable pleasures; and Elizabeth admired the command of countenance with which Charlotte talked of the healthfulness of the exercise, and owned she encouraged it as much as possible. (pp 156)

So the natural antithesis which separates simple from complex, and which should separate one from the other absolutely in the closest human relationship, can be upset and annulled by economic pressure.

Elizabeth's continual mistake is to ignore, or to set aside as uninfluential, the social context. It is a question not merely of individuals and marriage, but of individuals and marriage in an acquisitive society. Elizabeth expects nothing except comfort or amusement from simplicity, but she likes to believe that complexity means a categorically free will, without social distortion of qualification.

When complexity and a pleasing manner combine, as they do in Wickham, Elizabeth is at her least cautious. Wickham is clever and charming, a smooth social being, and for these qualities Elizabeth is ready to believe his long, unsolicited tale of being wronged and even to imagine herself falling in love with him. What she never allows, until much later, to cast a doubt upon his testimony is the fact that he is a dispossessed man in an acquisitive society. It is true that Wickham is very persuasive, and that Elizabeth's prejudice against Darcy (which has grown out of her failure to take into account his social context) has prepared her to accept Wickham's accusation. Still, she has reason to reconsider when Wickham turns his attentions to a Miss King, concerning whom the "sudden acquisition of ten thousand pounds was the most remarkable charm." (pp 149) If, instead, she refuses to begrudge him his change of heart, his "wish of independence," (pp 150) and acknowledges to her aunt that she is "open to the mortifying conviction that handsome young men must have something to live on, as well as the plain," (pp 150) she remains quite in character, less perceptive than usual out of her appreciation of Wickham's cleverness and manner, ready to believe that an unknown Miss King can scarcely be as bad as Charlotte's too well known Mr. Collins, that at any rate so charming a man cannot be altogether wrong.

It is with Wickham, nevertheless, that Jane Austen's directing and organizing irony—which functions doubly, at the same time through and upon Elizabeth—begins to fail; and the area of failure, as with Willoughby, is the sexual experience outside marriage.

The first flattening of tone occurs in Darcy's letter (pp 195ff.), in which Wickham's infamy is revealed. Wickham has attempted to seduce Darcy's sister, Georgiana; and it is this specific attempt, beyond any other evidence of profligacy, that automatically makes him a villain from Darcy's point of view, and from Elizabeth's also as soon as she can accept the truth of the letter. The curious fact is, not that Elizabeth and, here at least, Jane Austen regard seduction as infamous, but that, into an ironic atmosphere elaborated and intensified out of the difficulty of interpreting motive, Jane Austen pushes a standard black-and-white seduction-scene, with all the appurtenances of an ingenuous young girl, a scheming profligate, a wicked governess, and an outraged brother, and with no trace of doubt, shading, or irony. It is hardly enough to say, with Miss Lascelles,[2] that Jane Austen clings to this novelistic convention through almost all her work as to a usable climax, which she met in Richardson and for which she could find no adequate substitute. Why she retained this threadbare revelation when, as early as *Pride and Prejudice*, she could demonstrate the most subtle and resourceful skill in representing every other particular of the action, remains a question.

The answer seems to be that, though the nature of her subject makes an approach to the sexual experience inevitable, Jane Austen will not allow herself (as she did in "Love and Friendship" and continues to do in her letters[3]) to assimilate extra-marital sex to her characteristic unifying irony, and that her only other possible response is conventional. She must truncate, flatten, falsify, disapprove, all in the interests of an external morality; and the process in *Pride and Prejudice* is so out of key with its surroundings as to be immediately jarring.

Lydia is the outstanding victim. Not that Lydia is not throughout a wholly consistent and living character. On the solid and simple foundations of her personality she works up to her triumphant end in marriage to Wickham. If she acts from her sensual nature, it is Elizabeth and the author themselves who have proved to us that Lydia, being among the simple spirits who are never really aware and who act only upon their single potentiality, cannot do otherwise. She is fulfilling herself, as Mr. Collins fulfills himself in marriage and at Rosings, as Jane and Bingley fulfill themselves. The irony is, or should be, in her unawareness, in her powerlessness to change, in the incongruity between her conviction of vitality and her lack of choice. This irony, though, Jane Austen quite cuts off. She is herself silent, but it is clear that she allows Elizabeth to define the proper attitude toward Lydia. Elizabeth can feel, at first, no sympathy for Lydia at all—only shame and self-pity however altruistically phrased:

> Lydia—the humiliation, the misery, she was bringing on them all, soon swallowed up every private care; and covering her face with her handkerchief, Elizabeth was soon lost to everything else.... (pp 278)

It is true that this occurs in Darcy's presence, and in her growing consciousness of Darcy's worth. Later, however, when the moment of shame is long past, her attitude has not changed except to harden into sarcastic resentment. Lydia, back at Longbourn, suggests to her mother that the family visit her and Wickham at their new home:

> "... when you go away, you may leave one or two of my sisters behind you; and I dare say I shall get husbands for them before the winter is over."
>
> "I thank you for my share of the favour," said Elizabeth; "but I do not particularly like your way of getting husbands." (pp 317)

And when Lydia offers to give Elizabeth an account of the wedding,

"No really," replied Elizabeth; "I think there cannot be too little said on the subject." (pp 318)

Elizabeth's ill-tempered efforts to shame Lydia are fruitless, as Elizabeth should have known they would be while Lydia is Lydia still. What, they amount to is a kind of floating moral judgment. It seems that both Jane Austen and her heroine feel uneasily that a moral lesson must be taught, though they have already proved that Lydia is incapable of learning it:

> ... how little of permanent happiness could belong to a couple who were only brought together because their passions were stronger than their virtue, she could easily conjecture. (pp 312)

So Jane Austen suspends her irony, suspends her imagination altogether, while Wickham is engaged in seducing Georgiana or Lydia. Yet, apart from this temporary suspension, Wickham fits admirably into the large pattern of Elizabeth's social education. Not only is he, like Charlotte, an example of the complex personality discarding scruples, discarding candor, making the wrong choice under economic pressure; he is also an evil agent, quite willing to corrupt others as well, to involve them in public disgrace if he can thereby assure his own security. What he uses deliberately is what Mrs. Bennet used, much less deliberately, in her conquest of her husband: sexual attractiveness. It is, then, Wickham who by exploiting sex sets off that other intricate character who passively succumbed to it—Mr. Bennet.

It is, in fact, easy to imagine that when Mr. Bennet calls Wickham his favorite son-in-law (pp 379) he is not merely indulging in habitual paradox, but ironically recognizing the painful contrast between Wickham's awareness, however directed, and his own self-delusion, in the same emotional circumstance. Mr. Bennet made his mistake many years before, and must now stand by it because his class recognizes no respectable way out:

> ... captivated by youth and beauty, and that appearance of good humour, which youth and beauty generally give, he had married a woman whose weak understanding and illiberal mind, had very early in their marriage put an end to all real affection for her. Respect, esteem, and confidence, had vanished for ever; and all his views of domestic happiness were overthrown. But Mr. Bennet was not of a disposition to seek comfort for the disappointment which his own imprudence had brought on, in any of those pleasures which too often console the unfortunate for their folly or their vice. He was fond of the country and of

books; and from these tastes had arisen his principal enjoyments. To his wife he was very little otherwise indebted, than as her ignorance and folly had contributed to his amusement. This is not the sort of happiness which a man would in general wish to owe to his wife; but where other powers of entertainment are wanting, the true philosopher will derive benefit from such as are given. (pp 236)

Mr. Bennet has become an ironic spectator almost totally self-enclosed, his irony rigidly defensive, a carapace against the plain recognition of his own irrevocable folly. He observes, he stands apart "in silence ... enjoying the scene," (pp 103) he likes to make blunt comments on the silliness of his daughters, especially of Lydia and Kitty:

"From all that I can collect by your manner of talking, you must be two of the silliest girls in the country. I have suspected it some time, but I am now convinced." (pp 29)

and, equally, when Charlotte accepts Mr. Collins:

... it gratified him, he said, to discover that Charlotte Lucas, whom he had been used to think tolerably sensible, was as foolish as his wife, and more foolish than his daughter! (pp 127)

He likes to upset, in small ways, the social decorum which has overwhelmed him in its massive and permanent way, he enjoys pointing the contrast between what he ought to think and what he does think. It is a very minor social victory, but the only one now possible for him. His most dependable source of amusement is, of course, his wife; and he exploits her comic potentialities with a ruthlessness proportional to her unawareness of his purpose.

At the very beginning he is baiting her about Bingley. He baits her continually on the subject of Mr. Collins and the entail, as she raises her continued uncomprehending objection:

"I cannot bear to think that they should have all this estate. If it was not for the entail I should not mind it."
"What should you not mind?"
"I should not mind any thing at all."
"Let us be thankful that you are preserved from a state of such insensibility." (pp 130)

He even baits her about her death (pp 130), and so finds the only effective way to sidetrack her—the reason, perhaps, why he never tries it again, since her uninterrupted nonsense is more diverting than her fear.

It is true that Lydia's elopement shocks him into exposing himself for as long as it takes him to transact the unpleasant business. When he returns from his futile search in London, in acknowledgment of Elizabeth's

> ... briefly expressing her sorrow for what he must have endured, he replied, "Say nothing of that. Who should suffer but myself? It has been my own doing, and I ought to feel it."
> "You must not be too severe upon yourself," replied Elizabeth.
> "You may well warn me against such an evil. Human nature is so prone to fall into it! No, Lizzy, let me once in my life feel how much I have been to blame. I am not afraid of being overpowered by the impression. It will pass away soon enough." (pp 299)

It does soon enough, or at least the impulse to articulate it. With Lydia and Wickham safely married, Mr. Bennet restores himself to what he has been—rather, to what he has seemed. He needs only another letter from Mr. Collins to reaffirm all his amused detachment, to make explicit the only code by which he can tolerate the vacuity, the hopeless failure of sympathy, in his life.

> "... For what do we live, but to make sport for our neighbours, and laugh at them in our turn?" (pp 364)

If Elizabeth cannot answer, it is because she recognizes that there is nothing else left for her father, that his choice was made long ago, that he cannot withdraw or alter it, that he must live by it in the only way endurable for him. Of course his mistake and his despair might be decently masked; things would be better, for his children at least, if he could put up a front of quiet respectability concerning his relations with his wife:

> Elizabeth ... had never been blind to the impropriety of her father's behaviour as a husband. She had always seen it with pain; but respecting his abilities, and grateful for his affectionate treatment of herself, she endeavoured to forget what she could not overlook, and to banish from her thoughts that continual breach of conjugal obligation and decorum which, in exposing his wife to the contempt of her children, was so highly reprehensible. (pp 236)

But the damage to himself is done and cannot be remedied. Elizabeth knows her father: of the complex characters in the story, he is the only one whom she has known long and well enough to judge accurately from the outset. She has learned from his example that a complex personality may yield to the pressure of sensuality; that marriages made by sex—as well as those made by economics—represent, for the free individual, an abdication of choice, an irremediable self-degradation and defeat.

In his social context, in his status as a gentleman of independent means, Mr. Bennet was lulled into believing that choice was easy, a matter of simple and unexamined inclination; and in the same society Mrs. Bennet could not believe otherwise than that any gentleman of means must make a desirable husband. This much Elizabeth recognizes about the pressures of an acquisitive society, even upon a free individual like her father. The shock of Charlotte's marriage to a fool makes Elizabeth recognize that these pressures act decisively upon other free individuals as well. In spite of examples, however, it takes a long series of vexations and misunderstandings before she can be convinced that the imposed pride of rank and wealth, perhaps the strongest pressure in an acquisitive society, may act, not yet decisively—for the area of decision is marriage—but conditionally upon a free individual like Darcy, to make him behave with an overconfident and unsympathetic obstinacy, to make him seem far different from what he is capable of being behind the façade of pride.

It is the social façade of the complex person that deceives Elizabeth. She can penetrate her father's, out of sympathetic familiarity and concern; but Charlotte's has deceived her. Wickham's takes her in altogether; and by contrast with Wickham's, by the contrast which Wickham himself takes care to emphasize in his own support, Darcy's façade seems disagreeable indeed, or rather a clear window on a disagreeable spirit.

Darcy's function as the character most difficult for the heroine to interpret, and yet most necessary for her to interpret if she is to make a proper decision in the only area of choice her society leaves open, his simultaneous role as the heroine's puzzle and her only possible hero, is clearly marked out during the action. From Elizabeth's point of view, in fact, the process of the interpretation of Darcy's personality from disdain through doubt to admiration is represented with an extraordinarily vivid and convincing minuteness.[4] Nevertheless, Darcy himself remains unachieved: we recognize his effects upon Elizabeth, without recognizing that he exists independently of them.

Mrs. Leavis has persuasively documented her belief that *Pride and Prejudice* is an effort to "rewrite the story of *Cecilia* in realistic terms";[5] and she observes, more particularly, that Darcy fails because he does not transcend his derivation: he is a character out of a book, not one whom Jane Austen created or reorganized for her own purpose. But why Darcy alone: why is he, among the major figures in *Pride and Prejudice*, the only one disturbingly derived and wooden?

The reason seems to be the same as that which compelled Jane Austen to falsify her tone and commentary concerning Wickham's seductions and to supply Elinor and Marianne Dashwood with such nonentities for husbands. The socially unmanageable, the personally involving aspects of sex, Jane Austen can no longer treat with irony, nor can she as yet treat them straightforwardly. Darcy is the hero, he is the potential lover of a complex young woman much like the author herself; and as such Jane Austen cannot animate him with emotion, or with her characteristic informing irony. She borrows him from a book; and, though she alters and illuminates everything else, she can do nothing more with him than fit him functionally into the plot.

Even here the author is so uncharacteristically clumsy as to rely on inconsistencies of personality to move her story along. However difficult Elizabeth's task of interpreting Darcy, it is clear from the beginning that, in his consistent functional impact upon the story, he is a proud man with a strong sense of at least external propriety and dignity, and with no taste whatever for his aunt's vulgar condescension or the kind of sarcasm dispensed by Mr. Bennet. Yet on his first appearance he initiates Elizabeth's prejudice by speaking with a simple vulgarity indistinguishable from his aunt's, and in a voice loud enough to be overheard by the object of his contempt:

> ... turning round, he looked for a moment at Elizabeth, till catching her eye, he withdrew his own and coldly said, "She is tolerable; but not handsome enough to tempt *me*; and I am in no humour at present to give consequence to young ladies who are slighted by other men...." (pp 11f.)

In spite of his rigid and principled reserve, in spite of Elizabeth's having just turned down his arrogant proposal, he makes his explanation to Elizabeth in a thoroughly frank and unreserved letter, which—more appropriate to a Richardsonian correspondent than to Darcy as he has been presented— seems an author's gesture of desperation to weight the scales in favor of her predetermined hero. Later, Miss Bingley is allowed to sink herself entirely by spitefully recalling to Darcy a remark he made about Elizabeth:

"... I particularly recollect your saying one night, after they had been dining at Netherfield, '*She* a beauty!—I should as soon call her mother a wit.'..." (pp 271)

This sounds like something left over from Mr. Bennet's stock; at any rate, we have no cause to believe that Darcy, in his dignified and self-conscious pride, would even have thought it, much less ever expressed it to a woman eager for the indulgence of her spite.

Out of inconsistency, Darcy emerges into flatness. Only in his sparring with Elizabeth, and then only occasionally, does he establish himself with a degree of solidity, of independent reference, as when Elizabeth tries to tease him into communicativeness while they are dancing:

"... One must speak a little, you know. It would look odd to be entirely silent for half an hour together, and yet for the advantage of *some*, conversation ought to be so arranged as that they may have the trouble of saying as little as possible."

"Are you consulting your own feelings in the present case, or do you imagine that you are gratifying mine?"

"Both," replied Elizabeth archly, "for I have always seen a great similarity in the turn of our minds.—We are each of an unsocial, taciturn disposition, unwilling to speak, unless we expect to say something that will amaze the whole room, and be handed down to posterity with all the eclat of a proverb."

"This is no very striking resemblance of your own character, I am sure," said he. "How near it may be to *mine*, I cannot pretend to say.—You think it a faithful portrait undoubtedly." (pp 91)

In dialogue, at least when Elizabeth is an enlivening participant, Jane Austen seems able now and then to overcome her awkwardness in handling Darcy. Otherwise, however, she can only make him serve: he interests us chiefly because he is the center of Elizabeth's interest; and because, in a book in which the individual must choose and in which marriage is the single area of choice, Darcy represents Elizabeth's only plausible, or almost, plausible, mate. But Elizabeth's catalogue of his admirable qualities resembles an author's anxious trick to underscore this plausibility:

She began now to comprehend that he was exactly the man who, in disposition and talents, would most suit her. His understanding and temper, though unlike her own, would have

> answered all her wishes. It was an union that must have been to
> the advantage of both; by her ease and liveliness, his mind might
> have been softened, his manners improved, and from his
> judgment, information, and knowledge of the world, she must
> have received benefit of greater importance. (pp 312)

And when Darcy is ironed out into the conventionally generous and altruistic
hero, making devoted efforts to shackle Wickham to Lydia, expending
thousands of pounds to restore peace of mind to Elizabeth's family, and all
for the love of Elizabeth when he does all this, with no more of personal
depth than Jane Austen allows of moral depth in the whole Lydia–Wickham
episode, he comes very close to forfeiting even the functional plausibility that
Elizabeth's interest lends him.

The last third of the book, as R. A. Brower has pointed out,[6] does in
fact diminish suddenly in density and originality: that is, beginning with
Lydia's elopement. We get a conventional chase by an outraged father, a
friendly uncle, and a now impeccable hero; we get outbursts of irrelevantly
directed moral judgment, and a general simplification of the problems of
motive and will down to the level of the Burneyan novel. Jane Austen herself,
routed by the sexual question she has raised, is concealed behind a fogbank
of bourgeois morality; and the characters, most conspicuously Darcy, must
shift for themselves, or, rather, they fall automatically into the grooves
prepared for them by hundreds of novels of sentiment and sensibility.

Only Elizabeth does not. She may yield temporarily to a kind of
homeless moralizing on Lydia's disgrace, she may be rather obvious and stiff
in acquainting herself with Darcy's virtues at last; but the lapses are minor,
and they never seriously dim her luminous vigor, her wit; curiosity,
discrimination, and independence. If the novel does not collapse in the
predictabilities of the denouement, it is because Elizabeth has from the
outset been presented in a depth specific and vital enough to resist flattening,
because she remains what she has been—a complex person in search of
conclusions about people in society, and on the way to her unique and crucial
choice.

She observes, and her shield and instrument together is irony. Like
Mary Crawford later, Elizabeth is a recognizable and striking aspect of her
author; but, unlike Mary's, her sins are all quite venial, her irony unclouded
by the author's disapproval and—after a few detours—grandly vindicated in
its effect. Jane Austen has not yet made her first unqualified capitulation to
the suspicious sobriety of her class, and surrendered her values in exchange
for its own. She can, in fact, embody her personal values in her heroine and
be delighted with the result; so she writes to her sister about Elizabeth: "I

must confess that I think her as delightful a creature as ever appeared in print, and how I shall be able to tolerate those who do not like *her* at least I do not know." (L II 297, 29 Jan. 1813)

Elizabeth's third dimension is irony; and it is her irony that fills out and sustains the action. Her slightest perception of incongruity reverberates through the scene, and from it out into the atmosphere of the book. When Lydia, having informed Elizabeth that Wickham's wealthy catch has got away, adds:

> "... he never cared three straws about her. Who could about such a nasty little freckled thing?"
> Elizabeth was shocked to think that, however incapable of such coarseness of *expression* herself, the coarseness of the *sentiment* was little other than her own breast had formerly harboured and fancied liberal! (pp 220)

At Pemberley, she listens as the housekeeper eulogizes Darcy, until her uncle asks:

> "Is your master much at Pemberley in the course of the year?"
> "Not so much as I could wish, sir; but I dare say he may spend half his time here; and Miss Darcy is always down for the summer months."
> "Except," thought Elizabeth, "when she goes to Ramsgate."
> (pp 248)

recalling by this most astonishing economy of means—like a flashback in intent but with none of its deadening machinery—the whole charged atmosphere of Wickham's earlier attempt at seduction (more successfully than Darcy's letter, our original source of information, had created it at first), recalling the tension of Darcy's insulting and rejected proposal, the excitement of his letter and the depression and change of heart it inevitably brought: and all this richness and clarity of reference out of a single and immediately irrelevant ironic thought. There is, above all, the perpetual exuberant yet directed irony of her conversation, especially as she uses it to sound Darcy. When Miss Bingley assures her that Darcy cannot be laughed at, Elizabeth exclaims:

> "That is an uncommon advantage, and uncommon I hope it will continue, for it would be a great loss to me to have many such acquaintance. I dearly love a laugh."

"Miss Bingley," said he, "has given me credit for more than can be. The wisest and the best of men, nay, the wisest and best of their actions, may be rendered ridiculous by a person whose first object in life is a joke."

"Certainly," replied Elizabeth—"there are such people, but I hope I am not one of them. I hope I never ridicule what is wise or good. Follies and nonsense, whims and inconsistencies *do* divert me, I own, and I laugh at them when I can.—But these, I suppose, are precisely what you are without." (pp 57)

Darcy protests that his failings are, not of understanding, but of temper:

"... My temper would perhaps be called resentful.—My good opinion once lost is lost for ever."

"*That* is a failing indeed!" cried Elizabeth. "Implacable resentment is a shade in a character. You have chosen your fault well.—I really cannot *laugh* at it. You are safe from me."

"There is, I believe, in every disposition a tendency to some particular evil, a natural defect, which not even the best education can overcome."

"And *your* defect is a propensity to hate every body." (pp 58)

Whether Elizabeth is teasing him about his silence at dancing (pp 271), or, in Lady Catherine's drawing room, explaining her lack of skill at the piano to refute Darcy's claim of having no talent for sociability:

"My fingers," said Elizabeth, "do not move over this instrument in the masterly manner which I see so many women's do. They have not the same force or rapidity, and do not produce the same expression. But then I have always supposed it to be my own fault—because I would not take the trouble of practising ..." (pp 175)

she draws him out in the only ways in which he can be drawn out at all, by a challenging indirection just short of impudence, by the appeal of an intelligence as free and aware as that on which he prides himself, by the penetration of a wit which makes its own rules without breaking any significant ones, which even establishes its priority over simple truth:

"You mean to frighten me, Mr. Darcy, by coming in all this state to hear me? But I will not be alarmed...."

"I shall not say that you are mistaken," he replied, "because you could not really believe me to entertain any design of alarming you; and I have had the pleasure of your acquaintance long enough to know that you find great enjoyment in occasionally professing opinions which in fact are not your own." (pp 174)

If Darcy, finally sounded and known, hardly differs from the stiff-jointed Burneyan aristocratic hero, except as Darcy is provided with a somewhat more explicit personality, the fault is not Elizabeth's, but her author's. Elizabeth has learned what can be learned about him; she has even learned, with Miss Bingley, that Darcy is not to be laughed at—not, at least, in the matter of his influence over Bingley:

> Elizabeth longed to observe that Mr. Bingley had been a most delightful friend; so easily guided that his worth was invaluable; but she checked herself. She remembered that he had yet to learn to be laught at, and it was rather too early to begin. (pp 371)

In the process of interpretation, moreover—with its deflections, its spurious evidence, its shocks of awareness and repentance—she has brought to a focus at last all the scattered principles which her overconfidence and lack of experience continually obliged her to underestimate, forget or abandon.

She never gives up her first principle: to separate the simple personality from the complex, and to concentrate her attention and interest on the latter. Her point of reference is always the complex individual, the individual aware and capable of choice. Her own pride is in her freedom, to observe, to analyze, to choose; her continual mistake is to forget that, even for her, there is only one area of choice—marriage—and that this choice is subject to all the powerful and numbing pressures of an acquisitive society.

Under pressure, Charlotte denies her choice while making it, degrades herself to the level of a fool in marrying one. Under pressure, Wickham squanders his choice in any opportunity, however unscrupulous and desperate, to make his fortune. Under pressure, Mr. Bennet was led to believe that choice was easy, and to marry a woman who made no demands upon his awareness. And under pressure, Darcy jeopardizes his freedom by believing that, for the man of breeding, choice is not individual but ancestral, narrowly predetermined by rank and family. The simple people—Mrs. Bennet, Lydia, Mr. Collins, Lady Catherine, Jane, Bingley—do not choose at all; they are led, largely unaware; we cannot even submit them to a moral judgment: and the irony, as Elizabeth recognizes about all of them except Jane, is in their illusion of choice, their assumption of will. The complex do, on the other hand, choose; yet it takes a long time for Elizabeth to recognize that choice is never unalloyed, and may indeed be nullified altogether.

The central fact for Elizabeth remains the power of choice. In spite of social pressures, in spite of the misunderstandings and the obstacles to awareness that cut off and confuse the individual, in spite of the individual's repeated failures, the power of choice is all that distinguishes him as a being who acts and who may be judged. There are, certainly, limitations upon his choice, the limitations of an imposed prudence, of living within a social frame in which material comfort is an article of prestige and a sign of moral well-being: since even Elizabeth, though an acute and critical observer, is no rebel, she cannot contemplate the possibility of happiness outside her given social frame. The author is, likewise, pointedly ironic in contrasting Elizabeth's charitable allowances, first for Wickham, and then for Colonel Fitzwilliam, an "Earl's younger son," (pp 184) when her relative poverty obliges them to regard her as ineligible. Yet the irony does not go so far as to invalidate choice or distinctions in choice. Fitzwilliam, no rebel, is prudent in the hope that both prudence and inclination may be satisfied together in the future; but Wickham's "prudence," rather than merely limiting his choice, has deprived him of it entirely. In Elizabeth's feeling, upon touring Darcy's estate, "that to be mistress of Pemberley might be something!" (pp 245) the irony is circumscribed with an equal clarity: Darcy gains by being a rich man with a magnificent estate; but Pemberley is an expression of Darcy's taste as well as of his wealth and rank, and the image of Pemberley cannot divert Elizabeth from her primary concern with Darcy's motives and the meaning of his façade. Pemberley with Mr. Collins, or even with Bingley, would not do at all.

The focus is upon the complex individual; the only quality that distinguishes him from his setting, from the forms of courtship and marriage in an acquisitive society, which otherwise standardize and absorb him, is also his unique function—choice. What Elizabeth must choose, within the bounds set by prudence, is an individual equally complex, and undefeated by his social role. The complex individual is, after all, isolated by his freedom, and must be seen so at the end; for even if pressures from without, from the social system and the social class, deflect or overwhelm him, they demonstrate not that he is indistinguishable from his social role, but that he is vulnerable to it. The fact of choice makes him stand, finally, alone, to judge or be judged.

In *Pride and Prejudice*, Jane Austen's irony has developed into an instrument of discrimination between the people who are simple reproductions of their social type and the people with individuality and will, between the unaware and the aware. The defensive—and destructive—

weapon of *Northanger Abbey* and *Sense and Sensibility* has here been adapted directly to the theme through the personality of Elizabeth Bennet, who reflects and illustrates her author's vision without ever becoming (except in her malice toward Lydia) merely her author's advocate. The irony is internal, it does not take disturbing tangents toward the author's need for self-vindication: even self-defensive, it is internal and consistent—Mr. Bennet's shying from the consequences of his disastrous mistake, Elizabeth's provocative parrying of Darcy. And if this new control over her irony permits Jane Austen only to be more clever (and not particularly more persuasive) in avoiding a commitment, by Elizabeth in love, for example:

> "... Will you tell me how long you have loved him?"
> "It has been coming on so gradually, that I hardly know when it began. But I believe it must date from my first seeing his beautiful grounds at Pemberley."
> Another intreaty that she would be serious, however, produced the desired effect; and she soon satisfied Jane by her solemn assurances of attachment. (pp 373)

the characteristic block of Jane Austen's against direct emotional expression has occasion only very rarely to operate in *Pride and Prejudice*: above all, in the talk and atmosphere of Darcy's proposals, and in his letter—passages which most nearly reproduce the flat or melodramatic textures of *Cecilia*, without any lift of emotion or of irony either. The moment is soon over; and irony is not only back, but back at its proper task of discrimination.

In *Pride and Prejudice*, the flaw of an irrelevant defensiveness has almost vanished; and the flaw of a too obvious personal withdrawal before a moral or emotional issue, as with Lydia and Darcy, is not obtrusive enough, to annul or seriously damage the sustained and organizing power of Jane Austen's irony. Irony here rejects chiefly to discover and illuminate; and, though its setting is the same stratified, materialistic, and severely regulated society, its new text and discovery—its new character, in fact, whom Jane Austen has hitherto allowed only herself to impersonate—is the free individual.

NOTES

1. One is tempted to believe that Henry Austen, though he was Jane's "favourite brother" (W. and R. A. Austen-Leigh, *Jane Austen: Her Life and Letters*, London, 1913, p. 48), may have provided her with a model for at least Mr. Collins' style in letters. On the acquittal of Warren Hastings (godfather of Henry's cousin Eliza), Henry wrote to Hastings: "Permit me ... to congratulate my country and myself as an Englishman; for

right dear to every Englishman must it be to behold the issue of a combat where fortes of judicature threatened to annihilate the essence of justice." (*Ibid.*, 79.) And he wrote to the publisher John Murray concerning *Emma*: "... The politeness and perspicuity of your letter equally claim my earliest exertion.... Though I venture to differ occasionally from your critique yet I assure you the quantum of your commendation rather exceeds than fall short of the author's expectation and my own...." (*Ibid.*, 310.)

2. M. Lascelles, *Jane Austen and Her Art*, Oxford, 1939, 72f.

3. She quite freely exercised her irony on sex, not only in her *juvenilia*, but as an adult in her letters also (for a few examples in her letters, see p. 2, this study). Publication—and the anticipation of social pressure—inhibited the response entirely; and she had no other defense against the potential involvement of sex except the conventional response of disapproval or silence.

4. "In *Pride and Prejudice*, particularly in the presentation of Darcy's character, Jane Austen shows an almost Jamesian awareness of the multiple ways of reading a man's behaviour. She conveys her sense of the possibility of very different interpretations of the 'same' action, as James often does, through dialogues which look trivial and which are extremely ambiguous. At the same time they are not merely confusing because Jane Austen defines so precisely the ironic implications of what is said and because she gradually limits the possibilities with which the reader is to be most concerned." R. A. Brower, "The Controlling Hand: Jane Austen and 'Pride and Prejudice,'" *Scrutiny*, XIII (September, 1945), 99. This essay brilliantly analyzes the process by means of which Elizabeth comes to an understanding of Darcy.

5. Q. D. Leavis, "A Critical Theory of Jane Austen's Writings," *Scrutiny*, X (June, 1941), 71ff.

6. R. A. Brower, *op. cit.*, 108ff.

ANDREW H. WRIGHT

Elizabeth Bennet

i. Elizabeth Bennet

At first glance, perhaps, the two elder Bennet sisters may seem to vie with each other for primacy in *Pride and Prejudice*; but Elizabeth is definitely the heroine: not only does she explicitly represent one of the words of the title of the story; she also quite thoroughly dominates the action—and, by comparison, Jane is a shadowy accessory. The relationship of Miss Bennet to Bingley, which parallels that of Elizabeth and Darcy, is treated much less fully, partly because it is much simpler, but partly because it is intended to be a comment on that of her younger sister and the proud man from Derbyshire. Yet Jane throughout the book has the unqualified approbation of Elizabeth, author, and reader—though we may, with Elizabeth, wish to speak to her with the following affectionate mock-exasperation:

> 'My dear Jane! ... you are too good. Your sweetness and disinterestedness are really angelic; I do not know what to say to you. I feel as if I had never done you justice, or loved you as you deserve.'[1]

Indeed it is because of—not despite—her perfection that we must reject Jane as the heroine: the author's concern is with the complexity, the

From *Jane Austen's Novels: A Study in Structure.* ©1953 by Chatto & Windus.

interrelationship, of good and bad—the mixture which cannot be unmixed. Jane is a simple character, but '"intricate characters are the *most* amusing"',[2] and Jane, like Bingley, is not intricate: she is heroic but minor—she is not a heroine. 'I must confess,' writes Jane Austen of Elizabeth Bennet, 'that I think her as delightful a creature as ever appeared in print, and how I shall be able to tolerate those who do not like *her* at least I do not know.'[3]

To say that Darcy is proud and Elizabeth prejudiced is to tell but half the story. Pride and prejudice are faults; but they are also the necessary defects of desirable merits: self-respect and intelligence. Moreover, the novel makes clear the fact that Darcy's pride leads to prejudice and Elizabeth's prejudice stems from a pride in her own perceptions. So the ironic theme of the book might be said to centre on the dangers of intellectual complexity. Jane Bennet and Bingley are never exposed to these dangers; they are not sufficiently profound. But the hero and the heroine, because of their deep percipience, are, ironically, subject to failures of perception. Elizabeth has good reason to credit herself with the ability to discern people and situations extraordinarily well: she understands her family perfectly, knows William Collins from the first letter he writes, comprehends the merits and deficiencies of the Bingleys almost at once, appreciates Lady Catherine de Bourgh at first meeting. Her failures are with 'intricate' people who moreover stand in a relationship of great intimacy to her: Charlotte Lucas, George Wickham, Fitzwilliam Darcy. And the book is given an added dimension because it shows that intimacy blurs perceptions: intelligence fails if there is insufficient distance between mind and object.

Charlotte Lucas is 'a sensible, intelligent young woman, about twenty-seven ... Elizabeth's intimate friend'.[4] But we very soon know that in an important respect she differs from Elizabeth—though Elizabeth herself does not know this fact. When, very early in the first volume, they discuss the possibility of an attachment between Jane and Bingley, Charlotte says Jane should make some efforts in this direction; but Elizabeth reminds her friend that Miss Bennet hardly knows him. This, however, does not deter Charlotte:

> 'I wish Jane success with all my heart; and if she were married to him tomorrow, I should think she had as good a chance of happiness, as if she were to be studying his character for a twelvemonth. Happiness in marriage is entirely a matter of chance. If the dispositions of the parties are ever so well known to each other, or ever so similar before-hand, it does not advance their felicity in the least. They always continue to grow sufficiently unlike afterwards to have their share of vexation; and

it is better to know as little as possible of the defects of the person with whom you are to pass your life.'[5]

But Elizabeth does not believe this statement:

> 'You make me laugh, Charlotte; but it is not sound. You know it is not sound, and that you would never act in this way yourself.'[6]

Why does she refuse to believe Charlotte (who will soon demonstrate quite shockingly that she means every word she says on the subject of marriage)? It is because a natural kindness and affection have blinded Elizabeth to the demerits of her friend; it is because, in the nature of things, involvement (which is so necessary and desirable, in Austenian terms) carries with it the inevitable consequence of obscuring the marvellous clarity and depth of understanding so necessary to success in personal association.

There is no evidence that Charlotte misunderstands William Collins, but there is much to show that Elizabeth does comprehend him perfectly. '"Can he be a sensible man, sir?"'[7] she asks her father rhetorically after hearing the orotund phrases of the clergyman's letter. Nor is she wrong. At the Netherfield Ball, after dancing with him twice, 'the moment of her release from him was exstacy',[8] but she derives some consolation in discussing his demerits with Charlotte. The next morning he proposes marriage to Elizabeth ('"And now nothing remains for me but to assure you in the most animated language of the violence of my affection"'),[9] and of course she refuses him summarily. Then she is flabbergasted to learn that Charlotte has accepted Mr. Collins's subsequent proposal of marriage to her.

> She had always felt that Charlotte's opinion of matrimony was not exactly like her own, but she could not have supposed it possible that when called into action, she would have sacrificed every better feeling to worldly advantage. Charlotte the wife of Mr. Collins, was a most humiliating picture![10]

And now, for the first time, she begins to see Charlotte as she really is: and 'felt persuaded that no real confidence could ever subsist between them again'.[11] Elizabeth has learned something from this experience, as is demonstrated in her conversation with Jane not long afterwards:

> 'Do not be afraid of my running into any excess, of my encroaching on your privilege of universal good will. You need

not. There are few people whom I really love, and still fewer of whom I think well. The more I see of the world, the more am I dissatisfied with it; and every day confirms my belief of the inconsistency of all human characters, and of the little dependence that can be placed on the appearance of either merit or sense. I have met with two instances lately; one I will not mention [it is Bingley's 'want of proper resolution']; the other is Charlotte's marriage. It is unaccountable! In every view it is unaccountable!'[12]

Elizabeth does not give Darcy a chance—or rather she does not give herself a chance to know how she really feels about him. The famous first encounter is comically disastrous; it occurs at the assembly where Darcy says to Bingley of Elizabeth, who is sitting down: '"She is tolerable; but not handsome enough to tempt *me*; and I am in no humour at present to give consequence to young ladies who are slighted by other men"'. And as a natural result, 'Elizabeth remained with no very cordial feelings towards him'.[13]

But at Netherfield, where she has gone to nurse the ailing Jane, Elizabeth makes her extraordinary and attractive personality felt—so strongly that Mrs. Hurst and Miss Bingley take an immediate dislike to her; so strongly that she finds Darcy staring at her.

> She hardly knew how to suppose that she could be an object of admiration to so great a man; and yet that he should look at her because he disliked her, was still more strange. She could only imagine however at last, that she drew his notice because there was a something about her more wrong and reprehensible, according to his ideas of right, than in any other person present. The supposition did not pain her. She liked him too little to care for his approbation.[14]

However, when she refuses to dance with him and says, '"despise me if you dare"', he replies in unmistakable accents, '"Indeed I do not dare"'.[15]

But the insult of the Ball fresh in her mind, she does not like him; she is even willing to overweigh the negative evidence, which now presents itself first from Darcy himself, then from the plausible and attractive Wickham. In the conversation at Netherfield, during which Elizabeth makes her well-known remark, that '"I hope I never ridicule what is wise and good"', she finds from Darcy that '"My good opinion once lost is lost for ever"'[16]—a chilling comment which she acknowledges to be a defect, but not a laughable one.

Then she meets Wickham, and finding him charming, very easily believes his allegations that Darcy has behaved abominably, that the latter has cast the young lieutenant from a promised living in the church, that in fact both Darcy and his sister suffer from very excessive pride. Elizabeth is vexed and even angry when Wickham fails to appear at the Netherfield Ball, again not trying to suppose that there may be something to be said on Darcy's side. Even so, there are signs that she willy-nilly succumbs to his charms—in the pertness of her conversation while they are dancing:

'It is *your* turn to say something now, Mr. Darcy.—*I* talked about the dance, and *you* ought to make some kind of remark on the size of the room, or the number of couples.'

He smiled, and assured her that whatever she wished him to say should be said.

'Very well.—That reply will do for the present.—Perhaps by and by I may observe that private balls are much pleasanter than public ones.—But *now* we may be silent.'

'Do you talk by rule then, while you are dancing?'

'Sometimes. One must speak a little, you know. It would look odd to be entirely silent for half an hour together, and yet for the advantage of some, conversation ought to be so arranged as that they may have the trouble of saying as little as possible.'

'Are you consulting your own feelings in the present case, or do you imagine that you are gratifying mine?'

'Both,' replied Elizabeth archly; 'for I have always seen a great similarity in the turn of our minds.—We are each of an unsocial, taciturn disposition, unwilling to speak, unless we expect to say something that will amaze the whole room, and be handed down to posterity with all the éclat of a proverb.'[17]

However, when she questions him about Wickham, he keeps silent—nor can she understand him, as she readily admits before their dance is finished. It is an artful irony of Jane Austen's that Miss Bingley immediately thereafter tells her that Wickham is entirely in the wrong, and Darcy in the right, in the breach between the two men. Elizabeth disbelieves her for two reasons: first, because she has correctly sized Miss Bingley up as an entirely unreliable source of information; and second, perhaps, because she wants to dislike Darcy in order to avoid any entanglement which will cost her her freedom. Nevertheless, she feels mortified when she realizes that Darcy is overhearing Mrs. Bennet boast that Jane and Bingley will soon be engaged.

In the second volume, the relationship of Darcy and Elizabeth is resumed in Kent, at Rosings and at Hunsford, the parsonage to which William Collins has taken his new wife. Everything is unpropitious, so far as Elizabeth herself is concerned: she has agreed to visit Charlotte only because of the memory of their close friendship—'all the comfort of intimacy was over'.[18] Mr. Collins is just as senseless as ever; Miss de Bourgh is '"sickly and cross.—Yes, she will do for him [Darcy] very well. She will make him a very proper wife"';[19] and Lady Catherine is quite as insufferable as Wickham has promised. Amongst all these displeasing people comes Darcy, who adds to her annoyance by looking confused when she asks whether he has seen Jane in London (for she suspects that he has warned Bingley off her); and, despite his calls at the parsonage and their 'chance' encounters in Rosings Park, her prejudice against him increases, for she finds apparent corroboration of her suspicions in the conversation with Colonel Fitzwilliam, during which he recounts the fact that Darcy has told him of saving an intimate friend recently from a very imprudent marriage.

And so she is bowled over when Darcy tells her he loves her:

> 'In vain have I struggled. It will not do. My feelings will not be repressed. You must allow me to tell you how ardently I admire and love you.'[20]

But she is more than astonished: she is gradually angered by the tone and implication of his remarks:

> His sense of her inferiority—of its being a degradation—of the family obstacles which judgment had always opposed to inclination, were dwelt on with a warmth which seemed due to the consequence he was wounding, but was very unlikely to recommend his suit.[21]

So—and not without recrimination for '"ruining, perhaps for ever, the happiness of a most beloved sister"' and for his ill—treatment of Wickham-she refuses and dismisses the proud Mr. Fitzwilliam Darcy.

But this is not the end; indeed it is only the beginning of Elizabeth's very gradually successful efforts to know herself thoroughly. The next day she is handed Darcy's justly famous letter, written in proud tones and offering some new light not only on the Jane–Bingley business but upon the supposed unfairness to Wickham's claims. As to the first, Darcy says he thought Jane seemed not much attracted to Bingley, whereas Bingley was strongly attached to Jane; and furthermore, Darcy acknowledges an objection to Miss Bennet's family—two considerations which led him both to conceal from Bingley the fact of Jane's presence in London and to persuade his friend that she did not feel much affection for him. As for Wickham, the young Meryton militiaman resigned all claim to a living, in return for which Darcy gave him £3000 to study law. Three years later, the incumbent of the living, the claim to which Wickham had resigned, died; and Wickham, having lived a dissipated and extravagant life in London, sought it. Darcy refused, and Wickham abused him violently; but, more than that, sought Georgiana Darcy out, and persuaded her to elope with him—though the plot was prevented.

Elizabeth reads the letter with great astonishment and—at first—with little comprehension. She is, however, even more completely stunned by the account of Wickham, and her first impression is to disbelieve Darcy on that score too. But then, in reflecting on Wickham's behaviour at Meryton (especially with regard to his sudden betrothal to the rich Miss King), she is inclined to think it very probable that Darcy is telling the truth after all.

> She grew absolutely ashamed of herself.—Of neither Darcy nor Wickham could she think, without feeling that she had been blind, partial, prejudiced, absurd.
>
> 'How despicably have I acted!' she cried.—'I, who have prided myself on my discernment!—I, who have valued myself on my abilities! who have often disdained the generous candour of my sister, and gratified my vanity, in useless or blameable distrust.— How humiliating is this discovery! Yet, how just a humiliation!— Had I been in love, I could not have been more wretchedly blind.'[22]

In this dramatic moment of self-revelation she has the honesty to see that there may be some justice in what Darcy has said about Jane, for 'she felt that Jane's feelings, though fervent, were little displayed, and that there was a constant complacency in her air and manner, not often united with great sensibility'.[23] She has learned much from the letter, very much indeed; but Jane Austen is too perceptive a reader of character to suppose that all comes clear at once: it is by a marvellous irony that Elizabeth is made to reflect, '"Had I been in love, I could not have been more wretchedly blind"'; nor, though Elizabeth does know herself henceforth much better, does she yet know herself completely.

It is even true that her attitude toward the letter is to undergo a further change—when she has had a better chance to think of it with some coolness. She almost completely reverses her first excited opinion:

His attachment excited gratitude, his general character respect; but she could not approve him; nor could she for a moment repent her refusal, or feel the slightest inclination ever to see him again. In her own past behaviour, there was a constant source of vexation and regret; and in the unhappy defects of her family a subject of yet heavier chagrin.[24]

So, in a half-way stage in her thinking and feeling, she yet refuses to look squarely at the consequences of a commitment to Darcy; she still rebels against involvement. Nevertheless, her uncompromising honesty causes her to realize that there is much justice in his views about her family—all of them but Jane.

Elizabeth does not see Darcy again until the unexpected encounter at Pemberley, to which she has gone with the Gardiners on vacation. Presumably she has had an opportunity to absorb the lesson of the letter; at least she is now more willing to believe good things about him—from Mrs. Reynolds, for instance, who is the housekeeper of Pemberley and has only warm praise for her master, whom she has known since he was four years old—'"and he was always the sweetest-tempered, most generous-hearted, boy in the world"'.[25]

Already softened towards Darcy by such unstinted praise, she meets him by chance (he has returned home a day early) and finds him more civil to her than ever before, unfailingly kind to the Gardiners, and urgently desirous to '"introduce my sister to your acquaintance"'.[26] She likes Georgiana, and after the meeting takes occasion to reflect on her own not very clear feelings:

> She certainly did not hate him. No; hatred had vanished long ago, and she had almost as long been ashamed of ever feeling a dislike against him, that could be so called. The respect created by the conviction of his valuable qualities, though at first unwillingly admitted, had for some time ceased to be repugnant to her feelings; and it was now heightened into somewhat of a friendlier nature, by the testimony so highly in his favour, and bringing forward his disposition in so amiable a light, which yesterday had produced. But above all, above respect and esteem, there was a motive within her of good will which could not be overlooked. It was gratitude.—Gratitude, not merely for having once loved her, but for loving her still well enough, to forgive all the petulance and acrimony of her manner in rejecting him, and all the unjust accusations accompanying her rejection.... She respected, she

esteemed, she was grateful to him, she felt a real interest in his welfare; and she only wanted to know how far she wished that welfare to depend upon herself, and how far it would be for the happiness of both that she should employ the power, which her fancy told her she still possessed, of bringing on the renewal of his addresses.[27]

It is in the anti-climax of the first paragraph quoted (respect, esteem—gratitude) that Jane Austen is able to indicate something of the complexity of Elizabeth's mind, and the entire passage shows the continued resistance which she is still putting up against the release of her own strong feelings.

A crisis is called for, something which will break the placidity of her reflections; and this comes in the stunning news that Lydia Bennet and George Wickham have eloped; in her anguish Elizabeth blurts the story out to Darcy, who is most consolatory and kind. Nevertheless, when she leaves Derbyshire—as now she must, hurriedly—she is certain she will never see him again. She feels genuine regret on departure: and her feelings have ascended to another level.

Now the focus of attention shifts from Darcy and Elizabeth to Lydia and the conscienceless militia officer—the search for them in London, the self-recriminations of Mr. Bennet, the marriage agreed upon. Elizabeth has little leisure to reflect on her own feelings for several weeks. Then she begins to regret telling Darcy about the elopement, for now that Lydia and Wickham are to be married, she feels that the first tawdry adventure might have been concealed from him, who would so strenuously disapprove—though no doubt he would not under any circumstances ally himself to a family connected in any way with the despicable Wickham.

> She began now to comprehend that he [Darcy] was exactly the man, who, in disposition and talents, would most suit her. His understanding and temper, though unlike her own, would have answered all her wishes. It was an union that must have been to the advantage of both; by her ease and liveliness, his mind might have been softened, his manners improved, and from his judgment, information, and knowledge of the world, she must have received benefit of greater importance.[28]

But now, she thinks, it is too late: such an alliance can never be—until she discovers that it has been Darcy who has been mainly instrumental in arranging the marriage between Lydia and Wickham, through motives which she must interpret in but one way: 'Her heart did whisper, that he had done it for her'.[29] But she still cannot quite believe that he would ever consent to be the brother-in-law of Wickham, even for her. Nevertheless, she refuses—with keen disdain—to promise Lady Catherine de Bourgh not to accept a proposal of marriage from Darcy: an interview which, as Darcy says, '"taught me to hope ... as I had scarcely ever allowed myself to hope before"'.[30] And so they are betrothed, at last. But why has it been so much easier for her to like George Wickham? It is certainly true that, on their first meeting, he is much more polite than Darcy; his façade is much smoother, and his wit just as sharp. Elizabeth herself says, '"I have courted prepossession and ignorance ..."'. But there is a further reason, that she feels no danger of a permanent attachment to him; and for this second reason, she yields all too willingly to the belief that Darcy is what Wickham says he is.

She deceives herself Mrs. Gardiner, who is much more perceptive in this matter than her niece, warns Elizabeth not to fall in love with the lieutenant. But Elizabeth promises only to go slowly. Nevertheless (and this, it seems to me, proves my second point) she feels not a single pang of regret when Wickham announces his engagement to Miss King, the girl with a dowry of £10,000. As she writes to her aunt,

> 'I am now convinced ... that I have never been much in love; for had I really experienced that pure and elevating passion, I should at present detest his very name, and wish him all manner of evil. But my feelings are not only cordial towards him; they are even impartial towards Miss King.... There can be no love in all this.'[31]

And she is right: so she can afford herself the luxury of deciding, before leaving for Kent, that Wickham 'must always be her model of the amiable and pleasing';[32] she can (or so she thinks) indulge herself in the imperception of denying to Mrs. Gardiner that Wickham's attachment discloses his mercenary motives.

The profundity of her mortification at knowing the truth about him comes, then, not merely from the knowledge that her perceptions, on which she has prided herself, have been beclouded by prejudice, but from the deeper reason that her relationship to him, because it has not engaged her much, has been able to afford the luxury of quasi-intimacy. Against clarity, in *Pride and Prejudice*, involvement is set: both are desirable, but each, ironically, works against the other—and the reader cannot believe that the marriage of Darcy and Elizabeth, however happy or beneficial, will ever quite close the breach between these two opposites.

ii. *Fitzwilliam Darcy and George Wickham*

In *Pride and Prejudice*, hero and villain have prominent, interesting, and convincing parts. Each is present throughout the novel, both attract the heroine, and both receive the marital fates which they deserve. Elizabeth Bennet is a complicated and penetrating heroine; the two men with whom she associates herself romantically must also be intricate and intelligent.

If (as we have shown) Elizabeth's prejudices are views in which she takes pride, so ought it be said that Darcy's pride leads to prejudice. But even this is an over-simplification: his austerity of manner, as we learn from his housekeeper at Pemberley, stems partly from an inordinate shyness. It is impossible, however, to explain away his famous remark about Elizabeth ('"... tolerable; but not handsome enough to tempt *me* ..."' [33]) on the grounds of diffidence alone—nor, indeed, the statement that '"My good opinion once lost is lost for ever"', [34] nor the first proposal to Elizabeth; nor his subsequent explanatory letter. He is a proud man.

One way in which Jane Austen delineates his character is through his relationship with Bingley. [35] It is partly through this friendship that a certain completeness is given to Darcy's character. Although we are struck, at the very beginning of the book, with Darcy's rudeness and with his pride, we may overlook the solidity of temperament implied in his affection for Bingley.

Despite his early bad impression of Elizabeth, he is soon constrained to like her better: for, ironically, the heroine by behaving disdainfully to him, does just what is necessary to captivate him. Thus at Sir William Lucas's party, her refusal to dance with him only sets him to thinking of her attractiveness; her piquancy at Netherfield leads to the famous conversation in which Elizabeth, while acknowledging that '"I dearly love a laugh"', insists that '"I hope I never ridicule what is wise or good"'. [36]—and from there to Darcy's increased awareness of 'the danger of paying Elizabeth too much attention'. [37]

The next appearance of Darcy comes when Elizabeth is visiting Hunsford, where she has gone to fulfil an unwilling promise of spending some time with Charlotte and William Collins. Besides the unfortunate first impression which the squire of Pemberley has made, there is now the insistent and plausible evidence against his character which Wickham has adduced. Elizabeth cannot understand the why of Darcy's repeated calls at the parsonage, nor can she comprehend the astonishing regularity of their 'unexpected' encounters in the Park. And she is stunned by his declaration of love, and proposal of marriage (critics who censure Jane Austen for an alleged lack of emotion should re-read this chapter).

Elizabeth's astonishment was beyond expression. She stared, coloured, doubted, and was silent. This he considered sufficient encouragement, and the avowal of all that he felt and had long felt for her, immediately followed. He spoke well, but there were feelings besides those of the heart to be detailed, and he was not more eloquent on the subject of tenderness than of pride. His sense of her inferiority—of its being a degradation—of the family obstacles which judgment had always opposed to inclination, were dwelt on with a warmth which seemed due to the consequence he was wounding, but was very unlikely to recommend his suit.

In spite of her deeply-rooted dislike, she could not be insensible to the compliment of such a man's affection, and though her intentions did not vary for an instant, she was at first sorry for the pain he was to receive; till, roused to resentment by his subsequent language, she lost all compassion in anger. She tried, however, to compose herself to answer him with patience, when he should have done. He concluded with representing to her the strength of that attachment which, in spite of all his endeavours, he had found impossible to conquer; and with expressing his hope that it would now be rewarded by her acceptance of his hand. As he said this, she could easily see that he had no doubt of a favourable answer. He *spoke* of apprehension and anxiety, but his countenance expressed real security. Such a circumstance could only exasperate farther....[38]

Elizabeth's angry refusal marks the beginning of the great change in Darcy: he is humbled, though there is but one sentence in the letter which he writes to her, to indicate that he has been mollified: 'I will only add, God bless you'.[39]

Now he disappears from view, until Elizabeth, together with the Gardiners, visits Pemberley. Here Elizabeth's opinion of him softens slightly. And in fact there are a series of circumstances which disclose him to be a much more human person than she has previously thought him.

But this is not all: he behaves heroically, for he hastens to London, seeks out Lydia and Wickham, makes a provision for them, and all but drags them to the altar. These things he does not out of admiration for the eloped couple, but out of love for Elizabeth—which, however, he does not again bring himself to declare, until after Lady Catherine de Bourgh's interview with Elizabeth. This '"taught me to hope"',[40] and so he is able to propose again, thus time with success.

George Wickham is at once the most plausible and the most villainous of Jane Austen's anti-heroes: he is handsome, persuasive, personable; disingenuous, calculating, and dishonourable. His appearance in the story comes just as Elizabeth, smarting from Darcy's disapprobation, willingly abrogates her critical faculties in favour of a pleasant countenance and manner. She all too readily believes the militia lieutenant's defamation of Darcy's character—though we, the readers, are expected to take note of the warning signals which Elizabeth ignores. In the first place, Jane Bennet declares:

> 'It is impossible. No man of common humanity, no man who had any value for his character, could be capable of it. Can his most intimate friends be so excessively deceived in him? Oh! no.'[41]

In the second place, Miss Bingley plainly warns Elizabeth about Wickham, and indicates his relationship to Darcy:

> 'So, Miss Eliza, I hear you are quite delighted with George Wickham!—Your sister has been talking to me about him, and asking me a thousand questions; and I find that the young man forgot to tell you, among his other communications, that he was the son of old Wickham, the late Mr. Darcy's steward. Let me recommend you, however, as a friend, not to give implicit confidence to all his assertions; for as to Mr. Darcy's using him ill, it is perfectly false; for, on the contrary, he has been always remarkably kind to him, though George Wickham has treated Mr. Darcy in a most infamous manner.'[42]

Jane Austen does not stack the cards, but she is not averse to throwing sand in her readers' eyes: both Jane and Miss Bingley are, as it happens, perfectly correct here; but Elizabeth does not believe either of them, for Jane's unwillingness ever to be unkind does sometimes blind her to people's faults, and Caroline Bingley's careless, insensitive stupidity often leads to complete misapprehension.

So Elizabeth continues to think well of Wickham, and ill of Darcy— even when the former announces his engagement to Miss King, whose dowry is £10,000. This time the heroine ignores the testimony—or rather, the conjecture—of one whose judgment she has always trusted: her aunt, Mrs. Gardiner.

> 'If [says Mrs. Gardiner] you will only tell me what sort of girl Miss King is, I shall know what to think.'

'She is a very good kind of girl, I believe. I know no harm of her.'

'But he paid her not the smallest attention, till her grandfather's death made her mistress of this fortune.'

'No—why should he? If it was not allowable for him to gain my affections, because I had no money, what occasion could there be for making love to a girl whom he did not care about, and who was equally poor?'

'But there seems indelicacy in directing his attentions towards her, so soon after this event.'

'A man in distressed circumstances has not time for all those elegant decorums which other people may observe. If *she* does not object to it, why should *we?*'

'*Her* not objecting, does not justify *him*. It only shews her being deficient in something herself—sense or feeling.'

'Well,' cried Elizabeth, 'have it as you choose. *He* shall be mercenary, and *she* shall be foolish.'[43]

Although she is still unbelieving, however, Elizabeth will remember the doubts which she quashed in her early enthusiasm for Wickham—which, after all, arose partly out of her disdain for Darcy. Her big change dates from her second reading of Darcy's letter; then she excoriates herself for her blindness—though she cannot be expected to have guessed the full measure of Wickham's evil: his complete misrepresentation of Darcy, his planned elopement with Georgiana, his dissipated existence in London.

He gets the fate which he deserves: he marries Lydia, after causing great distress to everyone concerned, except the foolish young girl herself. But, true to his character, he does not lose an ounce of aplomb. On this visit to Longbourn:

his manners were always so pleasing, that had his character and his marriage been exactly what they ought, his smiles and his easy address, while he claimed their relationship, would have delighted them all. Elizabeth had not before believed him quite equal to such assurance; but she sat down, resolving within herself, to draw no limits in future to the impudence of an impudent man.[44]

Darcy and Wickham are virtually perfect agents of illusionment and thus of the ironic theme, in *Pride and Prejudice*. Elizabeth is put off by Darcy's rudeness; her vanity is piqued: but she allows herself to overemphasize his pride, because she comes so dangerously near to involvement with him. She credits Wickham's testimony because it is congenial to her—she misapprehends him because she wants to avoid entanglement with Darcy, while in fact there is nothing to fear from her relationship to Wickham: she is essentially indifferent to him. Thus her clarity of perception, which she genuinely possesses, contains the germs of its own myopia—ironically, when engagement of her affections is threatened.

NOTES

1. *Pride and Prejudice*, pp. 134, 135.
2. *Pride and Prejudice*, p. 42.
3. *Letters*, II, 297 (to Cassandra Austen, 29 January 1813).
4. *Pride and Prejudice*, p. 18.
5. *Ibid.*, p. 23.
6. *Ibid.*, p. 23.
7. *Pride and Prejudice*, p. 64.
8. *Ibid.*, p. 90.
9. *Ibid.*, p. 106.
10. *Ibid.*, p. 125.
11. *Ibid.*, p. 128.
12. *Ibid.*, p. 135.
13. *Ibid.*, p. 12.
14. *Ibid.*, p. 51.
15. *Ibid.*, p. 52.
16. *Pride and Prejudice*, pp. 57, 58.
17. *Ibid.*, p. 91.
18. *Ibid.*, p. 146.
19. *Ibid.*, p. 158.
20. *Pride and Prejudice*, p. 189.
21. *Ibid.*, p. 189.
22. *Ibid.*, p. 208.
23. *Ibid.*, p. 208.
24. *Pride and Prejudice*, p. 212.
25. *Ibid.*, p. 249.
26. *Ibid.*, p. 256.
27. *Ibid.*, pp. 265, 266.
28. *Pride and Prejudice*, p. 312.
29. *Ibid.*, p. 326.
30. *Ibid.*, p. 367.
31. *Ibid.*, p. 150.
32. *Ibid.*, p. 152.
33. *Pride and Prejudice*, p. 12. This remark, however, does little more than show him to be out of humour. The reader should not make Elizabeth's mistake of judging him too hardly for it.
34. *Ibid.*, p. 58.

35. See above, p. 21.
36. *Pride and Prejudice*, p. 57.
37. *Ibid.*, p. 58.
38. *Pride and Prejudice*, p. 189.
39. *Ibid.*, p. 203.
40. *Ibid.*, p. 367.
41. *Ibid.*, p. 85.
42. *Ibid.*, p. 94.
43. *Pride and Prejudice*, p. 153.
44. *Ibid.*, p. 316.

C.S. LEWIS

A Note on Jane Austen

I begin by laying together four passages from the novels of Jane Austen.

1   Catherine was completely awakened ... Most grievously was she humbled. Most bitterly did she cry. It was not only with herself that she was sunk, but with Henry. Her folly, which now seemed even criminal, was all exposed to him, and he must despise her for ever. The liberty which her imagination had dared to take with the character of his father, would he ever forgive it? The absurdity of her curiosity and her fears, could they ever be forgotten? She hated herself more than she could express ... Nothing could be clearer than that it had been all a voluntary, self-created delusion, each trifle receiving importance from an imagination resolved on alarm, and everything forced to bend to one purpose by a mind which, before she entered the Abbey, had been craving to be frightened ... She saw that the infatuation had been created, the mischief settled, before her quitting Bath ... Her mind made up on these several points, and her resolution formed, of always judging and acting in future with the greatest good sense, she had nothing to do but forgive herself and be happier than ever.

Northanger Abbey, Cap. 25

From *Essays in Criticism* 4, no. 4 (October 1954). ©1954 by Oxford University Press.

2   'Oh! Elinor, you have made me hate myself forever. How
     barbarous have I been to you!—you, who have been my only
     comfort, who have borne with me in all my misery, who have
     seemed to be suffering only for me!' ... Marianne's courage soon
     failed her, in trying to converse upon a topic which always left her
     more dissatisfied with herself than ever, by the contrast it
     necessarily produced between Elinor's conduct and her own. She
     felt all the force of that comparison; but not as her sister had
     hoped, to urge her to exertion now; she felt it with all the pain of
     continual self-reproach, regretted most bitterly that she had
     never exerted herself before; but it brought only the torture of
     penitence, without the hope of amendment ... [Elinor later saw in
     Marianne] an apparent composure of mind which, in being the
     result, as she trusted, of serious reflection, must eventually lead
     her to contentment and cheerfulness ... 'My illness has made me
     think ... I considered the past: I saw in my own behaviour nothing
     but a series of imprudence towards myself, and want of kindness
     to others. I saw that my own feelings had prepared my sufferings,
     and that my want of fortitude under them had almost led me to
     the grave. My illness, I well knew, had been entirely brought on
     by myself, by such negligence of my own health as I felt even at
     the time to be wrong. Had I died, it would have been self-
     destruction. I wonder ... that the very eagerness of my desire to
     live, to have time for atonement to my God and to you all, did not
     kill me at once ... I cannot express my own abhorrence of myself.'
                                    Sense and Sensibility, Caps. 37, 38, 46

3   As to his real character, had information been in her power, she
     had never felt a wish of inquiring. His countenance, voice, and
     manner had established him at once in the possession of every
     virtue ... She perfectly remembered everything that had passed in
     conversation between Wickham and herself, in their first evening
     at Mr. Philip's ... She was *now* struck with the impropriety of such
     communications to a stranger, and wondered that it had escaped
     her before. She saw the indelicacy of putting himself forward as
     he had done, and the inconsistency of his professions with his
     conduct ... She grew absolutely ashamed of herself ... 'How
     despicably have I acted!' she cried; 'I, who have prided myself on
     my discernment! ... who have often disdained the generous
     candour of my sister, and gratified my vanity in useless or
     blamable distrust. How humiliating is this discovery! yet, how

just a humiliation! Had I been in love, I could not have been more wretchedly blind. But vanity, not love, has been my folly ... I have courted prepossession and ignorance, and driven reason away ... Till this moment I never knew myself.'

Pride and Prejudice, Cap. 36

4   Her own conduct, as well as her own heart, was before her in the same few minutes ... How improperly had she been acting by Harriet! How inconsiderate, how indelicate, how irrational, how unfeeling, had been her conduct! What blindness, what madness, had led her on! It struck her with dreadful force, and she was ready to give it every bad name in the world ... Every moment had brought a fresh surprise, and every surprise must be matter of humiliation to her. How to understand it all? How to understand the deceptions she had been thus practising on herself, and living under! The blunders, the blindness, of her own head and heart! She perceived that she had acted most weakly; that she had been imposed on by others in a most mortifying degree.

Emma, Cap. 47

Between these four passages there are, no doubt, important distinctions. The first is on a level of comedy which approximates to burlesque. The delusion from which Catherine Morland has been awakened was an innocent one, which owed at least as much to girlish ignorance of the world as to folly. And, being imaginative, it was a delusion from which an entirely commonplace or self-centred mind would hardly have suffered. Accordingly, the expiation, though painful while it lasts, is brief, and Catherine's recovery and good resolutions are treated with affectionate irony. The awakening of Marianne Dashwood is at the opposite pole. The situation has come near to tragedy; moral, as well as, or more than, intellectual deficiency has been involved in Marianne's errors. Hence the very vocabulary of the passage strikes a note unfamiliar in Jane Austen's style. It makes explicit, for once, the religious background of the author's ethical position. Hence such theological or nearly-theological words as *penitence*, even the *torture of penitence, amendment, self-destruction, my God*. And though not all younger readers may at once recognize it, the words *serious reflection* belong to the same region. In times which men now in their fifties can remember, the adjective *serious* ('Serious reading', 'Does he ever think about serious matters?') had indisputably religious overtones. The title of Law's *Serious Call* is characteristic. Between these two extracts, those from *Pride and*

Prejudice and *Emma* occupy a middle position. Both occur in a context of high comedy, but neither is merely laughable.

Despite these important differences, however, no one will dispute that all four passages present the same kind of process. 'Disillusionment', which might by etymology be the correct name for it, has acquired cynical overtones which put it out of court. We shall have to call it 'undeception' or 'awakening'. All four heroines painfully, though with varying degrees of pain, discover that they have been making mistakes both about themselves and about the world in which they live. All their *data* have to be reinterpreted. Indeed, considering the differences of their situations and characters, the similarity of the process in all four is strongly marked. All realize that the cause of the deception lay within; Catherine, that she had brought to the Abbey a mind 'craving to be frightened', Marianne, that 'her own feelings had prepared her sufferings', Elizabeth, that she has 'courted ignorance' and 'driven reason away', Emma, that she has been practising deceptions on herself. Self-hatred or self-contempt, though (once more) in different degrees, are common to all. Catherine 'hated herself'; Elinor abhors herself; Elizabeth finds her conduct 'despicable'; Emma gives hers 'every bad name in the world'. Tardy and surprising self-knowledge is presented in all four, and mentioned by name in the last two. 'I never knew myself,' says Elizabeth; Emma's conduct and 'her own heart' appear to her, unwelcome strangers both, 'in the same few minutes'.

If Jane Austen were an author as copious as Tolstoi, and if these passages played different parts in the novels from which they are taken, the common element would not, perhaps, be very important. After all, undeception is a common enough event in real life, and therefore, in a vast tract of fiction, might be expected to occur more than once. But that is not the position. We are dealing with only four books, none of them long; and in all four the undeception, structurally considered, is the very pivot or watershed of the story. In *Northanger Abbey*, and *Emma*, it precipitates the happy ending. In *Sense and Sensibility* it renders it possible. In *Pride and Prejudice* it initiates that revaluation of Darcy, both in Elizabeth's mind and in our minds, which is completed by the visit to Pemberley. We are thus entitled to speak of a common pattern in Jane Austen's four most characteristic novels. They have 'one plot' in a more important sense than Professor Garrod suspected. This is not so clearly true of *Sense and Sensibility*, but then it has really two plots or two 'actions' in the Aristotelian sense; it is true about one of them.

It is perhaps worth emphasizing what may be called the hardness—at least the firmness—of Jane Austen's thought exhibited in all these undeceptions. The great abstract nouns of the classical English moralists are unblushingly and uncompromisingly used; *good sense, courage, contentment, fortitude,* 'some duty neglected, some failing indulged', *impropriety, indelicacy, generous candour, blamable distrust, just humiliation, vanity, folly, ignorance, reason.* These are the concepts by which Jane Austen grasps the world. In her we still breathe the air of the *Rambler* and *Idler.* All is hard, clear, definable; by some modern standards, even naively so. The hardness is, of course, for oneself, not for one's neighbours. It reveals to Marianne her 'want of kindness' and shows Emma that her behaviour has been 'unfeeling'. Contrasted with the world of modern fiction, Jane Austen's is at once less soft and less cruel.

It may be added, though this is far less important, that in these four novels, self-deception and awakening are not confined to the heroines. General Tilney makes as big a mistake about Catherine as she has made about him. Mrs. Ferrars misjudges her son. Mr. Bennet is forced at last to see his errors as a father. But perhaps all this does not go beyond what might be expected from the general nature of human life and the general exigencies of a novelistic plot.

The central pattern of these four has much in common with that of a comedy by Molière.

Two novels remain. In *Mansfield Park* and *Persuasion* the heroine falls into no such self-deception and passes through no such awakening. We are, it is true, given to understand that Anne Elliot regards the breaking off of her early engagement to Wentworth as a mistake. If any young person now applied to her for advice in such circumstances, 'they would never receive any of such certain immediate wretchedness and uncertain future good'. For Anne in her maturity did not hold the view which Lord David Cecil attributes to Jane Austen,[1] that 'it was wrong to marry for money, but it was silly to marry without it'. She was now fully 'on the side of early warm attachment, and a cheerful confidence in futurity, against that overanxious caution which seems to insult exertion and distrust Providence'. (Notice, in passing, the Johnsonian cadence of a sentence which expresses a view that Johnson in one of his countless moods might have supported.) But though Anne thinks a mistake has been made, she does not think it was she that made it. She declares that she was perfectly right in being guided by Lady Russell who was to her 'in the place of a parent'. It was Lady Russell who had erred. There is no true parallel here between Anne and the heroines we have been considering. Anne, like Fanny Price, commits no errors.

Having placed these two novels apart from the rest because they do not use the pattern of 'undeception', we can hardly fail to notice that they share another common distinction. They are the novels of the solitary heroines.

Catherine Morland is hardly ever alone except on her journey from

Northanger Abbey, and she is soon back among her affectionate, if placid, family. Elinor Dashwood bears her own painful secret without a confidant for a time; but her isolation, besides being temporary, is incomplete; she is surrounded by affection and respect. Elizabeth always has Jane, the Gardiners, or (to some extent) her father. Emma is positively spoiled; the acknowledged centre of her own social world. Of all these heroines we may say, as Jane Austen says of some other young women, 'they were of consequence at home and favourites abroad'.

But Fanny Price and Anne are of no 'consequence'. The consciousness of 'mattering' which is so necessary even to the humblest women, is denied them. Anne has no place in the family councils at Kellynch Hall; 'she was only Anne'. She is exploited by her married sister, but not valued; just as Fanny is exploited, but not valued, by Mrs. Norris. Neither has a confidant; or if Edmund had once been a confidant as well as a hero to Fanny, he progressively ceases to be so. Some confidence, flawed by one vast forbidden topic, we may presume between Anne and Lady Russell; but this is almost entirely off stage and within the novel we rarely see them together. Both heroines come within easy reach of one of the great archetypes—Cinderella, Electra. Fanny, no doubt, more so. She is almost a Jane Austen heroine condemned to a Charlotte Brontë situation. We do not even believe in what Jane Austen tells us of her good looks; whenever we are looking at the action through Fanny's eyes, we feel ourselves sharing the consciousness of a plain woman.

Even physically, we see them alone; Fanny perpetually in the East Room with its fireless grate and its touching, ridiculous array of petty treasures (what Cinderella, what Electra, is without them?) or Anne, alone beside the hedge, an unwilling eavesdropper, Anne alone with her sick nephew, Anne alone in the empty house waiting for the sound of Lady Russell's carriage. And in their solitude both heroines suffer; far more deeply than Catherine, Elizabeth, and Emma, far more innocently than Marianne. Even Elinor suffers less. These two novels, we might almost say, stand to the others as Shakespeare's 'dark' comedies to his comedies in general. The difference in the lot of the heroines goes with a difference in the 'character parts'. Mrs. Norris is almost alone among Jane Austen's vulgar old women in being genuinely evil, nor are her greed and cruelty painted with the high spirits which make us not so much hate as rejoice in Lady Catherine de Burgh.

These solitary heroines who make no mistakes have, I believe—or had while she was writing—the author's complete approbation. This is connected with the unusual pattern of *Mansfield Park* and *Persuasion*. The heroines stand almost outside, certainly a little apart from, the world which the action of the novel depicts. It is in it, not in them, that self-deception occurs. They see it, but its victims do not. They do not of course stand voluntarily apart, nor do they willingly accept the role of observers and critics. They are shut out and are compelled to observe: for what they observe, they disapprove.

It is this disapproval which, though shared both by Fanny and Anne, has perhaps drawn on Fanny, from some readers, the charge of being a prig. I am far from suggesting that Fanny is a successful heroine, still less that she is the equal of Anne. But I hardly know the definition of *Prig* which would make her one. If it means a self-righteous person, a Pharisee, she is clearly no prig. If it means a 'precisian', one who adopts or demands a moral standard more exacting than is current in his own time and place, then I can see no evidence that Fanny's standard differs at all from that by which Marianne condemns herself or Anne Elliot corrects Captain Benwick. Indeed, since Anne preaches while Fanny feels in silence, I am a little surprised that the charge is not levelled against Anne rather than Fanny. For Anne's *chastoiement* of poor Benwick is pretty robust; 'she ventured to recommend a larger allowance of prose in his daily study, and ... mentioned such works of our best moralists, such collections of the finest letters, such memoirs of characters of worth and suffering, as occurred to her at the moment as calculated to rouse and fortify the mind by the highest precepts and the strongest examples of moral and religious endurances' (cap. 11). Notice, too, the standards which Anne was using when she first began to suspect her cousin, Mr. Elliot: 'she saw that there had been bad habits; that Sunday travelling had been a common thing; that there had been a period of his life (and probably not a short one) when he had been, at least careless on all serious matters.' Whatever we may think of these standards ourselves, I have not the least doubt that they are those of all the heroines, when they are most rational, and of Jane Austen herself. This is the hard core of her mind, the Johnsonian element, the iron in the tonic.

How, then, does Fanny Price fail? I suggest, by insipidity. *Pauper videri Cinna vult et est Pauper.* One of the most dangerous of literary ventures is the little, shy, unimportant heroine whom none of the other characters value. The danger is that your readers may agree with the other characters. Something must be put into the heroine to make us feel that the other characters are wrong, that she contains depths they never dreamed of.

That is why Charlotte Brontë would have succeeded better with Fanny Price. To be sure, she would have ruined everything else in the book; Sir Thomas and Lady Bertram and Mrs. Norris would have been distorted from credible types of pompous dullness, lazy vapidity and vulgar egoism into fiends complete with horns, tails and rhetoric. But through Fanny there would have blown a storm of passion which made sure that we at least would never think her insignificant. In Anne, Jane Austen did succeed. Her passion (for it is not less), her insight, her maturity, her prolonged fortitude, all attract us. But into Fanny, Jane Austen, to counterbalance her apparent insignificance, has put really nothing except rectitude of mind; neither passion, nor physical courage, nor wit, nor resource. Her very love is only calf love—a schoolgirl's hero-worship for a man who has been kind to her when they were both children, and who, incidentally, is the least attractive of all Jane Austen's heroes. Anne gains immensely by having for her lover almost the best. In real life, no doubt, we continue to respect interesting women despite the preposterous men they sometimes marry. But in fiction it is usually fatal. Who can forgive Dorothea for marrying such a sugarstick as Ladislaw, or Nellie Harding for becoming Mrs. Bold? Or, of course, David Copperfield for his first marriage.

Fanny also suffers from the general faults of *Mansfield Park*, which I take to be, if in places almost the best, yet as a whole the least satisfactory, of Jane Austen's works. I can accept Henry Crawford's elopement with Mrs. Rushworth: I cannot accept his intention of marrying Fanny. Such men never make such marriages.

But though Fanny is insipid (yet not a prig) she is always 'right' in the sense that to her, and to her alone, the world of *Mansfield Park* always appears as, in Jane Austen's view, it really is. Undeceived, she is the spectator of deceptions. These are made very clear. In cap. 2 we learn that the Bertram girls were 'entirely deficient' in 'self-knowledge'. In cap. 3 Sir Thomas departs for Antigua without much anxiety about his family because, though not perfectly confident of his daughters' discretion, he had ample trust 'in Mrs. Norris's watchful attention and in Edmund's judgement'. Both, of course, failed to justify it. In cap. 12 when Crawford was absent for a fortnight it proved 'a fortnight of such dulness to the Miss Bertram's as ought to have put them both on their guard'. Of course it did not. In cap. 16 when Edmund at last consents to act, Fanny is forced to raise the question, 'was he not deceiving himself'. In 34 when Crawford (whose manners are insufferable) by sheer persistence pesters Fanny into speech when she has made her desire for silence obvious, she says, 'Perhaps, Sir, I thought it was a pity you did not always know yourself as you seemed to do at that moment.' But deception is most fully studied in the person of Mary Crawford, 'a mind led astray and bewildered, and without any suspicion of being so: darkened, yet fancying itself light.' The New Testament echo in the language underlines the gravity of the theme. It may be that Jane Austen has not treated it successfully. Some think that she hated Mary and falsely darkened a character whom she had in places depicted as charming. It might be the other way round; that the author, designing to show deception at its height, was anxious to play fair, to show how the victim could be likeable at times, and to render her final state the more impressive by raising in us false hopes that she might have been cured. Either way, the gap between Mary at her best and Mary in her last interview with Edmund is probably too wide; too wide for fiction, I mean, not for possibility. (We may have met greater inconsistency in real life; but real life does not need to be probable.) That last interview, taken by itself, is an alarming study of human blindness. We may—most of us do—disagree with the standards by which Edmund condemns Mary. The dateless and universal possibility in the scene is Mary's invincible ignorance of what those standards are. All through their conversation she is cutting her own throat. Every word she speaks outrages Edmund's feelings 'in total ignorance, unsuspiciousness of there being such feelings' (cap. 47). At last, when we feel that her ghastly innocence (so to call it) could go no further, comes the master stroke. She tries to call him back by 'a saucy, playful smile'. She still thought that possible. The misunderstanding is incurable. She will never know Edmund.

In *Persuasion* the theme of deception is much less important. Sir Walter is, no doubt, deceived both in his nephew and in Mrs. Clay, but that is little more than the mechanism of the plot. What we get more of is the pains of the heroine in her role of compelled observer. Something of this had appeared in Elinor Dashwood, and more in Fanny Price, constantly forced to witness the courtship of Edmund and Mary Crawford. But Fanny had also, at times, derived amusement from her function of spectator. At the rehearsals of *Lovers' Vows* she was 'not unamused to observe the selfishness which, more or less disguised, seemed to govern them all' (cap. 14). It is a kind of pleasure which we feel sure that Jane Austen herself had often enjoyed. But whether it were that something in her own life now began to show her less of the spectator's joys and more of his pains, forcing her on from 'as if we were God's spies' to 'break my heart for I must hold my tongue', or that she is simply exploring a new literary vein, it certainly seems that Anne's unshared knowledge of the significance of things she hears and sees is nearly always in some degree painful. At Kellynch she has 'a knowledge which she often wished less, of her father's character'. At the Musgroves 'One of the least agreeable circumstances of her residence ... was her being treated with too much confidence by all parties, and being too much in the secret of the complaints of each house' (cap. 6). One passage perhaps gives the real answer to any charge of priggery that might lie against her or Fanny for the judgments they pass as spectators. Speaking of Henrietta's behaviour to Charles Hayter, Jane Austen says that Anne 'had delicacy which must be pained' by it (cap. 9). This is not so much like the Pharisee's eagerness to condemn as the musicians' involuntary shudder at a false note. Nor is it easily avoided by those who have standards of any sort. Do not our modern critics love to use the term 'embarrassing' of literature which violently offends the standards of their own group? and does not this mean, pretty nearly, a 'delicacy' on their part which 'must be pained'? But of course all these spectator's pains sink into insignificance beside that very special, almost unendurable, pain which Anne derives from her understanding of Wentworth's every look and word. For *Persuasion*, from first to last, is, in a sense in which the other novels are not, a love story.

It remains to defend what I have been saying against a possible charge. Have I been treating the novels as though I had forgotten that they are, after all, comedies? I trust not. The hard core of morality and even of religion seems to me to be just what makes good comedy possible. 'Principles' or 'seriousness' are essential to Jane Austen's art. Where there is no norm, nothing can be ridiculous, except for a brief moment of unbalanced provincialism in which we may laugh at the merely unfamiliar. Unless there is something about which the author is never ironical, there can be no true irony in the work. 'Total irony'—irony about everything—frustrates itself and becomes insipid.

But though the world of the novels has this serious, unyielding core, it is not a tragic world. This, no doubt, is due to the author's choice; but there are also two characteristics of her mind which are, I think, essentially untragic. The first is the nature of the core itself. It is in one way exacting, in another not. It is unexacting in so far as the duties commanded are not quixotic or heroic, and obedience to them will not be very difficult to properly brought up people in ordinary circumstances. It is exacting in so far as such obedience is rigidly demanded; neither excuses nor experiments are allowed. If charity is the poetry of conduct and honour the rhetoric of conduct, Jane Austen's 'principles' might be described as the grammar of conduct. Now grammar is something that anyone can learn; it is also something that everyone must learn. Compulsion waits. I think Jane Austen does not envisage those standards which she so rigidly holds as often demanding human sacrifice. Elinor felt sure that if Marianne's new composure were based on 'serious reflection' it 'must eventually lead her to contentment and cheerfulness'. That it might lead instead to a hair-shirt or a hermitage or a pillar in the Thebaïd is not in Jane Austen's mind. Or not there. There is just a hint in *Persuasion* that total sacrifice may be demanded of sailors on active service; as there is also a hint of women who must love when life or when hope is gone. But we are then at the frontier of Jane Austen's world.

The other untragic element in her mind is its cheerful moderation. She could almost have said with Johnson, 'Nothing is too little for so little a creature as man.' If she envisages few great sacrifices, she also envisages no grandiose schemes of joy. She has, or at least all her favourite characters have, a hearty relish for what would now be regarded as very modest pleasures. A ball, a dinner party, books, conversation, a drive to see a great house ten miles away, a holiday as far as Derbyshire—these, with affection (that is essential) and good manners, are happiness. She is no Utopian.

She is described by someone in Kipling's worst story as the mother of Henry James. I feel much more sure that she is the daughter of Dr. Johnson: she inherits his commonsense, his morality, even much of his style. I am not a good enough Jamesian to decide the other claim. But if she bequeathed anything to him it must be wholly on the structural side. Her style, her system of values, her temper, seem to me the very opposite of his. I feel sure that Isabel Archer, if she had met Elizabeth Bennet, would have pronounced her 'not very cultivated'; and Elizabeth, I fear, would have found Isabel deficient both in 'seriousness' and in mirth.

NOTE

1. *Jane Austen*, Cambridge, 1936, p. 33.

HENRIETTA TEN HARMSEL

Pride and Prejudice

II

As noted in the chapter on *Sense and Sensibility*, the success of a Jane
Austen novel depends to a large extent upon her success in creating an
engaging and credible heroine. The strong, conventional antithesis
demanded between Elinor and Marianne results in the unpleasant ambiguity
already indicated—an ambiguity which leaves the reader wavering between
the sympathy the author arouses for Marianne and the moral approval she is
evidently trying to arouse for Elinor. A concomitant ambiguity evolves about
the identification of the real heroine of the piece—is it Elinor or is it
Marianne? There is no such ambiguity in *Pride and Prejudice*. Even though
Jane Bennet's romance parallels Elizabeth's, every reader realizes that
Elizabeth is the real heroine of the novel. But has the antithesis of *Sense and
Sensibility* disappeared completely? Obviously, there is not the corresponding
relationship to the abstractions of the title, for Jane Bennet represents
neither pride nor prejudice. Neither is there the stifling moral necessity to
approve of the one and to disapprove of the other. But there is an antithesis
nevertheless. R. A. Brower is right when he says that "Jane is conventionally
in love with a conventional lover".[16] But now the distinction has become
much more subtle than it was before. Jane is a conventional heroine, but she
is not necessarily morally reprehensible: she may have her Bingley in the end.

From *Jane Austen: A Study in Fictional Conventions*. ©1964 by Mouton & Co.

Neither is she necessarily to be burlesqued as unreal: she might very well exist in real life. But, as the heroine of a novel, she is uninteresting and inadequate. She is certainly included in that class of characters who, according to Elizabeth, are "easily seen through" (*PP*, 42). Elizabeth goes on, at that point, to set forth what may be called the basic principle of characterization in *Pride and Prejudice*: in the first place, a simple character is not necessarily evil nor is an intricate character necessarily good, for "It does not necessarily follow that a deep, intricate character is more or less estimable" than a simple one. But, in the second place, the "intricate characters are the *most* amusing" (*PP*, 42). It is in the simple category that Jane falls, together with the throng of eighteenth-century heroines like Pamela, Harriet Byron, Emily St. Aubert, and Emmeline. They are beautiful, accomplished, serene, and morally irreproachable. They intuitively discover and captivate their noble lovers. They deservedly live happily ever after. But for the centrally significant role of a heroine they do not have the qualifications which will unify a novel artistically and bring it to life. Therefore, in continual subtle contrast to the charming but simple and conventional Jane, her author sets her new creation, Elizabeth Bennet. In her, probably for the first time, the conventional Cinderella-heroine comes to full artistic maturity. She is still the typical heroine who overcomes all obstacles to win her hero in the end. But within this framework she is being transformed into a complex character who stands at the center of a well-unified fictional world. And the characterization of this "transformed" heroine—Elizabeth Bennet—becomes particularly forceful because it constantly runs parallel to the characterization of the "conventional" Jane Bennet.

A common trait of the Richardsonian eighteenth-century heroine is her passivity. Joyce Tompkins notes this when she states that the "heroines feel, but they do not initiate; they can resist but do not attack ...".[17] An application of these contrasted qualities to Jane and Elizabeth respectively shows how subtly the passivity of the conventional heroine forms a shadowy but continuous background to the lively action of the real heroine. At the initial Netherfield ball the "most beautiful" Jane dances serenely in the background while the only "tolerable" Elizabeth receives a challenging insult which arouses all the fighting spirit of her "lively, playful disposition" (*PP*, 11–12). During the enforced visit to Netherfield, Jane lies sick and inactive in her room while Elizabeth engages the reader's constant attention by her characteristic action—from the moment of her arrival "with weary ancles, dirty stockings, and a face glowing with the warmth of exercise", through the four lively and "loaded" conversations with Darcy and the Bingleys, to the time of their departure, which Jane finally demands only after Elizabeth has "positively resolved" upon it (*PP,* 32–59). Jane's attitude, throughout the period of Bingley's "desertion" remains serenely tolerant while Elizabeth's "is totally different" in its active condemnation of Miss Bingley's and Darcy's machinations (*PP,* 118; 147; 149; 185). Their respective attitudes toward the snobbish relatives who object to their possible marriages is completely characteristic: Jane tries sweetly to excuse Miss Bingley's duplicity by attributing it to her natural love for her brother—"whatever anxiety she may feel on his behalf is natural and amiable", she says (*PP,* 148). Elizabeth, on the other hand, is far from conciliating in her attitude towards Lady Catherine. In response to her rude inquiries she says: "You may ask questions, which I shall not choose to answer." In response to the insinuation that with her "arts and allurements" she may have drawn Darcy into an engagement, Elizabeth answers: "If I have, I shall be the last person to confess it." When threatened with the absolute censure of all of Darcy's relatives if she should marry him, Elizabeth responds with characteristic and spirited irony:

> "These are heavy misfortunes.... But the wife of Mr. Darcy must have such extraordinary sources of happiness necessarily attached to her situation, that she could, upon the whole, have no cause to repine." (*PP,* 354–55)

The behavior of the two sisters when their respective love affairs are approaching happy conclusions is again characteristic. Jane declares with naive propriety that her attitude will reveal that she and her lover "meet only as common and indifferent acquaintances" (*PP,* 339). The irrepressible Elizabeth, meanwhile, is not afraid to hasten Darcy's proposal by actively rebelling against Lady Catherine and finally and frankly expressing her gratitude to him for his intervention in the marriage of Lydia and Wickham (*PP,* 365). And Elizabeth's final description of her own happiness touches aptly upon the real difference between her and Jane. Like Jane, and hundreds of heroines before her, she says: "I am the happiest creature in the world." But she goes on to point out the difference: "Perhaps other people have said so before, but not one with such justice. I am happier even than Jane, she only smiles. I laugh" (*PP,* 382–83). When viewed in the light of Elizabeth's preceding action, her laughter is revealed to be not only the kind that sees comedy in every character and situation of life, but also the kind that triumphs because it has won what it has worked for. Very subtly, then, Jane Austen does use Jane Bennet as a conventional heroine throughout *Pride and Prejudice.* And nothing could display more authentically the artistic inadequacy of such a heroine than the constant contrast established between the simple passivity of Jane and the complex activity of her sister Elizabeth.

It is chiefly through the characterization of Elizabeth Bennet that *Pride and Prejudice* achieves artistic unity and greatness. Into the relatively simple outlines of the conventional Cinderella-heroine, Jane Austen pours the full strength of all her "transforming agents". Steadily developing character reveals both good and bad traits and results in the highest degree of psychological realism. In contrast with the "disconnection between character and action" so common to the novels of the late eighteenth century,[18] Elizabeth functions not only as the isolated heroine but also as the artistic unifying element whose influence and action reverberate through every character and scene in the book. Above all, the characterization of Elizabeth reveals a multitude of ironies—those which her astuteness discovers in the situations of others, those which she discovers in her growing knowledge of herself, and even those of which she seems to remain delightfully unaware. In using all of her transforming agents—psychological realism, developing character, variety of function, and irony—to create a truly great heroine, and in contrasting Elizabeth's bright colors with the shadowy outlines of her conventional sister, Jane Austen reaches a high point in her literary achievement.

First of all, the lack of ideal beauty, of extraordinary accomplishment, and of moral perfection combine to form a realism that makes of Elizabeth Bennet a psychologically credible heroine. Mrs. Bennet initially informs the reader that Elizabeth "is not so handsome as Jane" (*PP*, 4), and soon Darcy pronounces a similar judgment when he says at the ball that Jane is "the only handsome girl in the room" and that Elizabeth is only "tolerable" and not handsome enough to tempt him (*PP*, 11–12). When Elizabeth plays and sings, her performance is "pleasing, though by no means capital" (*PP*, 25). Such deliberate emphasis upon her lack of surpassing beauty and accomplishment almost gives Elizabeth a touch of the "anti-heroine" quality of Catherine Morland.

Mr. Bennet, who naturally favors Elizabeth over all his other daughters, defends her by saying that she has "more of quickness than her sisters" (*PP*, 5), but the reader soon notes that she also possesses more of asperity and cynicism than they do. When Mrs. Gardiner expresses the hope that Jane will not be embarrassed by meeting Darcy and the Bingleys in London, Elizabeth answers with a sharp sarcasm quite devoid of her usual innate graciousness:

> My dear aunt, how could you think of it? Mr. Darcy may perhaps have *heard* of such a place as Gracechurch Street, but he would hardly think a month's ablution enough to cleanse him from its

impurities, were he once to enter it; and depend upon it, Mr. Bingley never stirs without him. (*PP,* 141)

While contemplating her visit to the Collins' Parsonage, Elizabeth reflects a bitterness quite equal to that which she herself decries in her father:

> Thank heaven! I am going tomorrow where I shall find a man who has not one agreeable quality, who has neither manner nor sense to recommend him. Stupid men are the only ones worth knowing, after all. (*PP,* 154).

When Maria Lucas excitedly calls her downstairs to see Miss De Bourgh in her phaeton at the door of the Parsonage, even Elizabeth's most sympathetic admirer must recognize the momentary crudeness she displays in her comment:

> "And is this all? ... I expected at least that the pigs were got into the garden, and here is nothing but Lady Catherine and her daughter!" (*PP,* 158)

And when, having inadvertently promised to dance with Darcy, Elizabeth hears Charlotte's consoling suggestion that she may find him "very agreeable" her mocking answer reveals genuine prejudice in spite of its exaggerated playfulness:

> "Heaven forbid!—*That* would be the greatest misfortune of all!— To find a man agreeable whom one is determined to hate!—Do not wish me such an evil." (*PP,* 90)

Such unpleasant cynicism persuades the reader that Elizabeth displays deep-seated and genuine weaknesses which she must somehow recognize and correct:

As always in *Pride and Prejudice,* a painful irony will suffuse the changes of attitude which cause Elizabeth to eat the words cited in the passages above. Later Mr. Darcy will not only brave the "impurities" of the street where the Gardiners live but also perform there, in behalf of Lydia and Wickham, the gracious and tactful services which poignantly arouse Elizabeth's true gratitude and love. In spite of Elizabeth's insinuation that a stupid man like Collins is preferable to Darcy himself, it is that very Darcy of whom she later "honestly felt that she could have loved him ... now, when all love must be vain" (*PP,* 278). The very Lady Catherine whom she crudely

classifies lower than "pigs in the garden" she will later see fit to entertain as
her own aunt at Pemberley (*PP*, 388). And it is her emphatic and public
determination to hate Darcy that makes the irony painfully keen when she
finally reveals her engagement to him. Mr. Bennet is distressingly frank in his
amazement:

> "Lizzy," said he, "what are you doing? Are you out of your senses,
> to be accepting this man? Have not you always hated him?" (*PP*,
> 376)

And when even the tolerant Jane is incredulous, the irony is complete:

> Jane looked at her doubtingly. "Oh Lizzy! it cannot be. I know
> how much you dislike him." (*PP*, 372)

Not only through the realism of "mixed" qualities and their constant ironic
interplay, but also through steadily developing character Jane Austen is
depicting in her "new" heroine a sustained contrast to the simple and static
conventional Jane in the background. The gradual change which occurs in
Elizabeth develops beautifully from the first subtle foreshadowing of it in her
perverse but unconsciously fascinated interest in Darcy; through the
overwhelming revelation of her prejudices on the receipt of his explanatory
letter; and to her final surrender to a sincere and mature love for him. This
gradual change reveals how—on the one hand—Elizabeth is much like her
fictional forebear, Pamela, but now—on the other hand—she is entirely
different. The changing relationship of Pamela toward Mr. B follows the
same general outlines: it is foreshadowed by her covert fascination with him;
it is brought to its climax by the revelatory and conciliatory letter which
turns the tide in favor of Mr. B; and it ends in her final love for him.[19] The
difference lies chiefly in the characterization of the heroine. Pamela is simple
and passive, like most eighteenth-century heroines, in that she is completely
virtuous throughout and in that she uses this virtue not in action but as a
defense. In Elizabeth, on the other hand, it is her own spirited and
delightfully impetuous action that sets in motion the multiple forces which
later reveal her own prejudices; and it is these forces which she has set in
motion that sustain not only all the subsidiary action and characterization in
the novel but also the gradual personal changes which result in her final
achievement of self-knowledge and happiness.

These gradually developing changes in Elizabeth's character are
rendered particularly powerful by the sly ironies which they subsequently
reveal. Many of the faults she sees in others, she later discovers in herself. In

her first inadvertently accepted dance with Darcy (which in itself subtly foreshadows her future love for him), Elizabeth argues archly and with evident mockery that there is "a great similarity" in the turn of their minds. She goes on a few moments later to catechize him pointedly on his prejudices (evidently concerning Wickham) revealing again, in spite of her annoyance with him, her unconscious fascination with his puzzling character:

> "I remember hearing you once say, Mr. Darcy, that you hardly ever forgave, that your resentment once created was unappeasable. You are very cautious, I suppose, as to its *being created.*"
>
> "I am", said he, with a firm voice.
>
> "And never allow yourself to be blinded by prejudice?"
>
> "I hope not."
>
> "It is particularly incumbent on those who never change their opinion, to be secure of judging properly at first."
>
> "May I ask to what these questions tend?"
>
> "Merely to the illustration of your character," said she.... (*PP,* 93)

With her usual ironic emphasis, Jane Austen reveals gradually that Elizabeth *is* much like Darcy; that she is perhaps more unjustly "blinded by prejudice", particularly in regard to Wickham, than he is; and that her arch but smug interest in diagnosing and reforming *his* character had to be applied just as thoroughly to her own.

Such ironies accompany almost every revealed change in Elizabeth. After reading Darcy's enlightening letter, she vigorously accuses herself of prejudice and despicable behavior: "Had I been in love, I could not have been more blind. But vanity, not love, has been my folly.... Till this moment I never knew myself" (*PP,* 208). In these very words of sincere and moving self-examination there still lurks her delightfully characteristic vanity. Now, she boasts, she finally knows herself! But the naive "Had I been in love" reveals ironically how far she is still removed from understanding herself completely. And so the ironies continue. Among the elegant surroundings at Pemberley Elizabeth "thinks and thinks and wonders" why Darcy should appear so amiable and civil (*PP,* 245–59)! When she suffers through her father's ridicule of the "idle report" that Darcy has proposed to her, Elizabeth realizes that her father's wit, to which she is usually so congenial, can be as painfully embarrassing as her mother's stupidity, which she has often ridiculed herself (*PP,* 362–64). And in the end, Elizabeth never really knows how much the "comfort and elegance" of Pemberley has made her eager to leave all of her family and friends to live with Darcy there (*PP,* 384).

Another feature of Jane Austen's "new" heroine is the variety of ways in which she functions to unify the whole novel artistically. All the action of the book is related somehow to her action; all the characters are related somehow to her character and to its development. This feature may be clearly illustrated by the dependence of all the subsidiary romances in the novel upon that of Elizabeth and Darcy. Even before Elizabeth has peremptorily refused the pompous Mr. Collins, Jane Austen is foreshadowing Charlotte Lucas' interest in him. At the Netherfield ball when Elizabeth is being "teazed by Mr. Collins" and his pointed attentions, she is, ironically enough, relieved by what she thinks to be only Charlotte's consideration for her comfort:

> She owed her greatest relief to her friend Miss Lucas, who often joined them, and good-naturedly engaged Mr. Collins's conversation to herself. (*PP*, 102)

This preparation for Charlotte's surprise engagement to Mr. Collies continues subtly as she stands in the background, detained "by a little curiosity" to hear Mrs. Bennet dolefully trying to console the pompous but definitely jilted Mr. Collins (*PP*, 114). For the rest of the day it is Charlotte who engages the attentions of Mr. Collins, assumedly to relieve the embarrassment of the whole household (*PP*, 115). Jane Austen finally allows the subtle ironies to come out in the open (*PP*, 121) by informing the reader that "Charlotte's kindness extended farther than Elizabeth had any conception of"; by hurrying Collins to Lucas Lodge "the next morning ... to throw himself at her feet"; and by finally having her go "to meet him accidentally in the lane" to receive and accept his proposal. Her marriage is made possible by Elizabeth's refusal of Mr. Collins. Elizabeth's relationship to the whole situation, however, functions not only through her action, but even more subtly through the comparisons and contrasts of character. Charlotte is her best friend—shrewd, good-natured, and able to manipulate situations and people to her own purposes as Elizabeth is. In spite of these similarities, however, she plainly succumbs to the social pressures of the period, shocking Elizabeth into painfully frank objections to her engagement (*PP*, 124), but also subtly informing the reader how powerful those pressures are, even to a girl so similar to Elizabeth herself.

The other romances in the book also depend upon Elizabeth for their culmination. It is only her charm that causes Darcy to "allow" Bingley's marriage to Jane; and it is for her sake that Darcy induces Wickham to marry Lydia. Even the "romances" which do not evolve successfully—those of Miss Bingley and Miss De Bourgh—obviously owe their failure to the all-pervasive character and action of the lively heroine.

In functioning so richly through all the action, characterization, and subtle irony of the novel, Elizabeth Bennet far outshines any other eighteenth-century heroine. Richardson's heroines are central to his novels, but they are essentially simple in their sole dependence upon virtue for their final but passive victory.[20] Moll Flanders comes alive as a kind of picaresque heroine, but certainly neither controls the episodic action in which she functions nor serves as the artistic key to the characterization and action of the other characters. The Gothic heroines, too, although their reactions to situations help to establish the atmosphere of the Gothic novels, are essentially simple and passive. In his study of Fanny Burney, Eugene White concludes, after careful consideration, that "In her characterizations ... Miss Burney works through incident, letting her people reveal themselves by their reactions to situations".[21] But Elizabeth Bennet, particularly as she contrasts with the passive and conventional Jane in the background, represents a new achievement in the characterization of fictional heroines—transformed by her mixed and developing character, her richly various artistic functioning, and her constant subjection to and revelation of subtle ironies. These ironies, as demonstrated above, operate continuously through all of the other transforming agents and include all of the characters, even Elizabeth, in their pointed disclosures. In her relationship to the conventional Jane, a final irony may be noted. It is Elizabeth and Darcy who are responsible for uniting Jane and Bingley at last. But undeniably, although quite. accidentally, it was Bingley and Jane who had brought them together at first.

III

One of the most common conventions in eighteenth-century fiction following Richardson is the connection of the heroine with the villain and the hero by means of the attempted seduction by the former and the timely rescue by the latter. Sir Charles Grandison nobly saves Harriet Byron from the wicked devices of the villainous Sir Hargrave Pollexfen. Lord Orville watchfully protects Evelina against the attempts of Sir Clement Willoughby. This is evidently the tendency that Fielding is burlesquing in *Joseph Andrews* in the various rescues of Fanny from attempted ravishings. Sometimes slight variations occur on the theme so that, as in *Camilla*, it is not the heroine herself but her pock-marked and cripple sister Eugenia who is abducted by the villainous Bellamy. Jane Austen herself has brought in the seduction motif obliquely in *Sense and Sensibility*, as noted in the preceding chapter. In *Pride and Prejudice* various adaptations of the convention occur. As in *Camilla*, it is the heroine's sister rather than the heroine herself who becomes a candidate for seduction by the villain—although in this case a very willing candidate. As in *Pamela*, the roles of villain and hero seem to merge in the character who begins by villainously insulting the heroine and ends by being her hero and lover. The conventional villain, hero, and seduction motifs in *Pride and Prejudice* are so skillfully transformed and merged that they fit very smoothly into the unified scheme of the novel.

As the plot evolves, it becomes very evident that Wickham, although charming, is a rather conventional villain. Reuben A. Brower notes his villainous role as the seducing rake, later pursued and forced to decent capitulation by the wealthy and noble hero.[22] Although Jane Austen has delicately moved this melodrama off to one side, the whole notorious intrigue figures importantly and variously in the novel. Elizabeth's initial attraction to Wickham proves that even she, in a sense, is not immune to his rakish charms. For Darcy, meanwhile, the fact that his own sister has barely been prevented from eloping with Wickham forbids his condemning Elizabeth because her sister succeeds in doing so. A delightful irony exists in Elizabeth's instinctive reaction to her sister's disgrace—she feels that Darcy will now cast her off permanently:

> ... never had she so honestly felt that she could have loved him, as now, when all love must be vain. (*PP*, 278)

The irony exists, of course, in the fact that the very opposite is true. Instead of estranging Elizabeth and Darcy, the disgraceful elopement of Lydia and Wickham brings them together at last. Wickham, then, is perhaps most sustainedly the villain of *Pride and Prejudice*. His role, however, functions in various ways to advance the plot, enrich the characterizations, and multiply the ironies of the whole novel.

Wickham, however, is not the only "villain" of the piece. In the first part of the novel Darcy also functions as a kind of villain. His role as a "villain-hero" displays a definite analogy with that of Mr. B in *Pamela*.[23] Like Mr. B, he appears briefly, upon his introduction, to be the man who will develop into Elizabeth's hero. With his "fine, tall person, handsome features, noble mien", and, above all, his "ten thousand a year" he seems made to outshine all other possible heroes. However, his abominable pride and his insufferable insult to Elizabeth soon indicate that he must be the villain instead. His reported injustices to Wickham and his officious interference in Jane and Bingley's romance turn Elizabeth against him in every way. Her antagonism to his aristocratic villainy reaches its height near the end of the rising action in Darcy's insulting proposal to her. His proposal, though more refined, is as insulting to Elizabeth's sensibilities as Mr. B's approaches are to Pamela in the second bedroom scene. When "to her utter amazement, she saw Mr. Darcy walk into the room" (*PP*, 188–89), Elizabeth's surprise is certainly equal to Pamela's. Darcy's words are proud and humiliating:

"In vain have I struggled. It will not do. My feelings will not be repressed. You must allow me to tell you how ardently I admire and love you." (*PP*, 189)

Their similarity to Mr. B's insults to Pamela is unmistakable:

"In vain, my Pamela, do I find it to struggle against my affection for you...." (*Pamela*, I, p. 274)

Darcy's arrogance is quite insufferable as he dwells on "His sense of her inferiority—of its being a degradation ..." (*PP*, 189). It seems almost to echo Mr. B's remark: "Consider the pride of my condition. I cannot endure the thought of marriage, even with a person of equal or superior degree to myself.... How then ... can I think of making you my wife?" (*Pamela*, I, p. 233).[24] In the "villainous" insults of the proud Mr. Darcy, then, Jane Austen is evidently reshaping the conventional seduction attempts of the typical Richardsonian villain.

In his subsequent transformation into Elizabeth's hero, the connections with the old seduction motif are clearer and more conventional. Like Colonel Brandon in *Sense and Sensibility*, Darcy plays a typical hero role: he leads the search for the runaway lovers, modestly settles all the financial problems, and finally wins the gratitude and love of the heroine.[25] Like Colonel Brandon, too, Darcy fails to make an ideal hero for the superb heroine Jane Austen has prepared for him. Her transformation of his earlier villainous assaults into brilliant verbal battles with Elizabeth presented a new and often stimulating type of villain. But after his revelatory letter begins to change Elizabeth's attitude toward him, Darcy becomes much less interesting. His dignified but rather stiff behavior towards Elizabeth and the Gardiners at Pemberley; his modest heroics behind the scenes in manipulating the Lydia–Wickham affair; his awkward behavior toward Elizabeth immediately preceding his second proposal (which *her* initiative must elicit)—all of these support the judgment that Jane Austen made of him a better villain than a hero. The reader sympathizes completely with Elizabeth's rather rueful decision that she had better not tease Darcy about his delight in "controlling" Bingley for "She remembered that he had yet to learn to be laught at, and it was rather too early to begin" (*PP*, 371). Marvin Mudrick is substantially right, at least about Darcy, when he makes the following judgment:

The last third of the book ... does in fact diminish suddenly in density and originality: that is, beginning with Lydia's elopement. We get a conventional chase by an outraged father, a friendly uncle, and a now impeccable hero; we get outbursts of irrelevantly directed moral judgment, and a general simplification of the problems of motive and will down to the level of the Burneyan novel. Jane Austen herself, routed by the sexual question she has raised, is concealed behind a fogbank of bourgeois morality; and the characters, most conspicuously Darcy, must shift for themselves, or, rather, they fall automatically into the grooves prepared for them by hundreds of novels of sentiment and sensibility.[26]

In *Pride and Prejudice*, then, Jane Austen does use the conventional villain–hero–seduction triangle. Often she succeeds in transforming the material skillfully, especially through the richly various functioning of the seduction situations, the constant ironic implications inherent in them, and her initial use of the prospective hero as a kind of villain. After the climax, however, she uses the situations more conventionally and fails to integrate them so constantly by means of connecting and reverberating ironies, comparisons, and contrasts. However, chiefly because of the consistently skillful and rich characterization of Elizabeth, these imperfections only mar the surface, not the central effect of the novel itself. Since all subsidiary characters and motifs exist chiefly to form a part of Elizabeth's world, they always maintain their place in it, even though they may totter individually, because her rich characterization holds that world intact.

IV

The minor characters of *Pride and Prejudice* do not present a "Burneyan gallery" existing for the sake of extraneous social satire but always exist as integral parts of Elizabeth's world. In many of them Jane Austen is presenting transformations of stock fictional characters. In Mr. Collins she exploits the well-known figure of the moralizing clergyman. Each of her novels presents some version of the clergyman, but no other is so obviously a caricature of the didactic type, which McKillop cites as reaching a kind of climax in the preposterously pompous comments and letters of Mr. Collins.[27] His relationship to Dr. Bartlett and his moralizing role in *Sir Charles Grandison* is easily made apparent. His praise of the Grandisons is echoed, with mock pompousness, by Collins' praise of Lady Catherine. Collins refers to her as follows:

... I have been so fortunate as to be distinguished by the patronage of the Right Honourable Lady Catherine de Bourgh ... whose bounty and beneficence has preferred me to the valuable rectory of this parish, where it shall be my earnest endeavor to demean myself with grateful respect towards her Ladyship.... (*PP*, 62–63)

This tendency to flatter "especially those to whom he owes his preferment" (*PP*, 101) is an evident burlesque of such flatteries as Dr. Bartlett pours out to Charlotte Grandison concerning both Sir Charles and herself:

Your ladyship will not accuse me of flattery, when you read this ... I know that you love to have justice done to my lord ... if you receive his praises with some little reluctance, it is with such a modest reluctance as you would receive your own.... (*Sir Charles Grandison*, V, Letter 51)

Certainly, Mr. Collins might well have prefaced any of his remarks or letters with these words directly from the pen of Dr. Bartlett:

Forgive me ... if sometimes I am ready to preach: it is my province. (*Sir Charles Grandison*, V, Letter 51)[28]

As usual in her characterizations, Jane Austen uses Mr. Collins for a variety of functions. He serves, in various ways, as a kind of villain in the novel. Like Mr. Williams, the clergyman in *Pamela*, he is offered as a possible marriage prospect for the heroine. Mr. Collins' proposal, however, is "villainous" like Darcy's in that it insults Elizabeth in its pompous complacency and represents all of the pressures that might "seduce" her into a socially politic but personally degrading marriage. It appears in the rising action at a corresponding point with Mr. B's humiliating approaches to Pamela in the first bedroom scene—a correspondence which underlines the seductive force of the proposal. Charlotte Lucas' prompt acceptance of Collins' obviously artificial proposal, immediately after Elizabeth refuses it, is another evidence of its seductive force.

Mr. Collins' marriage to Charlotte Lucas also functions very naturally in creating the setting in which Elizabeth may next meet Darcy—this time among his relatives and their sumptuous surroundings. Collins' obsequious catering to Lady Catherine also prepares for a shifting emphasis in his villainy. It can obviously no longer try to induce Elizabeth to marry him, but turns now in new directions: first, a pompous parading of all the advantages of situation which she has forfeited by not becoming his wife; later, his officious attempt to prevent her marriage to the hero Darcy by warning her by means of a letter to her incredulous father "of what evils ... [she] may incur, by a precipitate closure with this gentleman's proposals, which, of course, ... [she] will be inclined to take immediate advantage of" (*PP*, 363). Of the hidden irony that Elizabeth has long ago "of course" rejected the proposal of this very gentleman, the pompous Collins remains blissfully unaware!

Besides these functions as "moralizer" and as "villain" Collins serves to illustrate beautifully the connections which link him with various other characters in the novel. As Elizabeth's cousin, he forms one of the family who, it appears to her, often "made an agreement to expose themselves as much as they could" to the scorn of the disdainful Darcy (*PP*, 101). His resemblance to Mrs. Bennet is slily displayed by Jane Austen at the time when he makes, at Mrs. Bennet's suggestion, the quick—and to both of them completely proper—switch of his "violent affections" from Jane to Elizabeth:

> Mr. Collins had only to change from Jane to Elizabeth—and it was soon done—done while Mrs. Bennet was stirring the fire. (*PP*, 71)

The minds of both are so shallow that they are sublimely unconscious of the lurking ironies of the situation. Mrs. Bennet's smug success in "stirring the fire" of his love into flaming suddenly for Elizabeth, is destined to turn very bitter when Charlotte Lucas on the very same day will exploit his vacillating affections by stirring up a "flame" in her own behalf! As for Mr. Collins, he can have no objections to switching his love from Jane to Elizabeth, for he is complacently certain of quick acceptance by either one.

But it is not only with Elizabeth's embarrassing relatives that Mr. Collins may be compared. He stands also as a subtle link between Mrs. Bennet at Longbourne and Lady Catherine at Rosings. One need only hear a few of Lady Catherine's officious remarks to realize how much she is like the pompous Collins. On first meeting Elizabeth, she feels free at once to insist that she and her sisters should have had a governess:

> Five daughters brought up at home without a governess!—I never heard of such a thing.... I always say that nothing is to be done in education without steady and regular instruction, and nobody but a governess can give it. (*PP*, 164–65)

If Mrs. Bennet's resemblance to Mr. Collins is no compliment to her, surely Lady Catherine's resemblance to him is no recommendation either. If the ridiculous Mr. Collins can feel at home with both, perhaps the distance between Longbourne and Rosings is, after all, not incapable of being bridged. By thus relating the role of Mr. Collins to the plot, the setting, and the other characters of the novel, Jane Austen creates a minor character who is not a mere "extra" but an indispensable part of the whole.

Not only the clergyman Collins, but also the other conventional minor characters assume new dimensions under Jane Austen's transforming touch. Mr. Bennet plays, in the Lydia–Wickham affair, the role of the irate father. In regard to Elizabeth, he presents, in his complete disapproval of Darcy, a new version of the objecting parent. It is, however, as a reflector of Elizabeth's own personality, as an example of the costly matrimonial mistakes she may make, and as an explanation for the almost incredible differences in the personalities of his children, that Mr. Bennet's role is especially revealing. The evident resemblance between him and Elizabeth remains a consistent tribute to her keen intelligence and delightful humor. His cynicism, however, is open to criticism, even by Elizabeth herself:

> Elizabeth ... had never been blind to the impropriety of her father's behavior as a husband ... she endeavored to forget what she could not overlook, and to banish from her thoughts that continual breach of conjugal obligation and decorum which, in exposing his wife to the contempt of his own children, was so highly reprehensible. (*PP*, 236)

Yet Elizabeth's faults are much the same as his. The cynicism she reveals in describing herself to Jane has surely grown from innate resemblance to her father and constant and congenial association with him:

> There are few people whom I really love, and still fewer of whom I think well. The more I see of the world, the more am I dissatisfied with it; and every day confirms my belief of the inconsistency of all human characters, and of the little dependence that can be placed on the appearance of either merit or sense. (*PP*, 135)

There is no doubt that Elizabeth's enjoyment of intricate characters because they are "most amusing" is related to her father's philosophy: "For what do we live, but to make sport for our neighbors, and laugh at them in our turn?" (*PP*, 364). Elizabeth's triumph, of course, lies in her being able to restrain this cynical tendency so that she is not, like her father, "a person whose first

object in life is a joke" (*PP*, 57). She openly condemns that attitude and
realizes her own danger of succumbing to it:

> ... there are such people, but I hope I am not one of *them*. I hope
> I never ridicule what is wise or good. Follies and nonsense, whims
> and inconsistencies *do* divert me, I own, and I laugh at them
> whenever I can. (*PP*, 57)

Elizabeth never joins her father in hoping that all new acquaintances may be
ridiculous in order to cause her amusement. She merely asks her father, upon
reading Mr. Collins' first absurd letter: "Can he be a sensible man, sir?" But
Mr. Bennet's answer indicates the depths to which his cynicism penetrated
when he says:

> "No, my dear; I think not. I have great hopes of finding him quite
> the reverse. There is a mixture of servility and self-importance in
> his letter, which promises well. I am impatient to see him." (*PP*,
> 64)

In Elizabeth, developing character and, especially, developing love bring her
to the point were she can check even her almost irrepressible desire to laugh
at Darcy:

> Elizabeth longed to observe that Mr. Bingley had been a most
> delightful friend; so easily guided that his worth was invaluable;
> but she checked herself. She remembered that he had yet to learn
> to be laught at, and it was rather too early to begin. (*PP*, 371)

Mr. Bennet would not so have checked himself. For what should have been
love in his life has turned out to be a tragic mistake—a mistake which results
in such incongruities in his own family that he is unable to keep his balance
within it. The final irony, however, of Elizabeth's congeniality with her father
comes when he ridicules the possibility of her ever loving Darcy. After
reading Mr. Collins' letter aloud, Mr. Bennet notices Elizabeth's mixed
reactions and is evidently disturbed that she is not laughing as amusedly as
he is:

> ... But, Lizzy, you look as if you did not enjoy it. You are not
> going to be *Missish*, I hope, and pretend to be affronted at an idle
> report. For what do we live, but to make sport for our
> neighbours, and laugh at them in our turn?"

"Oh!" cried [or *lied*] Elizabeth, "I am excessively diverted. But it is so strange!"

"Yes—*that* is what makes it so amusing. Had they fixed on any other man it would have been nothing, but *his* perfect indifference, and *your* pointed dislike, make it so delightfully absurd...." (*PP*, 364)

The ironies with which Jane Austen has transformed the typical "objecting father" situation are abundant and obvious. His deepening cynicism is a reflection of what Elizabeth might have become had she not avoided unsuitable marriages and learned through bitter experience to recognize her own true love. Simultaneously, his cynicism has so blinded him that he completely misinterprets the feelings of the daughter whom, of all people, he should have been able to understand. For Elizabeth, meanwhile, her own former and very public denouncement of Darcy's arrogance is reaping its full and bitter effects:

Elizabeth had never been more at a loss to make her feelings appear what they were not. It was necessary to laugh, when she would rather have cried. Her father had most cruelly mortified her, by what he said of Mr. Darcy's indifference, and she could do nothing but wonder at such a want of penetration, or fear that perhaps, instead of his seeing too *little*, she might have fancied too much. (*PP*, 364)

In introducing Mrs. Bennet to her readers, Jane Austen makes clear at once that she is a complete contrast to her husband:

Her mind was less difficult to develope. She was a woman of mean understanding, little information, and uncertain temper. When she was discontented she fancied herself nervous. The business of her life was to get her daughters married; its solace was visiting and news. (*PP*, 5)

In her eagerness "to get her daughters married" and in the constant embarrassments to which she subjects Elizabeth, Mrs. Bennet is evidently related to the ubiquitous chaperones that always hover about eighteenth-century heroines. Like Catherine Morland's Mrs. Allen, she is gossipy and unintelligent. Like Evelina's Madame Duval, she is crude and painfully embarrassing. But, like her husband's, her characterization assumes a variety of functions in its intimate connections with the incongruities within her family and with the constant ironies surrounding their romances. Obviously, Lydia is as much like her as Elizabeth is like Mr. Bennet. The differences between husband and wife make the differences between their daughters seem quite credible. The painfully embarrassing situations she creates for Elizabeth, especially in Darcy's presence, reveal the difference between her "mean understanding" and Elizabeth's intelligent sensitivity. But they serve also as early and subtle hints that Elizabeth is subconsciously determined to make a good impression on the "horrid" Mr. Darcy. After her mother's first tactless criticism of Darcy in his presence, Elizabeth automatically speaks in his defense:

> "Indeed, Mama, you are mistaken," said Elizabeth, blushing for her mother. "You quite mistook Mr. Darcy...." (*PP*, 43)

At a later occasion her reactions are, as they continue to be, very similar:

> Elizabeth blushed and blushed again with shame and vexation. She could not help frequently glancing her eye at Mr. Darcy, though every glance convinced her of what she dreaded; for though he was not always looking at her mother, she was convinced that his attention was invariably fixed by her. The expression of his face changed gradually from indignant contempt to a composed and steady gravity. (*PP*, 100)

These painful exposures of ill-breeding on the part of Mrs. Bennet, however, also serve to demonstrate sly ironies. When Elizabeth later visits Pemberley, Lady Catherine's officious condescension to her is fully as crude as Mrs. Bennet's rudeness had been to Darcy. When Lady Catherine suggests that Elizabeth come to practice on the "piano forte in Mrs. Jenkinson's room" because she will "be in nobody's way, you know, in that part of the house", Darcy's reaction is much like Elizabeth's had been before:

> Mr. Darcy looked a little ashamed of his aunt's ill breeding, and made no answer. (*PP*, 173)

Certainly his honest nature must have suggested to him that Elizabeth's crude relatives are no reason for his snubbing her when his own are just as crude! And a final irony is evidenced by the fact that in spite of—even because of—Mrs. Bennet's crude plotting and stupid bungling, three of her daughters are finally married to the very men she herself most wants for them. It *is* her first insistence upon Bingley's visit at Longbourn, her plotting to have Jane become ill at Netherfield, and her final maneuvering to leave Jane and Bingley alone in the drawing room at Longbourn that initiates, encourages, and finally climaxes their romance. It *is* her dearest wish that Lydia be allowed to go to Brighton, where the events begin that culminate in her final—and to Mrs. Bennet most propitious—marriage to Wickham. And, most ironically of all, it *is* her unwitting but pointed attempts to send Elizabeth off with Darcy to "get him out of the way" that allow them the leisure to enjoy their first moments of courtship and make arrangements for their marriage:

> "I am quite sorry, Lizzy, that you should be forced to have that disagreeable man all to yourself. But I hope you will not mind it: it is all for Jane's sake, you know...." (*PP*, 375)

But Mrs. Bennet's raptures, when she finds out that Elizabeth is to marry Darcy, reveal clearly that she never had really considered him a "disagreeable man" at all, but only an unattainable one:

> "Good gracious ... Mr. Darcy! Who would have thought it! And is it really true? Oh! my sweetest Lizzy ... I am so pleased—so happy. Such a charming man!—so handsome! so tall! ... Oh, Lord! What will become of me. I shall go distracted." (*PP*, 378)

As Jane Austen comments drily, "this was enough to prove that her approbation need not be doubted...". The ironies, however, upon which she makes no comment operate even more subtly to indicate that in spite of Elizabeth's likeness to her father and her difference from her mother, the latter has done at least as much as the former to bring Elizabeth and Darcy together.

If the roles of Mr. Bennet and Mrs. Bennet are related obliquely to those of the objecting father and the cruel and embarrassing chaperone respectively, that of Lady Catherine de Bourgh is undoubtedly related to the conventional aristocratic objecting relative who opposes the marriage of the aristocratic or rich gentleman to the lower-class girl. In her preface to *Cecilia*, Annie Raine Ellis notes the similarity between Lady Catherine and the Mrs. Delvile who objects to Cecilia's marriage to her son:

> Lady Catherine de Burgh [sic] is more openly insolent than Mrs. Delvile, and without her direct claim to authority, but there are so many analogies between the scene in "Pride and Prejudice," and that in "Cecilia," that as we read one, we think of the other.[29]

Lady Catherine's arrogant attitude toward Elizabeth Bennet when she angrily demands her to promise not to marry Darcy is certainly an echo of Mrs. Delvile's attitude.[30] But the similarity to a corresponding scene in *Pamela* is much more marked. Although there were no doubt real-life objections for rich and aristocratic relatives in eighteenth-century England to the marriage of their sons to poorer or lower-class girls, it is Richardson from whom the widely imitated literary convention originally stemmed. The similarities between the two scenes verify the fact that Jane Austen was intimately acquainted with Richardson's work.[31] The scenes both introduce indignant lady relatives—Lady Davers, Mr. B's sister; and Lady Catherine, Darcy's aunt. Although Lady Davers is more vulgar than Lady Catherine, the two are equally insulting. After offering various lewd suggestions, Lady Davers says to Pamela: "I suppose you would have me conclude you my brother's wife ..." (*Pamela*, II, p. 154). Lady Catherine is just as offensively indignant, as she dares Elizabeth to verify the shocking rumor that Darcy— her own nephew Darcy—is soon to marry her (*PP*, 353). Both heroines betray an admirable and almost impertinent obstinacy in their responses. Richardson's scene, as usual, stresses the fact that virtue is winning over vice. Jane Austen's scene, as usual, performs a variety of functions. Ironically, reversing the effect which Lady Catherine desires, her visit soon encourages Darcy to propose to Elizabeth. More subtle still is the fine balance the scene creates between Lady Catherine and Mrs. Bennet. Their similarly ridiculous attempts to arrange the marriages they desire remove class distinctions and make fools of them both. Certainly his aunt's rudeness must have made it a good deal easier for Darcy to forgive Elizabeth for having a mother like Mrs. Bennet. As Elizabeth remarks later: "Lady Catherine has been of infinite use, which ought to make her happy, for she loves to be of use" (*PP*, 381). A superficial reading fails to reveal of what "infinite use" Lady Catherine has really been. But careful reading reveals how variously Jane Austen has used this conventional figure to display the inadequacy of social distinctions in judging character; to set hidden ironies in motion; and, quite against her will, to bring about the "happy ending".

Just as the conventional descendant of the Richardsonian heroine is most often portrayed as being "perfect", so the outcome of her romance is most often perfectly happy. Here, too, the difference between Pamela and Elizabeth Bennet reveals how Jane Austen's sense of realism colors the conventional happy ending. Within the framework of her final happiness with her hero there still exist the many limitations to it which have existed throughout the book. This is perhaps the reason that Jane Austen is more successful than Richardson is in creating a victorious but still engaging heroine. Pamela's virtuous victory seems to justify in her an insufferable smugness. Her pious moralizing, her condescension to the adoring servants, her coy acceptance of the adulation of Mr. B and his aristocratic friends—all of these prove her victory to be complete but rather offensive. When her father arrives to share her happiness, she paints a typically sentimental picture of herself with him and Mr. B, sitting "in the happiest place I ever was blest with, between two of the dearest men in the world to me, and each holding one of my hands ..." (*Pamela*, II, p. 49). Elizabeth's victory, on the other hand, makes her neither perfect nor perfectly happy. The painfully honest ridicule of Darcy by Mr. Bennet; the constant potential mortification of Elizabeth by the vulgarity of her relatives; the brazen request that Lydia makes for money; the condescension of Lady Catherine's visits to Pemberley in spite of the way its shades have been "polluted"—all of these limit Elizabeth's happiness and demand of her a continual blending of sympathetic understanding with amused and critical analysis. Certainly, the gay, perceptive, and victorious Elizabeth makes no pretensions to smugness or perfection. Perhaps this is because she has learned that the "truth universally acknowledged, that a single man in possession of a good fortune, must be in want of a wife" (*PP*, 3) includes everyone, even herself, in its irony. She has been victorious, it is true, in convincing an aristocratic man "in possession of good fortune" that she is the wife he wants. But the very fortune which Darcy possesses will always keep her from smugness and pride, for even she will never fully know how much it and the whole aristocratic world it represents helped Darcy to win a victory over her.

In *Pride and Prejudice*, then, Jane Austen again draws freely upon the conventional features of popular eighteenth-century fiction. In it, however, she uses her "transforming agents"—psychological realism, developing character, variety of function, and especially irony—to such advantage that the novel presents a high point in her artistic production. In this achievement the characterization of Elizabeth Bennet is the unifying and overwhelmingly successful element. The merging of villain and hero roles in Darcy is only partially successful, but demonstrates, together with the minor characterizations, how ironic comparisons, contrasts, causes, and effects educate and finally unite the hero and the heroine. As their romance unfolds, even the minor conventional figures and motifs grow in significance and reveal themselves as meaningful parts of Elizabeth Bennet's world. In spite of the weakening of the novel by the more melodramatic uses of conventional material after its climax, the consistently fine characterization of the heroine continues, contributing to the novel a unity and richness which make it indubitably great.

NOTES

16. R. A. Brower, "The Controlling Hand: Jane Austen and 'Pride and Prejudice'", *Scrutiny*, XIII (September, 1945), 108.

17. Tompkins, p. 253.

18. See Tompkins, pp. 346–47. She refers to this as the "greatest weakness of the eighteenth-century novel". The complicated plots of the Gothic novels and the interrelated situations of the Burney novels had made contributions but had not made action "so directly referable to character" as Jane Austen does.

19. For a detailed analysis of these similarities see "*Pamela* and *Pride and Prejudice*", cited in note 6 of this chapter.

20. I do not mean here in any way to deny the psychological power of the characterization of Clarissa. It depends, however, upon the unchanging virtue of her character. Moreover, her characterization is essentially tragic and is therefore hardly amenable to comparison with Elizabeth Bennet's.

21. Eugene White, *Fanny Burney, Novelist* (Hamden, Connecticut, The Shoe String Press, Inc., 1960), p. 78.

22. Brower, p. 108.

23. See "*Pamela* and *Pride and Prejudice*", cited in note 6 of this chapter.

24. Note E. E. Duncan-Jones, "Proposals of Marriage in 'Pride and Prejudice' and 'Pamela'", *Notes and Queries*, IV (February, 1957), 76. He indicates these same similarities very briefly. The citations from Richardson are from the Yale edition, cited in note 6 of my chapter II, on p. 15.

25. Cf. Brower, p. 108.

26. Mudrick, pp. 119–20. Cf. here also Brower, pp. 108ff.

27. McKillop, "Critical Realism", p. 37.

28. Such "moralizers" as Fanny Burney's Rev. Villars in *Evelina*, Albany in *Cecilia*, and Dr. Marchmont in *Camilla* all belong to this didactic, and most often ministerial, line.

29. Frances Burney, *Cecilia*, I (London, G. Bell and Sons, Ltd., 1914), p. ix. Jane Austen's "borrowing" of the title of *Pride and Prejudice* from *Cecilia* (II, p. 462) is so well known that it needs no comment.

30. Cf. pp. 353–58 of *Pride and Prejudice* with pp. 175–82 of *Cecilia*, II.

31. The rest of this chapter draws many ideas from the article "*Pamela* and *Pride and Prejudice*", cited in note 6 of this chapter.

HOWARD S. BABB

Pride and Prejudice:
Vitality and a Dramatic Mode

Few readers would question that *Pride and Prejudice* is the most brilliant of Jane Austen's novels. Perhaps it is less neatly turned than *Emma*, to name a work which has recently found increasing favor among critics because of its technical finesse, but *Pride and Prejudice* has a vibrancy and a rich dramatic texture all its own. Especially through the first half of the novel, Jane Austen recreates the quality of our social experience, that sense we often have of the ambiguities inherent in behavior. She accomplishes this partly through engaging us, alongside the vivacious Elizabeth Bennet, in making out a number of characters largely on the basis of what they say and do in public. In addition, she shows us that the motives are themselves mixed which impel Elizabeth to misjudge the novel's hero for so long, to find Darcy insufferably arrogant and nothing more. But the author's major success here is with Darcy, who seems to me a far cry from the two-dimensional Fanny Burneyan figure that he is so often taken to be. For Jane Austen endows him with mixed motives of his own—pride, shyness; a liking for Elizabeth—at the same time that she keeps prompting us to share the prejudiced Elizabeth's flattened interpretation of him. And through the second half of the story, although Elizabeth and Darcy are now coming to terms with each other, Jane Austen refuses to thin the motives of either one. Elizabeth sacrifices none of her wit and charm in making her peace with Darcy's values, and Darcy attains a more

From *Jane Austen's Novels: The Fabric of Dialogue.* ©1967 by Ohio State University Press.

amiable manner without giving up the substance of his pride. In thus ripening, as it were, both Elizabeth and Darcy express the theme of *Pride and Prejudice*, which again is grounded in the heroine's progress from blindness to insight, and which again argues that the individual must mitigate the demands of personal feeling—whether Elizabeth's prejudice or Darcy's pride—and reconcile them with the claims of sense. Yet by ripening within the contours of personality established for them from the start of the novel, the hero and heroine bear witness to Jane Austen's integrity as an artist.

Both the variety of Darcy's character and Jane Austen's virtuosity in representing it are easy enough to overlook on our first reading of *Pride and Prejudice*, or even on later ones. For one thing, Elizabeth so wins the hearts of us all that we feel no urge to disagree with her, particularly about anyone as stuffy as Darcy appears to be. For another, Jane Austen must keep us pretty much in the dark about him—as she does by screening most of our impressions through Elizabeth—in order to bring off the chief dramatic effect of the story: overwhelming surprise at his first proposal. It is reactions like these, I suspect, that have combined to produce what seems to be the usual opinion of Darcy: that he is a cold man, implacably proud, who unexpectedly shows a new face from the first proposal on, yet remains altogether too unconvincing a character to make a fitting partner for the lively Elizabeth. But to my mind this opinion does no justice to the Darcy whom Jane Austen has created, and the main purpose of my chapter is to revise it. First off, as a kind of reintroduction to the story, I want to indicate how pervasively Jane Austen manipulates our view of Darcy. Next, I shall take up some of the novel's characters in greater detail, paying special attention to Elizabeth in hopes of showing that she readjusts herself at least as radically as Darcy does. Then, in the final section, we must turn to the most brilliant dialogues between Elizabeth and Darcy, where I shall aim at making the vitality of his courtship clear. If through all this I seem less than fair to other figures, particularly Elizabeth, it will be because of trying to make out as strong a case for Darcy as the novel allows.

II

In *Pride and Prejudice* our point of view is much more subtly managed than in either of the novels we have already examined. *Sense and Sensibility*'s Elinor proved reliable almost without exception. And though we saw the action of *Northanger Abbey* along with Catherine, Henry Tilney was always near at hand to correct any false impressions that might arise. But in *Pride and Prejudice* there is no one on whom we can depend for a true account. Rather, we are for the most part confined to Elizabeth's deeply biased perceptions, and Jane Austen tempts us to accept her heroine's view of Darcy at every turn, though just as consistently leaving the door open to a more favorable interpretation of his behavior.

At his introduction, we do not hear him speak until the "great admiration" he initially stirs has given way to a general "disgust" with his "manners"—that is, until Jane Austen has planted society's judgment, based wholly on appearances, in our minds, and perhaps in Elizabeth's as well. So the real ambiguity of his opening remarks catches us with our guard down. When Bingley urges him to dance, we overlook what may be Darcy's protestation of shyness in "You know how I detest it, unless I am particularly acquainted with my partner," even though it supplies a clear logic for the mention of Bingley's "sisters" that follows: "Your sisters are engaged, and there is not another woman in the room, whom it would not be a punishment to me to stand up with" (p. 11). Instead of entertaining the possibility that Darcy's tone reveals the instinctive irritation of a shy person at an aggressive invasion of his privacy, we seize on his whole reply as betraying an absolute contempt engendered by pride. Our listening to this with Elizabeth does not help a bit, for her prejudice is fixed when he goes on in as sharp a tone to reject Bingley's offer of introducing him to her—though it is an open question whether Darcy realizes that she can hear him.[1]

These first glimpses of him, so carefully slanted by Jane Austen, condition us to minimize every hint that he might be less of a monster than Elizabeth supposes. Thus her sister Jane's report—that Darcy "never speaks much unless among his intimate acquaintance. With *them* he is remarkably agreeable" (p. 19)—we discount readily enough, even though it echoes the ambiguity of Darcy's first speeches, because it has originated with the disagreeable Caroline Bingley. We refuse to set any store by Elizabeth's profession that she herself is biased, "... I could easily forgive *his* pride, if he had not mortified *mine*" (p. 20), because her phrasing sounds witty and open-minded. And by the time Darcy actually invites her to dance, first at the home of the Lucases and later at Netherfield, we have become so acclimatized to her dislike that we are almost as suspicious as she is of his intentions, as content to ignore the most plausible motive behind his requests, and as hopeful as she is that he will be discomfited by her ironic "Mr. Darcy is all politeness" (p. 26) or "... I do not want to dance a reel at all—and now despise me if you dare" (p. 52).[2]

Occasionally in these opening chapters Jane Austen lets us escape from Elizabeth's perspective to a more omniscient view of Darcy, but without encouraging us to give up Elizabeth's opinion. When the author describes Darcy's growing attachment, she narrates it in such a way that we are less aware of his affection than of his pride, less struck by his "discovery" of a "beautiful expression" in Elizabeth's eyes than by his finding the discovery "mortifying" (p. 23). Sometimes the rhetoric itself of Jane Austen's comments on Darcy inclines us toward Elizabeth's prejudice while it slyly permits him a richer blend of motives: for example, in stating that Elizabeth "attracted him more than he liked—and Miss Bingley was uncivil to *her*, and more teazing than usual to himself" (pp. 59–60), Jane Austen buries Darcy's sympathy for Elizabeth in the first half of the antithesis, completing the structure—as she has begun the sentence—with claims relating to his sense of himself. Even when she puts Darcy in action for us during Elizabeth's absence, as in his quarrels with Miss Bingley about Elizabeth's "fine eyes" (pp. 27, 36), we cannot tell for sure whether he wants to praise Elizabeth or to provoke her rival or to demonstrate haughtily that he is Miss Bingley's superior by turning down her bids to entangle him in a community of opinion.

Most of the time, however, Jane Austen forces us to look on with Elizabeth at what is happening, which means that Darcy is inevitably distorted. If Elizabeth notices, for instance, "how frequently Mr. Darcy's eyes were fixed on her," she immediately transforms the fact into a fancy that "there was a something about her more wrong and reprehensible according to his ideas of right, than in any other person present" (p. 51). Indeed we often hardly realize that what seems an objective account of Darcy's behavior by a detached author has really been filtered through Elizabeth's perceptions. When Mr. Collins leaves her to pay his respects to Lady Catherine's nephew, addressing himself to Darcy twice, we are told:

> —It vexed her to see him expose himself to such a man. Mr. Darcy was eyeing him with unrestrained wonder, and when at last Mr. Collins allowed him time to speak, replied with an air of distant civility.... Mr. Darcy's contempt seemed abundantly increasing with the length of his second speech, and at the end of it he only made him a slight bow, and moved another way. (p. 98)

The terms that color Darcy here—"wonder," "distant civility," and "contempt"—belong to Elizabeth, so to speak, and are perhaps heightened because she is "vexed" to start with.

By maneuvers like these, Jane Austen obscures Darcy's real nature through half of *Pride and Prejudice*. And, while we can no longer doubt his love for Elizabeth after the first proposal scene, the author tries to prevent us from settling his character decisively until the conclusion of the story. Thus, the housekeeper at Pemberley may commend him warmly, but Jane Austen undercuts the tribute by mentioning Mrs. Reynolds' "pride or attachment ...

in talking of her master" (p. 248). When Darcy himself turns up, Elizabeth keeps protesting about the amazing "alteration in his manner" (p. 252), although by this time we may well suspect that much of the alteration is in Elizabeth herself, who has been surrendering her prejudice against him. Even the favorable testimony of the Gardiners, who have given us for the first time in the novel a relatively unbiased reaction to Darcy (p. 257), is invalidated somewhat by their wish to see Elizabeth marry him (p. 264). Only at the end of *Pride and Prejudice* does Jane Austen permit Darcy to reveal his character completely and explicitly, although by restricting us still to her heroine's point of view in the closing chapters, she teases us about his feelings a good deal less than she does Elizabeth.

In detailing some of the tricks by which Jane Austen controls our perspective on Darcy, I am not implying that he is really without pride. Rather, I want to suggest how constantly in the interest of the novel's dramatic effect she highlights his pride, making him appear something of a humor character by keeping his other qualities hidden in shadow. But the very limitations of our point of view here should caution us to cling fast to the dialogues as our surest source of truth, about Darcy, Elizabeth, or anyone else. In them we can discover a three-dimensional Darcy, as I shall try to show more fully in the last section of this chapter. In the meantime, we must look closely at some of Elizabeth's verbal encounters, mainly to find out how she changes in the course of the novel, but partly to get a sense of some other figures as well, who display their own varieties of pride and prejudice.

III

Our best general guide to Elizabeth's development, and for that matter to Darcy's, is the insight she offers us late in the novel: "It was an union that must have been to the advantage of both; by her ease and liveliness, his mind might have been softened, his manners improved, and from his judgment, information, and knowledge of the world, she must have received benefit of greater importance" (p. 312). For the passage makes clear that Darcy changes in manner, not in essentials, and it implies that Elizabeth has been biased by her emotions. Yet she has always believed that she speaks cool sense, a sense which she thinks she can rely on because it owes so little to conventional opinion. Thus convinced that her mind is unclouded by prejudice of a sort, she invariably trusts herself to her immediate perceptions. And she is constantly exercising them to decide on some particular case, sure that her judgment will do fuller justice to its merits than any other. Of course, this assurance and unconventionality combine with the very real sense that she has to make almost everything she says sparkle with wit—though unfortunately I must ignore her wit from now on to make another point. For her speeches also reveal something that Elizabeth is quite unaware of: the fact that warm feeling rather than cool sense informs many of her decisions, and not only those concerning Darcy.

Early in the novel, for instance, when the relationship between Bingley and Jane Bennet engages the attention of most of the characters, Elizabeth has a set-to with her friend Charlotte Lucas about Jane's placid behavior to her suitor (pp. 21–23). The prudent Charlotte takes the position that Jane risks losing Bingley unless she shows her feelings more openly. Charlotte builds her case largely on hardheaded generalizations, though she sounds a more compassionate note in the first sentence that follows: "We can all begin freely—a slight preference is natural enough; but there are very few of us who have heart enough to be really in love without encouragement. In nine cases out of ten, a woman had better spew more affection than she feels." But Elizabeth brushes aside such reasoning to cite her own experience of the situation at hand: "If I can perceive her regard for him, he must be a simpleton indeed not to discover it too." She seems confident of uttering nothing but plain sense here, yet "simpleton" marks her typical intensity, and obviously the whole reply is inspired by sympathy for her sister. When Charlotte counters by observing rationally enough that Bingley cannot "know Jane's disposition as you do," Elizabeth refuses to retreat. Instead, she leaps to a generalization—"But if a woman is partial to a man, and does not endeavour to conceal it, he must find it out"—in order to confirm what she has said before, but surely this new claim stems at least as much from Elizabeth's private concern for Jane as it does from impartial reason. The exchange goes on in this vein, Elizabeth becoming so impatient with the prudence of her opponent that she finally breaks out in open sarcasm. This moves Charlotte to restate her position in generalizations that set out as severe version of marriage as ever, though they do not inhibit her own sympathy for Jane:[3]

> "Well ... I wish Jane success with all my heart; and if she were married to him to-morrow, I should think she had as good a chance of happiness, as if she were to be studying his character for a twelve-month. Happiness in marriage is entirely a matter of chance. If the dispositions of the parties are ever so well known to each other, or ever so similar before-hand, it does not advance their felicity in the least. They always continue to grow sufficiently unlike afterwards to have their share of vexation; and it is better to know as little as possible of the defects of the person with whom you arc to pass your life."

> "You make me laugh, Charlotte; but it is not sound. You know
> it is not sound, and that you would never act in this way yourself."

Again Elizabeth scoffs at Charlotte for being unreasonable, closing the argument with the splendid assertion that she knows Charlotte better than Charlotte knows herself. But the facts of the novel scoff at Elizabeth: one of Darcy's major reasons for intervening between Bingley and Jane is that she does not seem strongly attached; and Charlotte does adhere to her principles in marrying Mr. Collins. This is not by any means to say that we should approve of Charlotte's act or that she speaks more truly than Elizabeth in the passage under discussion. But it is to say that Elizabeth frequently misjudges, failing to recognize that her reasoning is biased by feelings, here her affection for Jane and her disdain for Charlotte's prudence.

The same motives and the same sort of misjudgment crop up when Elizabeth talks over with Jane the apparently permanent removal of Bingley to London, for which he has offered no explanation, and the engagement of Charlotte to Mr. Collins (pp. 134–37). Jane, of course, cannot bear to think badly of anyone, and she never speaks without revealing how completely her benevolent feelings determine her decisions. Indeed, a remark she makes at one point, "Let me take it in the best light, in the light in which it may be understood" (p. 137), might well serve as her motto. But refined as Jane's feelings are, her thoroughgoing dependence on them is a form of prejudice as settled as Charlotte's prudence. And Elizabeth is as eager to expose the one extreme as the other, still assured that her own sense is immune to any such error. So when Jane excuses Bingley much too charitably, blaming herself instead for having wrongly imagined that he liked her, Elizabeth first praises her sister as "angelic," but then proclaims her own superior wisdom in a rhetoric that assigns Jane to one camp and herself to another:

> "Do not be afraid of my running into any excess, of my encroaching on your privilege of universal good will.... There are few people whom I really love, and still fewer of whom I think well. The more I see of the world, the more am I dissatisfied with it; and every day confirms my belief of the inconsistency of all human characters, and of the little dependence that can be placed on the appearance of either merit or sense. I have met with two instances lately; one I will not mention; the other is Charlotte's marriage. It is unaccountable! in every view it is unaccountable!"

By distinguishing so dispassionately between the "few" whom she can "really love" and "still fewer of whom" she can "think well," Elizabeth presumably guards herself against Jane's emotional "excess." But the generalization about "inconsistency" actually arises from her dissatisfaction with "the world," and her "two instances" bear this out. Of Bingley she will say nothing at the moment out of affection for Jane, but Charlotte is another matter. Although Elizabeth protests, by "unaccountable" and "in every view," that her own verdict is purely rational, the repetition of phrase betrays her pique. And in fact the verdict is conditioned by her dislike for Mr. Collins and by her irritation with Charlotte—whom we saw accounting for herself in detail—for proving Elizabeth's earlier assessment of how her friend would behave quite incorrect. Perhaps it is mildly ironic that Jane should put her finger on the element endangering Elizabeth's judgment, begging her sister not to "give way to such feelings as these." In any event, Jane goes on typically enough to interpret the whole affair too generously:

> "Consider Mr. Collins's respectability, and Charlotte's prudent, steady character. Remember that she is one of a large family; that as to fortune, it is a most eligible match; and be ready to believe, for every body's sake, that she may feel something like regard and esteem for our cousin."

This is too much for Elizabeth, who belabors first Charlotte, then Mr. Collins, and concludes with a powerful array of conceptual terms to rebuke Jane for being irresponsible:

> "You shall not defend her, though it is Charlotte Lucas. You shall not, for the sake of one individual, change the meaning of principle and integrity, nor endeavour to persuade yourself or me, that selfishness is prudence, and insensibility of danger, security for happiness."

Again the effect of the rhetoric is to play off Jane's singularity against her own reliance on "principle and integrity," and certainly Jane deserves the rebuke. But the fundamental irony turns against Elizabeth once more. She is too irked by Jane's attitude and too positive of her oven integrity to realize that her fixed prejudice against Darcy lays her open to the same charge time and again through the first half of the novel at least, most obviously in her decisions about Darcy himself and in her misjudgment of Wickham.

About the first of her suitors, however, Elizabeth has no illusions. Only Mrs. Bennet could, and perhaps Lady Catherine de Bourgh, for Mr. Collins never deviates from absurdity. Certainly his overly formal rhetoric, constant polysyllables, and especially those notorious ripe metaphors are laughable enough, but we must look behind these traits to get at the essential absurdity of Mr. Collins' verbal manner. On one level he uses language quite consciously: we remember him telling Mr. Bennet about working out "little elegant compliments" in his spare moments. Yet Mr. Collins remains completely unaware that, by the time he has strung his phrases together, they develop an inflated tone which is at best ridiculously disproportionate to whatever he wants to say—and at the worst contradicts his claims. In his classic proposal to Elizabeth, for instance, he spins out a highly formal announcement about being in the grip of overpowering emotions: "And now nothing remains for me but to assure you in the most animated language of the violence of my affection" (p. 106). Diverting as this sort of verbal idiocy may be, the equivalent contradiction at the core of Mr. Collins' nature— humility become pride—makes him sometimes inane and sometimes frightening.[4] If he tries for sense, he comes closer to nonsense: "... I consider the clerical office as equal in point of dignity with the highest rank in the kingdom—provided that a proper humility of behaviour is at the same time maintained" (p. 97). And when he vents his feelings, as on learning of Lydia Bennet's elopement, the result is a ghastly parody of a clergyman's sympathy, his "comfort" for Mr. Bennet consisting in encouraging him to disown his daughter. But everything he says and does reflects his irresponsibility so clearly that Elizabeth never stands in danger of misreading him.

The case is rather different with Wickham, who also courts Elizabeth's favor. Her antagonism toward Darcy predisposes her to find "truth" in the "looks" of his enemy (p. 86), and she unhesitatingly accepts Wickham's story about being cut off from his rightful inheritance by a jealous Darcy. What does not register with Elizabeth until much later, after Darcy has told her the truth of the whole business, is that Wickham's verbal manner reveals a contradiction of its own. It is one more subtle than anything Mr. Collins can show, but just as firm a clue to irresponsibility. This false note is struck during Wickham's first conversation with Elizabeth. While he pretends to honor the demands of propriety in holding himself back, he in fact converts decorum into a backdrop to set off his own particular and unrestrained dislike for Darcy: "I have no right to give my opinion.... I am not qualified to form one. I have known him too long and too well to be a fair judge. It is impossible for me to be impartial" (p. 77). Wickham exploits these two roles throughout the scene. As soon as he knows that Elizabeth shares his dislike, he really opens up against Darcy, playing to the hilt the part of a man whose feelings are too strong to be kept back—indeed describing himself at one point as a person of "warm, unguarded temper" (p. 80). Along with these outbursts, sometimes almost in the same breath, Wickham makes a series of appeals to the generalizations of propriety, such as "I cannot pretend to be sorry ... that he or that any man should not be estimated beyond their deserts" (p. 78), or "A man of honour could not have doubted the intention, but Mr. Darcy chose to doubt it" (p. 79). But Wickham's emotional exhibitionism is simply incongruent with his professions of decorum, a fact which Elizabeth can formulate only when she has learned to think better of Darcy (p. 207). Until then, blinded by her prejudice, she is completely taken in by Wickham's artful inversions of his own appearance and reality, and of Darcy's.

All the encounters in which we have seen Elizabeth involved so far, however, seem like minor engagements when compared to her running battle with Darcy himself. In their clashes, she remains supremely confident of her perceptions as an individual. While Darcy does not undervalue his opinions either, he does go to work in a different fashion. No less interested than Elizabeth in arriving at the merits of the particular case, he starts out, at least, with generalizations, often those of society. And along the way he appears more careful than she to ally himself with objective reason. Certainly he sounds as self-assured in making his judgments as she does, though whether because of a peevish sense of superiority—as Elizabeth feels—or a proper pride is harder to determine. Their characteristic tones and methods are illustrated in various dialogues: the argument about Bingley's impetuosity (pp. 48–50), for example, or about Darcy's pride (pp. 57–58). But the scene in which ladies' accomplishments come up for discussion has some special advantages for our purposes. It will show us a little of two other characters, Bingley and his sister Caroline. More important, it will introduce us to the word that lies at the heart of the novel's meaning, *performance*, a concept we will be much concerned with in the final section of this chapter. For the present, though, we need only be aware that the sense of *performance* extends from a mere display of skill to a deed expressive of one's whole being, and that at the start of the conversation before us the word is equated with "accomplished," the alternate term thus acquiring exactly the same range of meaning and, in fact, taking the place of "performance" throughout this scene (pp. 38–40).

The words are put in play by Caroline Bingley, who sets out as usual to bind herself and Darcy together in an exclusive community of opinion, this time by rhapsodizing about his sister's "accomplished ... performance" on the piano:

> "Such a countenance, such manners! and so extremely accomplished for her age! Her performance on the piano-forte is exquisite."
>
> "It is amazing to me," said Bingley, "how young ladies can have patience to be so very accomplished, as they all are."

"All young ladies accomplished! My dear Charles, what do you mean?"

"Yes, all of them, I think. They all paint tables, cover skreens and net purses. I scarcely know any one who cannot do all this, and I am sure I never heard a young lady spoken of for the first time, without being informed that she was very accomplished."

Clearly Caroline means the words in a narrow sense only, to denote the skills of the aristocratic, so she becomes angry when her brother devalues such pursuits by allowing all "young ladies" to be "so very accomplished." Bingley himself speaks with that indiscriminating generosity which is so typical of him and which makes him the perfect partner for Jane. His generalizations flow straight from his feelings, but he praises the whole class of "young ladies" for trivial achievements.

As we might expect, Darcy seizes the opportunity to be discriminating about "accomplishments," yet we should beware of identifying his motives with Caroline's:

"Your list of the common extent of accomplishments ... has too much truth. The word is applied to many a woman who deserves it no otherwise than by netting a purse, or covering a skreen. But I am very far from agreeing with you in your estimation of ladies in general. I cannot boast of knowing more than half a dozen, in the whole range of my acquaintance, that are really accomplished."

He begins with Bingley's generalization and proceeds to test it in the light of his own observation. Maybe it would be risky to decide at the moment whether his distinction between "common extent" and "really accomplished" is inspired by a snobbish commitment like Caroline's to the superficial sense of the word or by a rational grasp of its whole meaning. But certainly when he replies to Elizabeth's "you must comprehend a great deal in your idea of an accomplished woman" with "Yes; I do comprehend a great deal in it," he accents the weight of the "accomplishments," though perhaps a chance remains that he is being merely haughty. His next remark, however, removes even this ambiguity. After Caroline has reeled off a host of refinements like "drawing," "the modern languages," and "a certain ... air and manner of walking" which the truly accomplished woman commands, thus hoping to deny the name to Elizabeth and all except the elegant, Darcy comments, "All this she must possess ... and to all this she must yet add something more substantial, in the improvement of her mind by extensive reading." His generalization insists on a fuller sense of "accomplished," the "more substantial" integrating refined behavior with the reason that comes from "reading." Yet Darcy's words strike a more personal note as well, for a little earlier Caroline has nastily characterized Elizabeth as "a great reader"; so this becomes a compliment to Elizabeth by offering her an entree into the select category that Caroline has been jealously hugging to herself.

But the only voice Elizabeth listens to is her antipathy toward Darcy, and characteristically, it compels her to translate his claim into an extreme:

> "I am no longer surprised at your knowing only six accomplished women. I rather wonder now at your knowing any."
>
> "Are you so severe upon your own sex, as to doubt the possibility of all this?"
>
> "*I* never saw such a woman. *I* never saw such capacity, and taste, and application, and elegance, as you describe, united."

Again Darcy assigns the richest meaning to "accomplished," and on one level his answer seems strictly rational. But it pays another compliment to the "sex" of which Elizabeth is a member. Furthermore, he echoes here one of her earlier attacks on him, "You are severe on us" (p. 24); thus Darcy may also be attempting to clear himself while hinting gently that she is the biased one. How much of this Elizabeth takes in we cannot tell; we can only be sure that she rejects both him and his sense of "accomplished" to assert the priority of her own experience. The dialogue has shown, however, that Darcy sets as high a value on personal experience in making judgments; that he seems, in addition, rather more scrupulous than Elizabeth about observing the place of reason in generalizations, either his own or those of others; finally, that he manages all this without slighting his particular feeling for her.

Darcy's feeling reaches its peak, of course, when he disregards Elizabeth's inferior social status and his low opinion of her family to propose to her, and Elizabeth's animosity comes to a boil at the same point. What she actually objects to, although she denies it to him (p. 192), is the mode of his proposal, to which she reverts again and again (pp. 193, 212, 224). And indeed the mode is all that Darcy ever really apologizes for (p. 367), having learned from Elizabeth's rebuff, not that he must change his convictions, but that he must modify the confidence and stiffness of his manner if he is to please. His letter explaining his dealings with Bingley and Wickham teaches Elizabeth, in her turn, how "wretchedly blind" her prejudice has made her too him and to herself. In fact, as she comes to see Darcy more clearly in the second half of the story, she even takes over from time to time something like his verbal method in presenting her judgments, though she remains quite capable of being witty. As for his opinion of her family, Elizabeth may resent it while he speaks, but she has censured them freely before the proposal (p. 101), and does so on several occasions later on, one of which we will glance at after a moment.

It is not very surprising that Elizabeth should feel a bit uncomfortable about all her immediate family except Jane, whom Darcy also exempts from his reproaches. Mrs. Bennet, to name first the most blatantly indecorous of the group, stands condemned every time she opens her mouth. Her fairly frequent metaphors, intensively particular terms, and abrupt rhythms show that she can never subdue her emotions—the source of her generalizations as well—and cannot therefore respond appropriately to the situations confronting her:

> "My dear, dear Lydia! ... This is delightful indeed!—She will be married!—I shall see her again!—She will be married at sixteen!—My good, kind brother!—I knew how it would be—I knew he would manage every thing. How I long to see her! and to see dear Wickham too! But the clothes, the wedding clothes! I will write to my sister Gardiner about them directly." (p. 306)

In the flow of her feelings, she treats Lydia, marriage "at sixteen," the aid of Mr. Gardiner, Wickham, and the "wedding clothes" as of equal importance. And obviously Mrs. Bennet is so possessed by her ruling passion, to get her daughters married as soon as possible, that she has no qualms at all about the circumstances of Lydia's elopement. Naturally Lydia herself has none. She shares, in fact, much of her mother's nature and most of her verbal traits, the only difference being that Lydia's tone usually sounds more unconcerned, rather as if she has not yet experienced the strain in satisfying her desires that Mrs. Bennet feels so often.

Although the wit of Mr. Bennet's conversation makes him a good deal more bearable than his wife or Lydia, his conduct really comes no nearer decorum than theirs. The emotional detachment which he cultivates so assiduously proves as crippling as their emotional involvement. Indeed he responds to life as predictably as they do, for whatever the situation, he encounters it with a joke—and pretty much the same joke at that. The essence of his wit lies in that literalistic manner by means of which he converts whatever is said to him and whatever happens into absurdity—thus indulging his superior wisdom. The trick is amusing enough when he plays it on the silly Mrs. Bennet, as in referring to her "poor nerves" as "my old friends" (p. 5). But he seems heartless, even imperceptive when he talks to

Elizabeth of Jane's separation from Bingley in the same fashion: "... your sister is crossed in love I find. I congratulate her. Next to being married, a girl likes to be crossed in love a little now and then. It is something to think of, and gives her a sort of distinction among her companions" (pp. 137–38). In the last analysis, Mr. Bennet's mode has the same effect as his wife's, prohibiting him from distinguishing between the trivial and the significant. It is peculiarly appropriate that his one attempt in the novel to express straight sense and straight feeling—when he dissuades Elizabeth from marrying Darcy (p. 376)—should coincide with Mr. Bennet's complete mistaking of his daughter, the person he has depended on knowing best.

The mind of Elizabeth, needless to say, is more flexible than her father's. She possesses altogether finer capacities than any of her family, and she has always behaved with a keener awareness of herself in relation to other people. Once Darcy's letter has cleared her insight, she does not hesitate to judge herself firmly. In the passage that follows, for instance, Elizabeth founds her generalizations in reason alone, and—in another reversal of her earlier ways with language—she levels the generalizations straight at her prejudice rather than considering herself an exceptional case beyond their reach:

> "And yet I meant to be uncommonly clever in taking so decided a dislike to him, without any reason. It is such a spur to one's genius, such an opening for wit to have a dislike of that kind. One may be continually abusive without saying any thing just; but one cannot be always laughing at a man without now and then stumbling on something witty." (pp. 225–26)

Here she may be remembering Darcy's previous warning, which she spurned at the time, about how easy it is for "a person whose first object in life is a joke" to render "ridiculous" the "wisest and the best of men" (p. 57).

But she adopts his verbal manner itself when she, alone among the Bennets, opposes Lydia's trip to Brighton and tries to persuade her father—who thinks Elizabeth selfishly hoping to preserve her own credit with her suitors—of its impropriety:

> "It is not of peculiar, but of general evils, which I am now complaining. Our importance, our respectability in the world, must be affected by the wild volatility, the assurance and disdain of all restraint which mark Lydia's character.... If you, my dear father, will not take the trouble of checking her exuberant spirits ... she will soon be beyond the reach of amendment. Her

character will be fixed.... A flirt ... in the worst and meanest
degree of flirtation; without any attraction beyond youth and a
tolerable person; and from the ignorance and emptiness of her
mind, wholly unable to ward off any portion of that universal
contempt which her rage for admiration will excite." (p. 231)

First Elizabeth differentiates carefully between the "peculiar" and the
"general"; then she sets out the moral generalization that covers the case; last
of all, she measures Lydia in the light of steadfast concepts. Method,
vocabulary, the decision itself-all might be Darcy's.

It seems especially fitting, though, that Elizabeth should use a method
approaching his—integrated with her own wit—to gain her brilliant triumph
over his aunt when that lady forbids her to think of marrying Darcy. Lady
Catherine de Bourgh represents the extreme of pride; we might say that her
motives really are what Elizabeth has imagined her nephew's to be during the
first part of the story. Obsessed with her rank, Lady Catherine cannot
distinguish between her own whims and general principles. This equation
dominates her speeches, perhaps never more unpleasantly than when she
berates Elizabeth for not giving way to her own project of uniting Darcy with
her daughter: "Are you lost to every feeling of propriety and delicacy? Have
you not heard me say, that from his earliest hours he was destined for his
cousin?" (p. 355). But Elizabeth puts Lady Catherine to rout by
discriminating between wishes, facts, and moral obligations:

"If there is no other objection to my marrying your nephew, I
shall certainly not be kept from it, by knowing that his mother
and aunt wished him to marry Miss De Bourgh. You both did as
much as you could, in planning the marriage. Its completion
depended on others. If Mr. Darcy is neither by honour nor
inclination confined to his cousin, why is not he to make another
choice? And if I am that choice, why may not I accept him?"
(p. 355)

Her controlled reasoning, here and throughout the dialogue, lays bare the
bias of her opponent's arguments in reducing them to nonsense. And of
course Elizabeth's victory in the scene, once Lady Catherine has reported
their discussion to Darcy, brings on his second, successful proposal.

As a result of failing the first time, however, Darcy has forsaken his
domineering manner for a mildness typified by his invitation to Elizabeth
when they next meet, at Pemberley:

> "There is also one other person in the party ... who more
> particularly wishes to be known to you,—Will you allow me, or
> do I ask too much, to introduce my sister to your acquaintance
> during your stay at Lambton?" (p. 256)

Indeed "Mr. Darcy is all politeness," almost excessively so in refusing to
presume on Elizabeth in any way and in reserving all wishes to his sister and
himself. Yet in spite of his more subdued tone, Darcy's habit of
differentiating remains unaltered, as is evident in one of his last talks with
Elizabeth:

> "Your retrospections must be so totally void of reproach, that the
> contentment arising from them, is not of philosophy, but what is
> much better, of ignorance. But with *me*, it is not so. Painful
> recollections will intrude, which cannot, which ought not to be
> repelled. I have been a selfish being all my life, in practice, though
> not in principle. As a child I was taught what was *right*, but I was
> not taught to correct my temper.... I was spoilt by my parents,
> who ... almost taught me to be selfish and overbearing ... to think
> meanly of all the rest of the world, to *wish* at least to think meanly
> of their sense and worth compared with my own.... You taught me
> a lesson, hard indeed at first, but most advantageous.... You
> shewed me how insufferable were all my pretensions to please a
> woman worthy of being pleased." (p. 369)

While he compliments Elizabeth by elevating "ignorance" above
"philosophy" and then proceeds to judge himself harshly, Darcy's speech still
bristles with discriminations: between "cannot" and "ought not," "practice"
and "principle," "to think" and "to wish," "hard" and "advantageous,"
appearance and reality. If the passage shows that Darcy has come to see
himself in a new light much as Elizabeth did, it also declares that his
fundamental beliefs have not altered.

IV

The verbal traits of all the characters whom we have been reviewing,
then, reveal how they form their judgments and how they behave. Bringing
the two together, we can go on to say that the theme of *Pride and Prejudice*
concerns judging from behavior and behaving with judgment. These crucial
issues are caught together in the word *performance*—whose meaning, as I
suggested earlier, ranges from a show, an exhibition, to a total act, a deed

integrated with one's entire nature. For the term amounts to more than a convenient ambiguity which allows Jane Austen to contrast Elizabeth and Darcy by associating her with the thinner sense and him with the deeper one. The word refers to behavior itself: a person can be known only by the qualities of his performance, whichever kind it may be, and in either sort of performance one mediates between society and oneself. The concept stands, in all its variety, at the very center of the novel's meaning, and it takes its life from the most brilliant dialogues between Elizabeth and Darcy. To these we must turn at last, searching out in them a Darcy who is less disagreeable and more emotional than we usually imagine.

The first conversation between them sets the tone of their relationship and introduces us to the pivotal concept (p. 24). After a moment we shall see Elizabeth interpreting it in a limited sense, but her immediate behavior makes the same point. For, urged on by Charlotte Lucas, she is provoked by the presence of Darcy to put on an exhibitionistic performance for him:

> "Did not you think, Mr. Darcy, that I expressed myself uncommonly well just now, when I was teazing Colonel Forster to give us a ball at Meryton?"
>
> "With great energy; but it is a subject which always makes a lady energetic."

She proclaims that she is unconventional by "uncommonly well" and that she is feminine by "teazing." Darcy's "great energy" acknowledges her uniqueness, but he then backs off to a generalization, either to avoid the impropriety of noticing her too personally or to pronounce sternly on the frivolity of ladies. Elizabeth reacts only to the second possibility and accuses him of being stuffy: "You are severe on us." Although her "us" may seem at first a decorous retreat to the anonymity of a class, it really flaunts the opposition of all her sex to Darcy.

Her antagonism swells when Charlotte, a little concerned for Darcy, teases her in turn about the actual performance that is to follow. Elizabeth may pretend to take account of propriety in calling Charlotte "strange," yet she directs attention to her own "vanity" in the act of denying that it has "taken a musical turn":

> "You are a very strange creature by way of a friend!—always wanting me to play and sing before any body and every body!— If my vanity had taken a musical turn, you would have been invaluable, but as it is, I would really rather not sit down before those who must be in the habit of hearing the very best

> performers.... Very well; if it must be so, it must." And gravely
> glancing at Mr. Darcy, "There is a fine old saying, which every
> body here is of course familiar with—'Keep your breath to cool
> your porridge,'—and I shall keep mine to swell my song."

Indeed she puts her individuality on parade all through the speech, closing with her most striking flourish at Darcy. Not content with having sneered at him obliquely by "any body and every body," Elizabeth becomes downright specific in her final saucy maxim—and whets its edge by the generalization that separates him from "every body here," from her circle of acquaintance. She is speaking ironically, of course, when she includes herself among the "performers" who entertain the idle rich with their skills. Nevertheless, Elizabeth clearly understands by *performance* nothing more than the kind of conscious self-display in which she has just been indulging.

We observed earlier in this chapter how Darcy identifies himself with the fuller sense of the concept in discussing ladies' accomplishments, and we saw that he does so without disregarding his own feelings for Elizabeth. In the dialogues that follow, we shall find him taking more and more delighted notice of her. When they meet at the Netherfield ball (pp. 91–94), for instance, Darcy surprises her into dancing with him, a high compliment if we recall his earlier comments on the pastime, but Elizabeth,

> suddenly fancying that it would be the greater punishment to her
> partner to oblige him to talk ... made some slight observation on
> the dance. He replied, and was again silent. After a pause of some
> minutes she addressed him a second time with
>   "It is *your* turn to say something now, Mr. Darcy. I talked about
> the dance, and you ought to make some kind of remark on the
> size of the room, or the number of couples."

She taunts him with another show of willfulness, weighing the silence that she reads as offensive pride against her own propriety, which she ironically pretends to, in conversing. Though she is off on another performance, Darcy yields to her with perfect politeness:

> He smiled, and assured her that whatever she wished him to
> say should be said.
>   "Very well.—That reply will do for the present.—Perhaps by
> and bye I may observe that private balls are much pleasanter than
> public ones.—But *now* we may be silent."
>   "Do you talk by rule then, while you are dancing?"

When she parodies decorum to make his stubbornness clear, he tries to cut through her exhibition to her real self, asking that they overthrow the "rule" of convention and be emotionally direct with each other.

Predictably, Elizabeth desires only to put Darcy in his place. Her first generalizations carefully set up the barrier of impersonal propriety again:

> "Sometimes. One must speak a little, you know. It would look odd to be entirely silent for half an hour together, and yet for the advantage of *some*, conversation ought to be so arranged as that they may have the trouble of saying as little as possible."

And her final generalization keeps Darcy apart from her by assigning them different standards, at the same time that it scarcely masks her disdain for him. Yet he responds with a more personal appeal, one that brushes aside the barrier of decorum to get at their private emotions:

> "Are you consulting your own feelings in the present case, or do you imagine that you are gratifying mine?"
>
> "Both," replied Elizabeth archly; "for I have always seen a great similarity in the turn of our minds.—We are each of an unsocial, taciturn disposition, unwilling to speak, unless we expect to say something that will amaze the whole room, and be handed down to posterity with all the eclat of a proverb."

But Elizabeth turns down his plea. She can spell out his arrogance if she condemns herself as well, though obviously she means her words to sound absurd when applied to herself.

Darcy rejects her typical move to the extreme in order to pursue the truth. But the compliment with which he begins and the warning in his last sentence that she is liable to error make no impression on her:

> "This is no very striking resemblance of your own character, I am sure," said he. "*How* near it may be to *mine*, I cannot pretend to say.—You think it a faithful portrait undoubtedly."
>
> "I must not decide on my own performance."

Elizabeth uses the term in its narrow sense only, carrying on the figure that "portrait" implies to announce her propriety once more. Yet the total meaning of the word measures her behavior to Darcy with sharp irony, for she is unaware that the role she keeps playing is itself a decision—or that this continuing performance expresses the opposition of her whole nature to

Darcy rather than controlled reason, as she supposes. And she remains oblivious through the rest of the scene, blithely acting out what she thinks of him while ignoring what he reveals of himself. When she presses him about Wickham, for example, she fails to realize that her advice is better suited to herself: "It is particularly incumbent on those who never change their opinion, to be secure of judging properly at first." Finally, Darcy resurrects "performance" to hint at her folly: "... I could wish, Miss Bennet, that you were not to sketch my character at the present moment, as there is reason to fear that the performance would reflect no credit on either." Nevertheless, he hopes to bring her nearer him by combining their senses of the word. The "performance" he mentions is surely a sketch, but to reproduce reality demands clear insight, which in turn depends on the artist's responsible, unbiased behavior. So, when Elizabeth insists on indulging her skill rather than judging the reality, Darcy shows his anger:

> "But if I do not take your likeness now, I may never have another opportunity."
> "I would by no means suspend any pleasure of yours," he coldly replied.

The word "pleasure" goes only with a light accomplishment. Since Elizabeth has blocked every advance toward mutual understanding and a community of feeling, Darcy ends their talk by handing her one-sided interpretation of the term back to her.

So far Jane Austen has used *performance* as something like a gauge for behavior, letting her characters define the range of the concept in their speeches. Throughout the scene at Rosings (pp. 174–76), she anchors the word in Elizabeth's actual playing of the piano. Now the speakers can keep up an appearance of decorum by pretending to talk of the literal situation, while in fact they treat it metaphorically, thus betraying their most intense emotions. It is the artistic device that we have observed Jane Austen working with in the earlier novels, and we will see it again in the novels to come, but she never manages the device more beautifully, with more moving effect, than she does here.

The conversation opens when Elizabeth accosts Darcy "at the first convenient pause" in her playing; as always, she assumes that he intends to be contemptuous:

> "You mean to frighten me, Mr. Darcy, by coming in all this state to hear me? But I will not be alarmed though your sister *does* play so well. There is a stubbornness about me that never can bear to

be frightened at the will of others. My courage always rises with every attempt to intimidate me."

Elizabeth's "hear me" and "play so well" maintain decorum, for they seem to speak only of piano-playing. Yet her final, fully emotional generalizations leave no doubt that she is challenging him personally. Although Darcy answers with conspicuous politeness, he also distinguishes—characteristically enough—between the real and the professed:

> "I shall not say that you are mistaken," he replied, "because you could not really believe me to entertain any design of alarming you; and I have had the pleasure of your acquaintance long enough to know, that you find great enjoyment in occasionally professing opinions which in fact are not your own."

Literally he is accusing Elizabeth of her usual self-willed performance, warning or begging her to recognize the truth about himself.

Elizabeth may appear to joke at this as a false sketch, ironically accepting what Darcy has said while she circumspectly addresses herself to Colonel Fitzwilliam. But she bitterly resents the thrust as another proof of Darcy's nastiness:

> Elizabeth laughed heartily at this picture of herself, and said to Colonel Fitzwilliam, "Your cousin will give you a very pretty notion of me, and teach you not to believe a word I say. I am particularly unlucky in meeting with a person so well able to expose my real character, in a part of the world, where I had hoped to pass myself off with some degree of credit. Indeed, Mr. Darcy, it is very ungenerous in you to mention all that you knew to my disadvantage in Hertfordshire—and, give me leave to say, very impolitic too—for it is provoking me to retaliate, and such things may come out, as will shock your relations to hear."

The phrase "pass myself off" reflects Elizabeth's view of what Darcy tried to do at Netherfield. And she couples "ungenerous" with the threat of laying bare his disagreeable past to attack him more directly. Her "impolitic" is just right, for it implies that she has more sense than Darcy, and it does so without weakening the emotional power of her assault. Yet he remains utterly polite, and something more: "'I am not afraid of you,' said he, smilingly." Darcy is "not afraid," either because he feels so confident of his integrity that he assumes it must win out over Elizabeth's willful misinterpretations or because he trusts in the ultimate integrity of her sense and feeling. In either case he puts himself completely in her hands, a real measure of his affection for her.

When Colonel Fitzwilliam invites her to go on, Elizabeth strikes a tone of parody that thinly disguises her indictment of Darcy:

> "You shall hear then—but prepare yourself for something very dreadful. The first time of my ever seeing him in Hertfordshire, you must know, was at a ball—and at this ball, what do you think he did? He danced only four dances! I am sorry to pain you—but so it was. He danced only four dances, though gentlemen were scarce; and, to my certain knowledge, more than one young lady was sitting down in want of a partner. Mr. Darcy, you cannot deny the fact."

Such phrases as "to my certain knowledge" and "the fact" allege that Darcy was haughty in refusing to dance with her, though Elizabeth still protects her own feelings by generalizing about "more than one young lady." This deed is the foundation of her prejudice, the reality that she is positive Darcy "cannot deny." But he does. At least he redefines what Elizabeth has always taken to be pride as shyness: "I had not at that time the honour of knowing any lady in the assembly beyond my own party." In effect he is saying, "You have interpreted my performance wrongly—as a mere exhibition—because you ignore my total character."

Elizabeth refuses his explanation, polishing him off with a clearly absurd generalization, and then she turns to his friend:

> "True; and nobody can ever be introduced in a ball room. Well, Colonel Fitzwilliam, what do I play next? My fingers wait your orders."
>
> "Perhaps," said Darcy, "I should have judged better, had I sought an introduction, but I am ill qualified to recommend myself to strangers."

Yet Darcy insists on his shyness, even admitting that feeling may have swayed his judgment. So, though Elizabeth keeps her tone light by speaking to Colonel Fitzwilliam, she attacks with even more authority, counting on her impersonal phrasing to provide an air of sense that will decide finally against Darcy:

"Shall we ask your cousin the reason of this?" said Elizabeth, still addressing Colonel Fitzwilliam. "Shall we ask him why a man of sense and education, and who has lived in the world, is ill qualified to recommend himself to strangers?"

. . . .

"I certainly have not the talent which some people possess," said Darcy, "of conversing easily with those I have never seen before. I cannot catch their tone of conversation, or appear interested in their concerns, as I often see done."

But the hostility of Elizabeth still lurks in the bias of her rhetorical question. And Darcy, because he remains unsatisfied that her formula takes account of his real nature, refers to his shyness for the third time, again declaring that he cannot put on a skilled performance, that he must enact his convictions.

Elizabeth finally resorts to her literal performance on the piano in order to carry the day. She uses it metaphorically so that her thrust may seem decorously oblique, yet she aims her words straight at Darcy's stubbornness:

"My fingers ... do not move over this instrument in the masterly manner which I see so many women's do. They have not the same force or rapidity, and do not produce the same expression. But then I have always supposed it to be my own fault—because I would not take the trouble of practising. It is not that I do not believe *my* fingers as capable as any other woman's of superior execution."

At the same time, of course, this is one of Elizabeth's typical self-displays. But there is a further point: since Elizabeth creates the metaphor consciously, making the social situation into a vehicle for illustration, she must still be thinking of *performance* in its flattest sense.

This allegiance on her part fills Darcy's reply with reverberations:

Darcy smiled and said, "You are perfectly right. You have employed your time much better. No one admitted to the privilege of hearing you, can think any thing wanting. We neither of us perform to strangers."

He expresses his deepest attachment to her in these sentences. The first refuses to dispute her judgment of him, which is to say that Darcy cheerfully sacrifices the real motives he has been explaining. His second sentence must be sheer feeling, for it contradicts the logic both of Elizabeth's metaphor and of what Darcy himself has said earlier: after all, he praises his sister at the beginning of the scene because she "practises very constantly," and Elizabeth has just reproached herself for not practicing more often. Darcy can only mean that her behavior toward him, no matter how prejudiced, is more valuable than her piano-playing. In the third sentence he reverts to the metaphor by "hearing you," which plainly stands for "being with you," but only to keep his extravagant generalization about her charm within the bounds of propriety. Yet his last sentence crowns the others. Perhaps, as a gallant gesture, he is straining to use "perform" in Elizabeth's narrow sense—straining fearfully, if he really wants this meaning, for she is indeed playing to "strangers." But actually, I think, Darcy is calling here on his deeper sense of the word while uttering his most impassioned plea for intimacy, a plea all the more fervent in that it quite irrationally disregards—as a paraphrase shows—the blindness which has marked Elizabeth all along: "We reserve our fullest selves, perfectly understood by both of us, for each other." It is his final, almost desperate attempt before the first proposal to come to terms with her.

But that proposal soon follows, and the letter revealing Darcy to Elizabeth. With both of them now making the necessary personal adjustments and becoming surer of one another's behavior, the play with *performance* disappears from the novel. By the last pages of *Pride and Prejudice*, the earlier tense misunderstandings between them have given way to an exchange like the following, begun by Elizabeth, which ends with them cozily enjoying a joke that takes their true motives for granted:

> "Why, especially, when you called, did you look as if you did not care about me?"
>
> "Because you were grave and silent, and gave me no encouragement."
>
> "But I was embarrassed."
>
> "And so was I."
>
> "You might have talked to me more when you came to dinner."
>
> "A man who had felt less, might."
>
> "How unlucky that you should have a reasonable answer to give, and that I should be so reasonable as to admit it!" (p. 381)

In spite of its lower tension, this bit of dialogue measures how far the characters have traveled since the start of the story. Darcy still defends himself by pointing to his shyness, but he can reckon the liabilities of his behavior. And Elizabeth, though she still puts on something of a show in ironically suggesting that she is disappointed in reason, nevertheless declares the reasonableness of them both. Certainly the lighter tone of the passage should not beguile us into imagining that Darcy has renounced his sense of status, of prudence, of reason, of decorum—those conventional social values which have prompted so many of his previous actions. Indeed, Elizabeth herself comes to endorse these values as I tried to suggest before, comes to approve the foundations of Darcy's performance.[5] What he has found out— and it is important enough—is that one's total performance may be unacceptable unless it is softened by a gracious display. And Elizabeth has discovered that her own behavior has been lacking in integrity—that the sort of performance in which she has so often acted out her judgment of Darcy has been grounded in a prejudice that distorts reason. The concept, which Jane Austen brings so vividly to life in dialogue, epitomizes the theme of the novel.

NOTES

1. Mary Lascelles speaks for many critics when she objects to this incident, contending that the Darcy it presents is "inconsistent" with the one "described and developed in the rest of the book" (*Jane Austen*, p. 22). But I think she misses the full psychology behind Darcy's remarks and the artistry of Jane Austen, who sets up here a hero antipathetic to Elizabeth without completely sacrificing his character in the process. Darcy's letter to Elizabeth after his first proposal has also been called in question by Miss Lascelles—and other critics—on much the same grounds: she feels it "not ... quite plausible" that "so much, and such, information would ... be volunteered by a proud and reserved man—unless under pressure from his author" (p. 162). But Darcy says himself in it that "my character required it to be written and read" (p. 196), that he will tell Elizabeth what he has done because an "explanation ... is due to myself" (p. 197). Indeed the letter seems to me almost the only unequivocal instance in the novel of the pride usually attributed to Darcy.

2. Reuben Brower has analyzed these dialogues magnificently in his essay on *Pride and Prejudice in The Fields of Light* (New York, 1951), pp. 164–81. His chapter contains the most exciting exposition of Jane Austen's methods that I know, and he is the only critic who has done justice to her portrait of Darcy. Brower shows how Darcy's offers to dance convey a variety of motives, ranging from insufferable pride to serious interest in Elizabeth.

3. By pointing out Charlotte's capacity to feel, which also shows up in other parts of *Pride and Prejudice*, I am hoping to suggest only that Jane Austen makes her a somewhat fuller character than we ordinarily imagine, influenced as we are by the hard attitude toward marriage that Charlotte preaches and then puts in practice by accepting Mr. Collins: "... it was the only honourable provision for well-educated young women of small fortune, and however uncertain of giving happiness, must be their pleasantest, preservative from want" (pp. 122–23). Perhaps it is worth noting, however, that such undeniably sympathetic characters as Mrs. Gardiner and Colonel Fitzwilliam advance a prudent view of marriage themselves (pp. 144, 183).

4. Dorothy Van Ghent makes out the most persuasive case for taking the verbal manner of Mr. Collins as an index to his character, noting at one point that "The elaborate

language in which Mr. Collins gets himself fairly *stuck* is a mimesis of an action of the soul, the soul that becomes self dishonest through failure to know itself, and that overrates itself at the expense of the social context, just as it overrates verbalism at the expense of meaning" (*The English Novel*, p. 106).

5. Although Mudrick acknowledges the pressures of society in *Pride and Prejudice*, the general tendencies of his commentary on the novel seem to me misleading. He divides its characters into the simple and the complex, arguing that this is the "first decision" Elizabeth makes about any person and that the decision "is not moral but psychological" (*Jane Austen*, p. 95). The simple personalities, he maintains, are beneath "moral judgment" (p. 123). The "complex individual" is marked by his capacity for "choice" and by his "freedom": a freedom which makes him at bottom "isolated" from his society; a choice which Elizabeth, at least, must exercise by settling on a husband who is "undefeated by his social role" (pp. 124–25). In all this Mudrick seriously underrates, so I think, both Elizabeth's responsiveness to the values of society and the influence of conventional morality in the novel. Dorothy Van Ghent takes a stand somewhat like Mudrick's in treating *Pride and Prejudice* as organized about a clash between the "feelings" of the individual and the "utility interests" of society (*The English Novel*, p. 102). She finds the latter embodied in Jane Austen's "materialistic" vocabulary and offers a number of wonderfully perceptive stylistic analyses. Yet I am not quite sure whether she means to suggest ultimately that Jane Austen was really reacting against such language and its implications, though tied down by history to the words and meanings "inherited from her culture" (p. 109), or that the author accepted her society and its language. The critic's closing judgment of what goes on in the novel itself is completely unequivocal, however, and I feel that it lies nearer to my own view than to Mudrick's: "The final fought-for recognitions of value are recognitions of the unity of experience—a unity between the common culture and the individual development" (p. 111).

STUART M. TAVE

Affection and the Mortification of Elizabeth Bennet

The first time Elizabeth Bennet sees Mr. Darcy, before they have ever spoken to each other, he mortifies her. It is the beginning of their action. His character has been decided already, by all the principal people in the room; Bingley has such amiable qualities as must speak for themselves, but—what a contrast between him and his friend!—Darcy is the proudest, most disagreeable man in the world. Before the action ends Elizabeth will have to discover that this is a really amiable man, to whom she must give her affection. She will have to define the differences between the agreeable and the amiable and to define the foundations of affection; and he will have to become worthy of that process of painful definition. It will be a mortifying experience for both of them. Elizabeth has wit and intelligence, a mind that runs with rapid play and liveliness. She finds life more amusing than others do because she is superior in discernment and abilities, so quick in observation and decisive in judgment at the first interview; she will discover a slower and seemingly "less interesting mode" far more interesting, more full of real life.

It will be a long time before she can say of Darcy that he is an "amiable" man, because it is a long time before she knows what the word means. It is a word that can be used lightly, as she has been using it, but not by those who weigh

From *Some Words of Jane Austen.* ©1973 by The University of Chicago.

their words. Before Frank Churchill comes to Highbury Emma and Mr.
Knightley are arguing about him and the argument, as Mr. Knightley
attempts unsuccessfully to give it some precision, turns upon a definition.
Emma has called Frank "an amiable young man" (E 148). Not only is she
unacquainted with him but she is, when she uses the phrase, offering a
general proposition about a young man of a certain type; to Mr. Knightley it
is a weak, indecisive type. There is in some weak people an amiability that is
an inactive, docile good temper; it is what Mr. Woodhouse has (7) and
Isabella, the daughter who is more like him (92); it is the kind of thing
Captain Wentworth finds in Henrietta Musgrove (P 86) and, when he knows
her faults better, in Louisa (182). But that is not what Mr. Knightley means
by real amiability. Nor is it quite what Emma meant, who had something
more agreeable in mind and, without realizing it, something more
dangerous. Emma is surprised at the heat of the reaction she has provoked in
Mr. Knightley, for several reasons, but she had spoken the word casually, as
a conventional epithet of praise. It had pervaded the fiction of the late
eighteenth century, densely populated by "amiable," "more than amiable"
and "most amiable" heroines and heroes.

Some awareness of this novelistic jargon adds a delight to a reading of
Jane Austen's juvenilia, because it adds force to the parodic use of the word.
One meets an absurdly endless number of amiable characters, like the
landlady of the little alehouse in Evelyn, "who as well as every one else in
Evelyn was remarkably amiable" (MW 180); one meets characters who are,
over and over, "the amiable Rebecca" (notwithstanding her forbidding
squint, greasy tresses, and swelling back) (6 ff.). Part of the joke of the
"History of England" is the application of the novelistic adjective to kings,
queens, and entire realms, with a scholarly exactness: in the reign of Charles
I ("This amiable Monarch") "never were amiable men so scarce. The
number of them throughout the whole Kingdom amounting only to *five* ..."
(148–49). The historian herself may be partial, prejudiced, and ignorant but
we must take confidence in the value of the History from her own assurance
that she is "my no less amiable self" (147). If we are told, in one of these early
pieces, that a character is amiable we know it to be perfect: "perfectly
amiable," like the young man who was addicted to no vice (beyond what his
age and situation rendered perfectly excusable) (74). It is a happy thing to
hear in a young lady's account of her education that "I daily became more
amiable, & might perhaps by this time have nearly attained perfection" (17).
The progress of the young Catherine Morland, from an unsuccessful
romantic heroine to a rather more sensible observer of humanity, can be
traced: from her beginning point, when she was surprised that she had
reached the age of seventeen "without having seen one amiable youth who

could call forth her sensibility" (NA 16); through her exceeding love for Isabella, as she swallows whole James Morland's estimate of that "thoroughly unaffected and amiable ... most amiable girl" (NA 50); to the end point where she can clear General Tilney from her grossly injurious suspicions of villainy and still be able to believe, upon serious consideration, that he is "not perfectly amiable" (200). The charming Augusta Hawkins, before she is ever seen by Highbury, is discovered to have every recommendation of person and mind, to be handsome, elegant, highly accomplished, and, it follows by the formula that denotes not a real person but a fiction, "perfectly amiable" (E 181). The vapid amiable character, familiar to Jane Austen and no danger to her from her earliest years, remained a staple product of novelists and it was one of the dangers she had to mark out for that beginning author, young Anna Austen. A character in Anna's manuscript is at first interesting to Jane Austen "in spite of her being so amiable" (L 387), obviously an unusual accomplishment; but Anna could not maintain that pitch, so, in a second letter, her aunt loses interest in that character and finds still another who worries her: "I am afraid [he] will be too much in the common Novel style— a handsome, amiable, unexceptionable Young Man (such as do not much abound in real Life)" (403).

To stupid Mr. Collins, a self-conscious master of complimentary terminology that has not much to do with real life, the word is a valuable all-purpose superlative. Miss De Bourgh, he rapidly informs the Bennets, is "perfectly amiable" (PP 67), though the details of her he has offered bear another tale. His cousin Elizabeth, as he tells her with clocklike solemnity during his proposal, also qualifies for the word, though, as he also assures her, there are many other amiable young women in his own neighborhood (105, 106, 107, 108); and when he transfers his affections to Charlotte he transfers the word as easily (128, 139). What is more amusing is that in Elizabeth's difficult brief period, following her rejection of Mr. Collins, Charlotte seems to her to be "very amiable" in accepting his attentions (121); she is thankful to her friend Charlotte for this obliging, kindness. Elizabeth has something to learn about amiability. It is something important enough to consider in multiple illustration because it keeps returning in almost all of Jane Austen's writing. To Mr. Knightley it is a point of reality that helps define the national character.

What Elizabeth has to learn is important, because there is a true amiability, not an insipid fictive perfection that offers itself for immediate admiration but a reality that frequently takes time to disclose itself or to be discovered by an observer who is unable to see it. An intelligent young woman, unlike a romantic heroine, will not meet much perfection in her experience but she may well make mistakes in understanding what is more difficult: the difference between those who are truly "amiable" and those who are only "agreeable." That is "an important distinction," Dr. Gregory warned his daughters, "which many of your sex are not aware of" (*A Father's Legacy to His Daughters*, 1774, and many later editions, into the nineteenth century, p. 37). Jane Austen makes the distinction in two of her letters, writing about the same young man: first in a passing observation to her sister Cassandra, and then, more than a year later, to Fanny Knight, on a critical occasion, which validates the large significance of the words. Mr. John Plumtre, she tells Cassandra, is someone she likes very much: "He gives me the idea of a very amiable young Man, only too diffident to be so agreeable as he might be" (L 342). He is lacking in the social manner that would make him complete, but a completeness cannot be expected often, and when there are choices to be made it is always the amiable that is to be chosen. Mr. Plumtre then attaches himself to Fanny Knight and Fanny encourages him until she finds that perhaps she has mistaken her own feelings; Jane Austen, as her aunt, tries to give her the best possible advice, not telling her what to do, but clarifying for her what the alternatives are. There is a strong case to be made for Mr. Plumtre, "above all his character—his uncommonly amiable mind, strict principles, just notions, good habits ... All that really is of the first importance." His manners are not equal to this excellence, but a comparison between him and Fanny's own "agreeable, idle Brothers" will show Fanny that it is Mr. Plumtre who has the sterling worth. He is not perfect, because he has a fault of modesty, and if he were less modest "he would be more agreeable, speak louder & look Impudenter," but it is a fine character of which this is the only defect (L 409–10). The conclusion is not that Fanny should marry him—and we'll come back to Mr. Plumtre—but her aunt's advice will lead her to understand her choices and enable her to decide for the right reasons, not reject a man of uncommonly amiable mind and all that is really of the first importance because she thinks it more important that the man be agreeable.

If agreeable men are likely to be suspect characters in Jane Austen there is good cause. Their agreeableness might be an initial value but it would improve upon acquaintance and reveal the mind, principles, notions, and habits that make the moral character, so that the agreeableness of manner and person would not remain the most notable quality. Mr. Elliot of *Persuasion* is that "exceedingly agreeable man," who makes his impression even before his identity is known, who is, in his regard for Anne, a source of agreeable sensation to her; he is offered as a suitable match. "Where could you expect a more gentlemanlike, agreeable man?" (P 104–5, 159–60, 196). But well before she learns the full story of his life Anne has real doubts because she can never find anything more in him. "Mr. Elliot was too generally agreeable," deliberately pleases even where he is contemptuous: even Mrs. Clay "found him as agreeable as anybody," a note in passing that makes the ending of the novel less surprising and more enjoyable (P 160–61). Henry Crawford is more interesting because he is a man who makes an effort to change himself to something better, from "the most agreeable young man" the Miss Bertrams had ever known (MP 44) to a man deserving of the affection of an amiable woman. There is much byplay at Mansfield Park about the mutual agreeableness of the Crawfords and the young Bertrams and even Sir Thomas is impressed by Henry's "more than common agreeableness," the address and conversation pleasing to everyone (316). Mrs. Price at Portsmouth "had never seen so agreeable a man in her life" (400). It will take more than this to win Fanny but she sees in his visit to Portsmouth that there are ways in which he really is acting differently. In his account of where he has been and what he has been doing there is more than the "accidental agreeableness" of the parties he has been in; he has done; good work in performing a duty, for the first time, among the tenants of his estate, thereby securing "agreeable recollections for his own mind"; that is certainly a better kind of agreeableness than he has ever known (404). She sees that he is much more gentle, obliging, and attentive to other people's feelings than he had ever been at Mansfield: "she had never seen him so agreeable—so *near* being agreeable" (406). Fanny is using the lower word in her own high sense, because he is now near being amiable, and she is making a fine distinction; but she is right, because the good impulse now moving Henry will not be enough. He lacks the principle to maintain the habit of right action. His moral character cannot rise above the agreeable manner. His story ends when he goes to the house of the family at Twickenham where Maria has grown intimate—a family of lively, "agreeable manners, and probably of morals and discretion to suit," for to that house Henry had constant access at all times (450). What he threw away when he entered that accessible house was the way of happiness, working for the esteem and tenderness that leads to "one amiable woman's affections" (467).

To recognize the one amiable woman, or man, is the first simple perception in making a marriage. In fact few can do it. The lady for whom Willoughby has jilted Marianne is very rich, Elinor learns, but what Elinor wants to know is what kind of woman she is: "Is she said to be amiable?" (SS 194). That is the question because it will determine what can be said for him and what are his chances of happiness, but it was never a question that touched his mind. Edward Ferrars is a better man because the question did concern him, but he had not been able to answer it: Lucy Steele had been successful with him because she "appeared everything that was amiable and obliging" (362). She was not really so, as Elinor has always known (129, 238), and the mistake he made could have been ruinous in time. The perception of a real amiability requires time. Mrs. Dashwood is correct in her opinion of Edward but her opinion is without much meaning: "It was enough for her that he appeared to be amiable"; to say that he is unlike Fanny Dashwood is enough: "It implies every thing amiable. I love him already" (15–16). Elinor's measured answer is the right one: "'I think you will like him,' said Elinor, 'when you know more of him,'" because time and knowledge measure possible degrees and truths of feeling. If, therefore, Edward had married Lucy he would have entered a future of great peril. The man who marries an unamiable woman may be made unhappy, but that is not the worst; if he falls in with her manner he may be happy, but he will become an unworthy man. It happened to John Dashwood, who "had he married a more amiable woman" might have improved, "might even have been made amiable himself," for he was very young when he married and very fond of his wife; but Mrs. John Dashwood was a caricature of himself, more narrow-minded and selfish (5). It happened to Mr. Elton. Emma recognizes that when she sees him as an old married man, to use his own phrase, deliberately hurting Harriet while smiles of high glee pass between him and his wife. "This was Mr. Elton! the amiable, obliging, gentle Mr. Elton" (E 328). He is not quite so hardened as his wife but he is growing very like her. There is a littleness about him that Emma had not discovered.

Emma's discovery is a long time in coming because the ability to recognize an amiable man is dependent on the ability to perceive with a moral clarity of definition. Harriet can look forward to being happily married to Mr. Elton, Emma assures her, because "here is a man whose amiable character gives every assurance of it" (E 75). With the advantage of her long intimacy with Miss Taylor Emma should be able to recognize a "truly amiable woman" (117); but if she can then say of Harriet that she has never met with a disposition "more truly amiable" (43) the word can have no real meaning for her. She finds Harriet very amiable because of that early and easy deference to herself (26). Emma cannot distinguish the amiable from the agreeable, uses the words indiscriminately. She has no doubt she has given Harriet's fancy a proper direction when she makes her aware that Mr. Elton is a "remarkably handsome man, with most agreeable manners" (42); but that is also the language of the talkative Miss Nash, head teacher at Mrs. Goddard's, telling Harriet that beyond a doubt Mr. Elton has not his equal "for beauty or agreeableness" (68). The question Emma puts to Harriet about Robert Martin is precisely the wrong one: "if you think him the most agreeable man you have ever been in company with, why should you hesitate?" (5 3). The intention of the question, as she points out, is to put another man into Harriet's mind, and it is successful, unfortunately. But it takes a blunt John Knightley to point out an obvious truth: "I never ... saw a man more intent on being agreeable than Mr. Elton" (111); Emma has been willing to overlook the labor and the affectation and the working of every feature because it fits her pleasure to think he is a man of good will. Only after he has astonished her by his proposal does she judge him "not ... so particularly amiable" (138), because at that point it is a great consolation to think so.

Emma needs the agreeable so that she can continue to be comfortable, think a little too well of herself, create her own world without being disturbed by examining it or herself too closely. It is Mr. Knightley, angry with her for misguiding Harriet, who prompts her better self by making things uncomfortable and being "very disagreeable" (E 65). It is he who gives her hints, that she is being neglectful in not visiting the Bateses, not contributing to their scanty comforts, and some hints have come from her own heart—but none is equal to counteract the persuasion of its all being "very disagreeable" (155). When she does call on them, with Harriet, it is not to bring comfort to them but to get rid of what is now the more tiresome subject of Mr. Elton.

The mistake with the agreeable Mr. Elton also makes her rejoice in the coming of Frank Churchill; she hopes to find him agreeable. It was the hope that she was defending against Mr. Knightley when she elicited his critical definition. She has called Frank amiable, but Mr. Knightley makes the distinction for her: "Your amiable young man," if he has not been following his duty instead of consulting expediency, "is a very weak young man." The young man writes fine flourishing letters but he has never exerted himself to pay the proper attention to his father and especially to Mrs. Weston, upon their marriage, so that he has all the external manner and none of the reality of action: "No, Emma, your amiable young man can be amiable only in French, not in English. He may be very 'aimable,' have very good manners, and be very agreeable; but he can have no English delicacy towards the feelings of other people: nothing really amiable about him." But those smooth, plausible manners will be enough, Emma says, to make him a treasure at Highbury, where "We do not often look upon fine young men, well-bred and agreeable"; we must not be nice and ask for virtue too. Her idea of him is that he can adapt his conversation to the taste of everybody and "has the power as well as the wish of being universally agreeable." If he is anything like this he will be insupportable, Mr. Knightley says (E 148–50). But when Frank arrives Emma's vanity gives him every support. She is directly sure that "he knew how to make himself agreeable," as he certainly does; he talks of Highbury as his *own* country and says he has had the greatest curiosity to visit: that he should "never have been able to indulge so amiable

a feeling before" passes suspiciously through Emma's brain, but it passes
(191). She only feels that he is agreeable and the rest must wait. The danger
to her of the man who knows how to make himself agreeable but who is not
amiable multiplies as the story progresses. He even arrives at the point where
he is sick of England, which means that in self-pity he is prepared to run
from the obligations he owes to the feelings of others. He is, Mr. Knightley
had guessed correctly, a weak young man; on the day at Box Hill Jane Fairfax
has come to recognize that fact and recognize that he therefore puts his own
happiness at the mercy of chance, and hers too. For Emma the moral dangers
are even greater because she is readily susceptible to, desirous of, his
agreeableness and blind to the rest. In the climactic two hours at Box Hill,
when to amuse her "and be agreeable in her eyes" seems all he cares for,
Emma is ignorant of his motives and is not sorry to be flattered (368). As the
pitch of the scene rises, in response to his lead Emma loses self-command
and insults Miss Bates, pains her, is herself unfeeling. There is an
extraordinary pathos and irony when Miss Bates can only reply, "I must make
myself very disagreeable, or she would not have said such a thing to an old
friend" (371).

The really amiable man, Mr. Knightley teaches us, is the man who is
strong in his action because fine in his emotion, who habitually exerts himself
to do his duty because he has a delicacy for the feelings of others. He will be
a man capable of love and worthy of love. The happiness of Elizabeth Bennet
turns upon her ability to recognize the really amiable man; one way of
marking her fortunes and progress is to follow her accuracy in assigning the
right adjective to the right man and all that it implies of quality of vision.
Darcy, we have said, enters the novel with a character quickly determined by
the assembly room at the first ball, when his fine person and fortune draw
admiration and then, just as quickly, his manners give a disgust. He is
discovered to have "a most forbidding, disagreeable countenance." "He was
the proudest, most disagreeable man in the world" (PP 10–11). The
immediate contrast is between him and Bingley, whose "amiable qualities
must speak for themselves": Bingley soon makes himself acquainted with all
the principal people in the room, is lively and unreserved, dances every
dance, talks of giving a dance himself at Netherfield. The evidence on either
side is hardly existent and Elizabeth will have to do better than all the
principal people. She will have to do so in spite of the man himself, in spite
of herself, and of their mutually disagreeable introduction. Bingley tries to
interest Darcy in Elizabeth as some one very pretty "and I dare say, very
agreeable," but he is not tempted (11). To her Darcy is then "only the man
who made himself agreeable no where, and who had not thought her
handsome enough to dance with" (23). When, some weeks later, he does ask

her to dance she is surprised into accepting him and she frets. "I dare say you will find him very agreeable," says Charlotte, with a small echo. "Heaven forbid!—That would be the greatest misfortune of all!—To find a man agreeable whom one is determined to hate!—Do not wish me such an evil" (90).

Bingley, it does develop, is "truly amiable," as Elizabeth later calls him (82); but even at the time she says that she doesn't know enough of him, and her opinion is still to undergo changes, because Bingley's is a soft amiability that makes him dependent on chance, susceptible to interference by others with his own happiness and therefore with the feelings of the woman he loves. More importantly, Elizabeth's praise of Bingley is offered to emphasize the contrast between him and Darcy and it is delivered to Wickham for that purpose. In response to Wickham's questioning the very first thing she had said of Darcy was "I think him very disagreeable" (77). For that reason she is ready to accept Wickham's story and to think of Darcy as cruel, malicious, unjust, inhumane. Wickham himself she trusts: he is a young man, she says to herself, "whose very countenance may vouch for your being amiable" (80–81); and if she thinks of herself as a better judge of character than Jane, she has done no better than Jane will do the next day: "it was not in her nature to question the veracity of a young man of such amiable appearance as Wickham" (85). Jane's less confident nature at least preserves her from Elizabeth's error of deciding the matter against Darcy. More than that, Jane has a good reason for suspending judgment for it is difficult to believe that an intimate friend like Bingley can be so deceived in Darcy's character. The very thought had just occurred to Elizabeth as she listened to Wickham and declared Bingley's amiability but, like several other true thoughts that had come and gone, it did her no good. She is not in love with Wickham, she tells Mrs. Gardiner, "But he is, beyond all comparison, the most agreeable man I ever saw," and the possibility of affection interests her (144–45). For all her superior intelligence Elizabeth is more blind than Jane. When Jane thinks that Bingley has departed from her life she has the steadiness not to repine though he "may live in my memory as the most amiable man of my acquaintance" (134). When Elizabeth parts from Wickham, who may now be marrying Miss King, she is convinced that "he must always be her model of the amiable and pleasing" (152). Only Jane has any evidence of the real character of the man she is talking about and Elizabeth has confused the most agreeable man with the model of the amiable. Jane has been crossed in love by the loss of Bingley, which gives her, says Mr. Bennet, a sort of distinction: "Let Wickham be *your* man." "Thank you, Sir," Elizabeth replies, "but a less agreeable man would satisfy me" (138). He would and he does. What she has still to discover is the identity and amiability of that less agreeable man.

Where Wickham has been able to deceive her by false information he has done what he could. As he was maligning Darcy he was also shaking his head over Miss Darcy, professing pain because he could not call her "amiable"—but she was too like her brother in being very, very proud (82); some months later, in Derbyshire, Elizabeth is prepared to see a "proud, reserved, disagreeable girl," then finds that Miss Darcy is "amiable and unpretending" (284). But Wickham's ability to mislead her where she has never seen the object of his lies is a small thing. The great humiliation is the discovery that she has believed all he says of Darcy because she has been pleased by his preference and offended by Darcy's neglect, therefore courted prepossession and ignorance and driven reason away. The discovery she makes in the receipt of Darcy's letter is less in the new information he offers than in a self-discovery that allows her to see what has always been before her. What she now begins to comprehend is a reality to which she has blinded herself because the appearance was so much more pleasing. That agreeableness, that false amiability of Wickham, had been a charm: it was a countenance, a voice, a manner; as to his "real character" she had never felt a wish of inquiring. She tries now to find some moral reality in her recollection of him, "some instance of goodness," some trait of integrity or benevolence, virtue; she, can see him instantly before her in every charm of air and address, but she can remember no "substantial good" beyond the general approbation of the neighborhood or the regard that his social powers had gained him (206).

The substantial good evaporates as one seeks it in Wickham; as it does in Willoughby, with his uncommonly attractive person and lively manner, which it was no merit to possess (SS 333); as it does in Mr. Elliot when Anne finds him sensible and agreeable but is still afraid to answer for his conduct (P 160–61). Anne has her own reasons for prizing a man of more warmth and enthusiasm, but the truth about Mr. Elliot's real character, that he has no feeling for others (199), is the truth about all the very well-mannered and very agreeable young men who, in Mr. Knightley's distinction, have no delicacy toward the feelings of other people, nothing really amiable about them. They can separate their agreeableness from their feeling, so that the pleasing sensations they offer turn terribly chilling. To miss the distinction, then, to be drawn to the agreeable, is shocking, is both an easy and a dangerous temptation, because it is to fall into that pleasing sensation of the unreality that flatters the self. The agreeable imitation of feeling becomes the instant welcome deception. But the real feeling of the amiable man expressing the principle of a life can be known only by the evidences of an earned experience. It may be hard to find that reality, when its appearance is not readily pleasing, and to acknowledge it, however disagreeable to the self.

It was this reality Elizabeth had denied Darcy, as she rejected him and grew more angry and told him directly, in the last sentence that drove him from the room: his manners impressed her with "the fullest belief of your arrogance, your conceit, and your selfish disdain of the feelings of others" (193). As she begins to make the discovery about her blindness she remembers that she has often heard Darcy speak "so affectionately of his sister as to prove him capable of come amiable feeling." It is a minimal fact but it has meaning as it follows a new realization of his character—that however proud and repulsive his manners, her acquaintance has given her an intimacy with Darcy's ways and she has never seen anything that betrayed him to be unprincipled or unjust, anything that spoke of irreligious or immoral habits. It has meaning as it precedes her new realization that had his actions been what Wickham represented them, there could be no friendship between anyone capable of those actions and "such an amiable man as Mr. Bingley" (207–8). She realizes now, when she receives his letter, that she has no evidence to bring against him; as she learns more of the history of his life, when she visits his home, she learns more positively what his behavior has been as child and man. Mrs. Reynolds can testify to his goodness of disposition and to his goodness of action as landlord to tenant and as master to servant. It is a new light on his character. "In what an amiable light does this place him!" Elizabeth thinks, "... so amiable a light" (249, 265). But above all she then knows by his conduct to her, who has given him such cause to be an enemy, his capacity for love. She questions him at the end of the story, wanting him to account for having ever fallen in love with her, when her behavior to him had been at least always bordering on the uncivil and when she never spoke to him without rather wishing to give him pain: "Had you not been really amiable you would have hated me for it." He knew no "actual good" of her, she adds; but in fact he did, certainly in her "affectionate behavior" to Jane in need (380). They are both of them people who are capable of actual good, of affection, really amiable, worthy of love. She knows what he has done for her and her family. By the time Darcy has made his second proposal Elizabeth has learned enough of him and his family (339, 369) to be able to answer her father's doubts of that proud, unpleasant man: "'I do, I do like him,' she replied, with tears in her eyes. 'I love him. Indeed he has no improper pride. He is perfectly amiable'" (376). It is astonishing praise, and a daring phrase for Elizabeth to use. It is a sign of the pressure of feeling upon her, because her earlier misjudgments and immoderate expressions have forced her into this awkwardness, that she should be so extravagant as to use a kind of novelistic jargon; and it is a sign of Darcy's real excellence that he does not sink under the weight of it. He really is amiable.

The accomplishment of amiability is unusual; it is earned by moral and intelligent effort and it cannot be distributed sentimentally as a reward. The narrator wishes it could be said that Mrs. Bennet's accomplishment of her earnest desire in marrying off her daughters produced so happy an effect as to make her "a sensible, amiable, well-informed woman"; but that could not be, and perhaps it was lucky for her husband, who might not have relished domestic felicity in so unusual a form (385).

The form in which domestic felicity comes to Elizabeth and Darcy is unusual and it is there not by luck. It comes, first, because both are amiable and that is a necessary foundation, but it comes because on that is built something more. Above all, as Elizabeth knows, there must be love, or to use the word Jane Austen prefers in such contexts, there must be "affection." It is the quieter, more general word, for an emotion of slower growth and more lasting therefor; but it is, in this context, a strong word for a deep emotion. It is the word Emma uses at the moment of her insight into her own heart when she is ashamed of every sensation but one, "her affection for Mr. Knightley" (E 412); it is the word Anne Elliot uses to describe her feelings for Captain Wentworth, when he is once again desirous of her affection: "her affection would be his for ever" (P 190, 192). It is, in general, Jane Austen's chiefest instance of how without the appropriate emotion there is no moral action; specifically it is the love that every marriage must have and without which no married life can stand. Elizabeth Bennet's closest friend calls it into serious question, both in talk and in action, with grave result both for herself and for Elizabeth.

To Charlotte affection is of no importance, except as an appearance that may be useful for getting a husband. She has advice for Jane Bennet, who is very much on the way to being in love but whose composure and cheerfulness do not disclose her real strength of feeling; her advice has nothing to do with the needs of that reality and of the particular characters of Jane and Bingley, for Charlotte's concern is the general method of exploiting the opportunity to fix a man by helping him on with a show of affection. "In nine cases out of ten, a woman had better shew *more* affection than she feels." The love may or may not follow the marriage, but if it does it is a casual supplementary decision that does not require any thought or feeling. "When she is secure of him, there will be leisure for falling in love as much as she chuses." In a word, affection has no real existence for Charlotte. The minor practicality of her advice is that she is right about Bingley's need for encouragement, but she would apply that to any man because the larger need of understanding one's own thoughts and feelings and a mutual understanding of character is what she denies in marriage. The time needed for a developed love is meaningless. To marry tomorrow, to marry after studying character for a twelvemonth, is all the same. "Happiness in marriage is entirely a matter of chance." Knowledge does not advance felicity and it is better to know as little as possible of the defects of the person with whom you are to pass your life. Elizabeth refuses to take her seriously, finds the opinion laughable because it is not sound, because Charlotte knows it is not sound and because Charlotte would never act in that way herself (21–23). But Charlotte acts precisely in that way.

There can be no question of any "affection" for or from Mr. Collins, a man to whom the word is known, and known only, as a word which it is customary to employ during a proposal. We have heard him declare himself to Elizabeth shortly before he is secured by Charlotte. "And now nothing remains for me but to assure you in the most animated language of the violence of my affection," where the words and the meaning of the sentence are so marvellously contradictory (106). Charlotte marries him. "I am not romantic you know," she tells Elizabeth. "I never was." She asks only a comfortable home and considering what she will get with Collins she is convinced that her chance of happiness with him is as fair as most people can boast of on entering the marriage state. Elizabeth's astonishment is so great that it overcomes the bounds of decorum and she cannot help crying out, "Engaged to Mr. Collins! my dear Charlotte,—impossible!" She could not have supposed it possible that when Charlotte's opinions on matrimony were called into action she could have sacrificed every better feeling to worldly advantage. It is, to Elizabeth, a humiliating picture (124–25).

One must not be misled by Charlotte's quiet declaration that she is not romantic to think that she is acting in a sensible way in a most difficult situation. What Charlotte does is wrong. But then what ought Charlotte do rather than marry Mr. Collins? She is without much money, she is not handsome, she is no longer young, and to be an old maid without money or position will be an unfortunate life. Miss Bates of *Emma* is an instance and Mr. Knightley lectures Emma on the special consideration Miss Bates's misfortune demands. Miss Bates is in worse condition than Charlotte would be because she has no abilities that can give her respect; Charlotte is intelligent. But that intelligence increases the magnitude of Charlotte's defection, because it makes her match with Mr. Collins the more unequal. He is stupid. He is neither sensible nor agreeable; his society is irksome; and his attachment to her must be imaginary. "But still he would be her husband." And that and his establishment are his total charm. Charlotte is interested in neither the man nor the relationship, only the marriage; and it is not the narrator's but Charlotte's reflection on marriage that "it was the only honourable provision for well-educated young women of small fortune, and however uncertain of giving happiness, must be their pleasantest preservative from want" (122–23).

There is more than enough evidence, elsewhere in Jane Austen and in this novel, to make clear how mistaken Charlotte is in a decision to marry without affection. The problem of that type of decision returns several times, in minor works and in major, and even in the letters, and the answer is always the same. It is in the first conversation Emma Watson has with her oldest sister. Elizabeth Watson tells bitter tales of their sister, Penelope, who has acted with rivalry and treachery to Elizabeth in the pursuit of a husband, for there is nothing Penelope would not do to get married; at present she is in pursuit of a rich old doctor attacked by asthma. Emma Watson's reaction is sorrow and fear and more than that: to be so bent on marriage, to pursue a man merely for the sake of a situation is shocking to her and she cannot understand it. "Poverty is a great Evil, but to a woman of Education & feeling it ought not, it cannot be the greatest.—I would rather be a Teacher at a school (and I can think of nothing worse) than marry a Man I did not like." Emma Watson is surprised because she is inexperienced, but there is no question that her principles are quite right and that if Elizabeth Watson thinks her too refined it is because Elizabeth herself is, though good-hearted, coarse. Elizabeth's reply, "I think I could like any good humoured Man with a comfortable Income," is one of many signs of her deficiencies (MW 318). In *Mansfield Park* the great temptation of Fanny Price is to accept the proposal of Henry Crawford, for which every pressure is brought to bear upon her and by those she loves most. But she knows she is doing right in refusing him and she hopes that her uncle's displeasure with her will abate when he considers the matter with more impartiality and comes to feel, as a good man must feel "how wretched, and how unpardonable, how hopeless and how wicked it was, to marry without affection" (324). We never have any doubt that she is right in this refusal and indeed the whole novel turns on it. It is wicked to marry without affection.

One of Jane Austen's more interesting letters is the advice she wrote to Fanny Knight in 1814 (just after the publication of *Pride and Prejudice* in 1813 and of *Mansfield Park* in 1814), that same letter about the amiable Mr. Plumtre. In it she replies to her niece's anxiety over a grievous mistake, because Fanny has encouraged the young man to such a point as to make him feel almost secure of her—and now her feelings have changed. It was a common mistake, her aunt comforts her, one that thousands of women fall into: he was the first young man who attached himself to her and that was a powerful charm. Furthermore, unlike most who have done the same, Fanny Knight has little to regret, because the young man is nothing to be ashamed of. Jane Austen then goes on to point out all his excellences—his mind, his principles, and all qualities which, as she says, are really of the first importance; the more she writes about him the warmer her feelings grow and the more strongly she feels the sterling worth of such a young man and the desirableness of Fanny's growing in love with him again. She takes up certain objections that Fanny has to him and tries to show her that they are false, that what her niece thinks are faults in him are really unimportant or even advantages. At that point, after such a lengthy, thoughtful, and feeling argument on behalf of the young man, Jane Austen puts into the other side of the balance the one thing that outweighs everything else:

> —And now, my dear Fanny, having written so much on one side of the question, I shall turn round & entreat you not to commit yourself farther, & not to think of accepting him unless you really do like him. Anything is to be preferred or endured rather than marrying without Affection; and if his deficiencies of Manner &c &c strike you more than all his good qualities, if you continue to think strongly of them, give him up at once. (L 409–10)

To return, then, from Jane Austen's "my dear Fanny" to Elizabeth Bennet's "my dear Charlotte" and Jane Bennet's "my dear Lizzy" (as they are all addressed in moments of similar crisis): when Elizabeth receives her second proposal from Darcy and accepts him, she seems to the intelligent members of her family, to her father and Jane, to be in a situation similar to Charlotte's when Charlotte accepted Mr. Collins. The similarity is emphasized by a verbal identity. Elizabeth's astonishment had been so great when Charlotte informed her of the engagement to Collins that she could not help crying out, "Engaged to Mr. Collins! ... impossible!" (124). When Elizabeth is engaged and opens her heart to Jane, the reaction is, untypically for Jane but understandably so, absolute incredulity: "engaged to Mr. Darcy! ... impossible" (372). Jane's disbelief, unlike Elizabeth's reaction to Charlotte's match, is not that she thinks Darcy without a single quality to make him a desirable husband; on the contrary, nothing could give Bingley or Jane more delight than such a marriage. But she thought it impossible because of Elizabeth's dislike, and even now she cannot approve, however great and desirable it seems, if Elizabeth does not really love him quite well enough. The appeal is direct and deep, and very like Jane Austen's words to Fanny Knight: "Oh, Lizzy! do any thing rather than marry without affection. Are you quite sure that you feel what you ought to do?" (373). So the answer to the question of what Charlotte Lucas ought to do rather than marry Mr. Collins is—"any thing." To be an impoverished old maid is a misfortune, but to marry Mr. Collins is immoral.

Nor is it true that because she has not made the romantic choice, Charlotte has made the practical choice for the comfortable home. The antithesis is false. She had said, in general, that happiness is entirely a matter of chance and she says, in particular, that considering what Collins is, in character, connections, and situation, her chance of happiness with him is as fair as most people can boast on entering the marriage state. But her chances are not even uncertain. That point emerges most convincingly because Charlotte makes the very best of her marriage state and manages it admirably. Elizabeth thinks that it will be impossible for her friend to be tolerably happy (125), but in her visit to Kent she sees how well Charlotte can do. Charlotte maintains her comfortable home and her married life by excluding her husband from it as much as she possibly can. She chooses for her own common use an inferior room with a less lively view because he is less likely to appear in it Elizabeth gives her credit for the arrangement (168). She encourages her husband as much as possible in his gardening, to keep him out of the house. When he says something of which she might reasonably be ashamed, which certainly is not seldom, she sometimes blushes faintly, but in general she wisely does not hear (156). The necessary wisdom for living with Mr. Collins, which Charlotte accepts, is to give up a piece of herself, suppress her shame, lose her ears, see less, diminish her life. As Elizabeth leaves her, at the end of the visit, Charlotte does not ask for compassion, but her prospect is a melancholy one. Her home, housekeeping, her parish and poultry have not yet lost their charms (216). Not yet. Neither is it a comforting later little note to hear that Mr. Collins's dear Charlotte is expecting a young olive branch. She no doubt will do the best she can, but the children of mismatches without respect or affection do not begin life with advantage.

With her eyes open Charlotte has miscalculated, because there are no fair chances of happiness in an inequality that makes affection impossible. Elizabeth's father can advise his child of this. Like Jane, Mr. Bennet may be mistaken in his facts but not in his principle when he warns Elizabeth to think better before having Mr. Darcy. He knows she cannot be happy or respectable unless she esteems her husband, that an unequal marriage would put her in danger, perhaps discredit and misery. "My child, let me not have the grief of seeing you unable to respect your partner in life" (376). He and his daughter know the living experience that speaks in these words. Captivated by youth and beauty and the appearance of good humor they generally give, he had married a woman whose weak understanding and illiberal mind "had very early in their marriage put an end to all real affection for her" (236). The results have been before the reader since the first chapter and before Elizabeth, with less amusement and more pain, all her life. She has felt strongly the disadvantages that must attend the children of so unsuitable a marriage, and Lydia's disaster has confirmed her judgment.

Lydia's affair is, for one thing, what can happen to the child of a marriage without affection. It is, for another, itself an instance of a marriage where neither person is capable of affection. "Her affections had been continually fluctuating" and it required only encouragement for her to attach herself to him in particular (280). His fluctuations have been apparent to Elizabeth from personal experience; his affection for Lydia, just as Elizabeth had expected, is not equal to hers for him (318) and it is only in fulfillment of the obvious that we hear at the end how "His affection for her soon sunk into indifference" (387). His last private conversation with Elizabeth, in which she makes embarrassingly clear that she knows all about him, ends as he kisses her hand "with affectionate gallantry, though he hardly knew how to look" (329): a very pretty touch that leaves his affection exposed for what it is in a shallow and losing gesture. But, furthermore, the affection of Lydia's Wickham was once something that interested Elizabeth for herself (144–45, 153), so that her own understanding of the meaning of affection has not always been what it is at last; it has taken time. If Charlotte Lucas thinks time is unimportant because affection is unimportant, Elizabeth has flirted with another mode in which time is unimportant because affection is so quickly seen. Lydia's affair helps her sister to better understanding.

The validity of the marriage between Darcy and Elizabeth is established by the time in which their affection grows, and by the capacity of the affection to withstand and to be strengthened by the proofs of time and crisis. Elizabeth is certain that the immediate effect of Lydia's disgrace will be that her own power with Darcy must sink, that everything must sink under such a proof of family weakness; it makes her understand her own wishes, and never has she so honestly felt how much she could have loved him as now when all love is vain. The whole of their acquaintance, as she can now review it, has been full of contradictions and varieties and she sighs at the perverseness of her own feelings, which have so changed. In the mode of romance Elizabeth's change is unreasonable or unnatural in comparison with the regard that arises on a first interview and even before two words have been exchanged; but she had given "somewhat of a trial" to this "method" with Wickham and its ill-success might perhaps authorize her to try the other "less interesting mode of attachment." The ironic language sounds like the language of experimental method, and it is that, in the sense of tested experience of common life as opposed to romantic prejudice, but the reality here is the reality of tried emotions. "If gratitude and esteem are good foundations of affection"—and the hypothesis has been tried by Elizabeth's mind and emotions—then the change of sentiment will be "neither improbable nor faulty" (279).

Henry Tilney had come to be sincerely attached to Catherine Morland, he felt and delighted in all the excellences of her character and "truly loved" her society, but, as we know, "his affection originated in nothing better than gratitude." That may be a new circumstance in romance, but not in common life (NA 243). "Gratitude" here is the response to the feeling of another, the natural obligation in return for having been thought worthy of being loved. It was this that led Fanny Knight into her mistake with her young man, whose powerful charm was that he was the first young man to attach himself to her. John Gregory, giving fatherly advice to his daughters, warns them that what is commonly called love among girls is rather gratitude and partiality to the man who prefers theirs to the rest of the sex, so that such a man they often marry with little personal esteem or affection. But the difference between Fanny Knight or Dr. Gregory's daughters and what happens to Elizabeth Bennet is the difference between the young miss and the woman who knows the meaning of affection. In the one the gratitude is the first pleasing stir of a self-love that confuses its object, in the other it is the feeling that initiates a self-discovery. The feeling develops if, as with Darcy, there is a continuing revelation of a character whose actions build more powerful causes of gratitude and if, as with Elizabeth, there is a continuing increase of a character who can perceive and respond to that revelation. Elizabeth's gratitude develops in a heightened vision of him, and in a properly chastened revision of her self-love. That irony, the coolness and detachment of her language, as she recollects how she has arrived at her present feelings by the less interesting mode of attachment, is directed not at her feelings but at herself. She sees in her affection the complicated history of herself. The slow preparation of the foundations creates for an affection its depth of interest and is the guarantee of its reality of meaning in a life. Four months earlier at his declaration of how ardently he admired and loved her she had not been willing to grant Darcy even the conventional gratitude: "In such cases as this, it is, I believe, the established mode to express a sense of obligation for the sentiments avowed, however unequally they may be returned. It is natural that obligation should be felt, and if I could *feel* gratitude, I would now thank you. But I cannot—I have never desired your good opinion" (190). Now she knows by extended experience what his good opinion is worth and what the value of his affection is. Having seen him at Pemberley in a new light, an amiable light, there was then above all, above the respect and esteem, another motive within her, the gratitude she felt for his love of her. It was gratitude not merely for his having loved her, but for loving her still well enough to forgive the petulance and acrimony of her manner in rejecting him and forgive all her unjust accusations. A man who had reason to be her enemy has been eager to preserve her acquaintance, solicit the good opinion of her friends, make her known to his sister. Such a change in such a man excites gratitude, for this is a man who knows something of love, of ardent love (265–66).

Furthermore, Darcy's response to the event which she fears has put an end to their acquaintance then becomes the severest test of his affection. He arranges for the marriage of Wickham and her sister and he does it because of "his affection for her" (326). At first she rebukes her vanity for putting so much dependence on the force of that affection, but she has underestimated it. It has remained unshaken (334), unchanged (366); when, at last, he can tell her of his feelings, they prove how important she has been to him, and they make "his affection every moment more valuable" (366). That is what enables her to answer her father's doubts of Darcy with "absolute certainty that his affection was not the work of a day, but had stood the test of many months suspense" (377). She is "in the certain possession of his warmest affection" (378).

They have come to that happy moment because each has suffered a change. If he has no improper pride and is perfectly amiable when she accepts him, he was not so when she rejected him. And if she is capable of the kind of affection she feels when she accepts him, she was not so when she rejected him. Each has changed because each has worked a change on the other. The happiness is deserved by a process of mortification begun early and ended late. Charlotte Lucas suggested at the start that Darcy is a man who has some right to be proud, and Elizabeth agrees. "I could easily forgive *his* pride, if he had not mortified *mine*" (20). As Mary Bennet, on the same page, draws upon her reading of synonym dictionaries to define pride, we can get some help from these sources in understanding mortification. It is more than the mere vexation of a contradictory will, it is a force that cuts into the understanding and evaluation of one's self. Mrs. Bennet is easily vexed—"You take delight in vexing me," she says in the first chapter. "You have no compassion on my poor nerves" (5)—but she cannot be mortified. Elizabeth will have to make the distinction. Vexation arises from the crossing our wishes and views, says Crabb's *English Synonymes* (1816, p. 760), "mortification from the hurting our pride and self-importance."

The hurt may not be significant when it is simply a proper return for the excessive self-opinion of a fool who is deceived but who will never be improved by the event: as, at the end of *Persuasion*, Elizabeth Elliot is mortified when Mr. Elliot withdraws, or both she and Sir Walter are "shocked and mortified" by the discovery of Mrs. Clay's deception (P 250, 251). Deliberately to inflict mortification on others is significant as the action of a small mind desirous of hurting another to gratify its own pride and insulting importance. It appears in "Volume the Second" in an early sketch for Lady Catherine de Bourgh (MW 158). Mrs. Ferrars and Mrs. John Dashwood of *Sense and Sensibility* are "anxious to mortify" (233). To be the victim of such mortification when one's conduct has not merited it is more significant, because that is a severe test. Elinor Dashwood cannot now be made unhappy by this behavior of Mrs. Ferrars, though a few months ago it would have hurt her exceedingly; a few months ago was before she had learned from Lucy of Edward's engagement. She cannot now be hurt because she is the mistaken object of attack, but she is stronger also because she had met successfully that earlier undeserved and much worse mortification. In Lucy's revelation she had faced an emotion and distress beyond anything she had ever felt before: "She was mortified, shocked, confounded." That is the effect on Sir Walter and Elizabeth at the end of *Persuasion*, but for Elinor this is early in the action, the end of only her first volume, and she exerts herself to struggle resolutely and to gain strength (SS 134–35). (It makes more comic, incidentally, our recollection of how Marianne blushes to acknowledge her sister's lack of strong affections—and the striking proof Marianne gives of the strength of her own affections by her ability to love and respect that sister "in spite of this mortifying conviction" [104]; the incident improves Marianne's opinion of herself.)

Misapplied mortifications, felt by those who do not need them, not understood by those who do, can be a source of touching, piercing emotion. In *Mansfield Park* the mortifications are almost always distorted. Some of them are gratuitous insults inflicted on Fanny, by the Miss Bertrams or even Sir Thomas (20, 33); she is undeserving of them, there is nothing she can do to improve under them, and she feels too to lowly to be injured by them; it is altogether painful and helps define the pain peculiar to *Mansfield Park*. Even Edmund, under the spell of Mary Crawford, mortifies Fanny when he turns from her, in their congenial moment of enthusiastic contemplation of nature, turns his back and rejoins Mary; the failure is not Fanny's and only the sigh is hers—and a scolding from Mrs. Norris (113). She who is pained by others is put in difficult circumstances where it is she who must bear the burden of not giving pain: if she does not wear the amber cross William has given her it might be mortifying him (254); but a few pages later if she does not wear Mary's necklace, Edmund says, it would be mortifying Mary severely (263). Always it is Fanny who feels for others what they are unable to feel for themselves; when she finds out that Henry has not changed as much as she had thought, that he is still the acquaintance and perhaps the flirt of Mrs. Rushworth, "She was mortified. She had thought better of him" (436). Those who most need the benefits are incapable of the pain. They feel it on the wrong occasions, for the wrong reasons, as when Maria, having lost the barouche box to her sister takes her seat within, "in gloom and mortification" (80). Mary Crawford, when Edmund refuses to accept the temptation that he take part in the play, moves away from him "with some feelings of resentment and mortification" (145); when she hears later that he is soon to take orders, this too "was felt with resentment and mortification" (227). The combination, emphasized by the identity of reaction on the two occasions, is especially bad, because it means that Mary cannot learn; she is thinking only of her own importance and far from turning the experience valuably upon herself she turns it weakly upon him, expends her emotion not in revising her own faults but in anger at his for making her think less of herself. Henry is worse. When, at the end, he is received by Mrs. Rushworth with a coldness that ought to have been repulsive and final, he is "mortified" because he cannot bear to be thrown off by the woman he had once commanded; "lie must exert himself" to subdue her "resentment" (468). There is a devilish reversal of terms.

Sweet Anne Elliot knows much of the poignancy of the lonely mortification. It is only Anne who has been able to see the mortifications hanging over her father and sister (P 212, 215), without being able to help because of their obtuse vanity; it is Anne who has to bear the mortification of their conduct (226) because they are insensitive to the effect of their own action. She has had long practice in bearing lonely feelings. Nobody appreciates her music, but Mr. and Mrs. Musgrove's fond partiality for their daughters' performance and total indifference to hers gives her more pleasure for their sake than mortification for her own (47). Anne bears the pain even when it is cruel, even when there is no way that she can respond by changing herself to avoid it. When she hears that Captain Wentworth thought her so altered that he should not have known her, a wound has been inflicted. But "Anne fully submitted, in silent, deep mortification" (60–61), a sentence in which every word is important and to which we will return. There is nothing Anne can do to reverse time, but she can accept the blow fully as it tells her a truth about herself that she must live with.

But the mortification that leads to a truth has its fullest value when it is part of an extended learning process, simple or complex. The tale of Catherine Morland is a tale of "hopes and fears, mortifications and pleasures" (NA 97) that are an initiation into the ways of life and the proper responses to it, though their interest, of course, is limited by the simplicity of the heroine. She cannot be aware of the full meaning of her actions or of what is done to her. When she is turned out of the Abbey, "It was as incomprehensible as it was mortifying and grievous" (226), so that there seems to be little she can do to meet it. Still, the little that Catherine does do is sufficient for her purposes. In the Upper Rooms at Bath "one mortification succeeded another" and from the whole she deduced a small but useful lesson," about the anticipations and the realities of going to a ball (55). She is teachable, and one of the best signs of this is that she does not answer mortification by trying to return it. Having been put by the Thorpes into a situation in which she has been impolite to Eleanor and Henry Tilney, she calls upon Miss Tilney to explain and be forgiven; she is told that Miss Tilney is not at home, only to see her walk out a moment later. Catherine's response to the denial is a "blush of mortification" and her response to the sight of Miss Tilney is "deep mortification" (91-92). Miss Tilney's conduct has been angry incivility, Catherine thinks, and she could almost be angry herself in return; "but she checked the resentful sensation; she remembered her ignorance" (92). That is a virtue and we can augur well for Catherine. At the end her "mortified feelings" at General Tilney's insolence are controlled in her letter to Eleanor, which is just, both to herself and her friend, "honest without resentment" (235). She can profit from her experience as the far more knowledgeable Mary Crawford never can.

The mortification becomes a fuller part of the learning when it comes to a conclusion, when it is the moment of final vision, the sort of epiphany announced by Reginald De Courcy at the end of *Lady Susan*: "The spell is removed. I see you as you are. Since we parted yesterday, I have received from indisputable authority, such an history of you as must bring the most mortifying conviction of the Imposition I have been under" (MW 304). There has not been much of a process here, Reginald being a silly stick, and the change occurring through the receipt of authoritative information about somebody else. Emma comes to a similar conviction, similar in words, that is, when she perceives that "she had been imposed on by others in a most mortifying degree"; but the difference is in the clause that follows directly— "that she had been imposing on herself in a degree yet more mortifying" (E 412)—and hers is a much more interesting history. Hers is a history of self-understanding and the mortifications have been an essential and continuing part of the process by which that understanding has been achieved. She has been an easy fool of others because she has been her own fool and the understanding of self and the understanding of others come to her as parts of the same experience. For her, when the spell is removed, the perception is a revision of what she is, head and heart, and of what she has valued—most notably what she has judged and felt to be worthy of love. What Emma sees for the first time, in that surprise and humiliation, is herself and the man she loves; then the knowledge of herself makes her ashamed of every sensation but one, "her affection for Mr. Knightley" (412). The mortification is the necessary condition of the affection; the beginning of the new and larger life asks the painful end of the old and blinded self. Which returns us to *Pride and Prejudice*.

Mortification, in Jane Austen's language, no longer has a religious force. She can use it in that sense only in jest—Jane Fairfax, for example, thinking of herself as a devoted novitiate resolved at one-and-twenty to complete the sacrifice and retire from all the pleasures of life to penance and mortification forever (E 165). But it can be, we know, much stronger than a social term for an embarrassment; it can still carry a moral, renovative, force. Elizabeth and Darcy change one another because each hurts the pride and self-importance of the other, humbling, humiliating, forcing a self-recognition that requires a giving up of part of the character for which each has always felt self-esteem and a taking on of a new character. That each is capable of the loss and the renewal by mortification is what makes the love valuable. The inception, the turning point, and then the resolution of the changing relationship of Elizabeth and Darcy are, each of them, marked by mortifications: the first rousing effect each has on the other; the unsuccessful proposal and the letter that follows; and the elopement of Lydia, the event necessary for a fitting successful proposal. Each signalizes a challenge that calls forth a revealing response either of self-protective failure or of self-conquest.

The process begins immediately upon the first occasion of their being together, when Darcy looks for a moment at Elizabeth, till catching her eye, then withdraws his own and coldly refuses to dance with her because she is not handsome enough to tempt "*me*": Elizabeth could easily forgive *his* pride, "if he had not mortified *mine*" (20). Without his intending it, and without her knowing it, he has indicated the sort of lesson Elizabeth must learn. Pride relates to our opinion of ourselves, Mary Bennet says, and it is that pride which now begins to be and will be more properly and more severely mortified. It is he, however, his withdrawn eye, which is most in need of education at this point, and the very next thing we hear of him is that she becomes an object of some interest in his eye; having scarcely allowed her to be pretty and looking at her, when they meet again, only to criticize, and making clear to himself and his friends that she has hardly a good feature in her face, he then finds the intelligence and beauty of her eyes. "To this discovery succeeded some others equally mortifying" (23). Though he has detected with critical eye more than one failure in the perfect symmetry of her form, he is now forced to acknowledge that it is light and pleasing; though he has asserted that her manners are not fashionable he is now caught by their easy playfulness. The return upon himself is just, as she, unknowingly, is catching and forcing him to admit that he has been mistaken.

The first important effect each has on the other is a mortification, a lowering of self-opinion. But neither has yet been able to benefit from the effect; the effect has not been strong enough, in good part because neither is in a moral position to make the other feel the effect.

The turning point of their developing relation is Darcy's proposal to Elizabeth and his rejection. He has no right to propose. Elizabeth is quite right to reject him; he would not be a good husband. He has not, even in proposing, behaved in a gentlemanlike manner and is startled to be told that truth, and more than startled: "You could not have made me the offer of your hand in any possible way that would have tempted me to accept it"; this he must hear from the woman whose pride he mortified by saying she was not handsome enough to tempt *him*. He looks at her with "mingled incredulity and mortification" (192–93). She goes on and begins to remove the incredulity by describing how from the first moment of their acquaintance his deficiencies of manner impressed her with that fullest belief in his arrogance, conceit, and selfish disdain of the feelings of others that formed the groundwork on which succeeding events have built so immovable a dislike. Her accusations are ill founded, formed on mistaken premises, but, as he later says, his behavior to her merited the severest reproach and the mortification remains. It is from this point that Darcy's life changes importantly. It takes time. The recollection of what he said, his conduct, his manners, his expression, is for many months inexpressibly painful. Her reproof, that he had not behaved in a gentlemanlike manner—the words remain with him—had been a torture; and it was some time before he was reasonable enough to allow their justice. To a man of principle the pain of realizing the pride and selfishness of a lifetime is a hard lesson and he owes much to her who taught him. "By you, I was properly humbled" (367–69).

What we see of Darcy, of course, is mainly the result of what has happened, not the many months of pain; we see him through Elizabeth's eyes and share with her the surprise of what has happened and understand it in retrospect as it moves her. As Elizabeth rejects Darcy, producing the mortification that changes his life, our interest, as always, is in what will happen to her, and what happens to her, painfully and fortunately, is the letter from him producing the mortification that changes her life. It comes as a particularly powerful blow to her because it makes her know the meaning of feelings she has experienced repeatedly and never understood; the causes of mortification have been at work and she has felt them without recognizing their import. They have been at work in what is closest to her, in her own family, in her friend, in the man she has found so agreeable, in herself.

Elizabeth has always been confident in knowing the truth, immediately and exactly. She has believed the history of himself that Wickham gave: there was truth in his looks. Jane finds it difficult to decide between the conflicting accounts she has heard—it is distressing—one does not know what to think. But Elizabeth knows: "I beg your pardon;—one knows exactly what to think" (86). It is the certainty that carries her straight to that extraordinary carnival of foolishness, so wealthy in detail, the Netherfield ball. She dances herself into what is, exactly, a dance of mortification, totally misunderstood by her. The prospect of that ball, extremely agreeable to every female of her family, brings to Elizabeth the pleasurable thought of dancing a great deal with Wickham and seeing a confirmation of everything in Darcy's looks and behavior. Her spirits are so high that they carry her away and though she does not often speak unnecessarily to Mr. Collins she cannot help asking whether he is going and whether he will think it proper to join the amusement. To her surprise he is not only prepared to dance but takes the opportunity she has offered by securing her for the first two dances. She feels herself completely taken in, is her own victim. She had fully proposed being engaged by Wickham for those very dances—and to have Mr. Collins instead! her liveliness had never been worse timed (86–87). She enters the dancing room at Netherfield to look for Wickham, a doubt of his being present having never occurred to her, certain of meeting him, dressed with more than usual care and prepared in the highest spirits for completing the conquest that evening. But he is not there. She suspects that it is Darcy who has caused his exclusion, then finds that it is Wickham who has wished to avoid Darcy and is thereby assured that Darcy is no less answerable for Wickham's absence than if her first surmise had been just. Pursuing that line of justice in her disappointment she is hardly able to reply with tolerable civility to Darcy's politeness, because attention, forbearance; or patience with him is injury to Wickham, and she turns from him in ill humor. She turns to Charlotte Lucas, tells that friend all her griefs, makes a voluntary transition to the oddities of her cousin Collins, whom Charlotte has not yet seen, and points him out to the particular notice of her friend. Charlotte takes particular notice (89–90).

Three sets of dances follow. The first dances are with Mr. Collins and bring distress, as in his awkwardness and solemnity and often moving wrong without being aware of it he gives her all the shame and misery a disagreeable partner can give: they are "dances of mortification." The moment of release from him is ecstasy. Wickham is not there but she next dances with a fellow officer of his and has the refreshment of talking of Wickham and hearing that he is universally liked. Then she finds herself suddenly addressed by Darcy, "who took her so much by surprise in his application for her hand, that, without knowing what she did, she accepted him." She is then left to fret over her presence of mind while Charlotte tries to console her by saying she will find him very agreeable (90). That is the succession of her partners, of the three men who will be, or seem to be, solicitous of her hand and who present to her problems of increasing complexity. She delivers herself into the hands of each with an increasing ironic ignorance, finally accepting Darcy in spite of her determination to hate that disagreeable man. Darcy had once rejected her as a partner, mortifying *her* (italicized) pride. It was her mother's advice then that at another time she should not dance with *him* and Elizabeth believed she could safely promise *never* to dance with him (20). It was a promise she kept, when the opportunity first offered, at Sir William Lucas's; her resistance to Darcy did not injure her with the gentleman (26–27). Now, at Netherfield, she accepts him and is unhappy she has lost that assured control of a mind which, a few pages before, knows exactly what to think. We never hear of her dancing with anyone else after that, but it will be a while before she will understand the meaning of what she has done. She dances badly, in fact, taking the occasion not to learn more of Darcy's mind and character but, in a sudden fancy, to punish him. She is unable to resist the temptation of forcing the subject of Wickham on him, even blaming herself for weakness in not going on with it more than she does. There are times when she literally does not know what she is saying because her mind is wandering to Wickham and she then asks searching questions of Darcy's character that are more immediately relevant to her own blindness. Elizabeth is perfectly satisfied that she knows his character and Wickham's, and contradictory information that evening, whether from Miss Bingley or from Jane, can only confirm her; she is acutely analytic in refusing to accept what they say, and she is wholly mistaken in her conclusion. Changing the subject then to Jane's modest hopes of Bingley's regard, Elizabeth, always confident, says all in her power to heighten Jane's confidence (91–96).

Perfectly satisfied with herself she is forced by the conduct of her family into a series of confused vexations and mortifications. Mr. Collins discovers wonderfully that Mr. Darcy is a nephew of Lady Catherine, insists on introducing himself, and though Elizabeth tries hard to dissuade him, determines to follow his own inclination; it "vexed" her to see him expose himself to such a man. She is then deeply "vexed" to find that her mother is talking openly of her expectation of Jane's marriage to Bingley; Elizabeth tries to check Mrs. Bennet or make her less audible, for to her "inexpressible vexation" she perceives that Darcy is overhearing; but nothing she says has any influence: "Elizabeth blushed and blushed again with shame and vexation." With a brief interval of tranquillity she then has the "mortification" of seeing Mary oblige the company by exhibiting herself in a song (98–100). Elizabeth suffers most painful sensations and agonies, until at her look of entreaty her father interferes, in a speech that makes her still more sorry. Mr. Collins takes the opportunity to make a worse fool of himself before Darcy, which amuses Mr. Bennet and draws a serious commendation from Mrs. Bennet. To Elizabeth it appears that had the family made an agreement to expose themselves as much as possible they could not have played their parts with finer success (101); and all she misses is her own even finer part. The greatest relief in all this she owes to her friend Charlotte, who often good-naturedly engages Mr. Collins's conversation to herself. Darcy never comes near enough to speak again and feeling it to be the probable consequence of her allusions to Wickham Elizabeth rejoices in it. It has been an evening of wonderfully compounded errors. Mrs. Bennet, like Elizabeth, is "perfectly satisfied" (103).

But from that point of satisfaction the series of vexations and mortifications, unprofitable because misunderstood, begins to work upon her. Mr. Collins's proposal the next day is vexing and embarrassing, but Elizabeth can overcome that problem; the private acknowledgment of Wickham, that his regret and vexation at having been absent was in fact a self-imposed necessity to avoid Darcy, meets with her approval; the possibility, in Bingley's sudden and unexpected departure, that he may never return to Jane, she treats with contempt. The first serious surprise to her is the revelation that Charlotte's continued kindness in keeping Mr. Collins in good humor, for which Elizabeth is more obliged than she can express, is a kindness that extends further than Elizabeth has any conception of. Elizabeth could not have supposed it possible that her friend could have sacrificed every better feeling to worldly advantage. "Charlotte the wife of Mr. Collins, was a most humiliating picture!" (125). The humiliation is hers. It then becomes clear that Bingley will not return and that Jane's hope is entirely over. The perfectly satisfied Elizabeth finds herself becoming dissatisfied, not with herself but with the world; every day confirms her belief of the inconsistency of all human characters and of the little dependence that can be placed on the appearance of either merit or sense; Bingley is one instance and Charlotte is the other. Nor will she allow Jane to defend Charlotte or for the sake of one individual change the meaning of principle and integrity, confuse selfishness with prudence. Finally the sole survivor of her apparent satisfactions at the Netherfield ball disappears, as Wickham's apparent partiality subsides and he becomes the admirer of someone else, someone whose most remarkable charm is the sudden acquisition of ten thousand pounds. But Elizabeth, so dissatisfied with the inconsistency of human character, less clear-sighted in this case than in Charlotte's, finds his wish of independence entirely natural. If she did not think so, if she did not think she would be his only choice if fortune permitted, that fortune denied him by that abominable Mr. Darcy, she would be forced to think differently of herself. She is not young in the ways of the world, she says, and she is "open to the mortifying conviction" that handsome young men must have something to live on (150). In her subsequent conversation about Wickham, with Mrs. Gardiner (153–54), she seems to have lost sight of the difference in matrimonial affairs between the mercenary and the prudent motive, a difference so clear to her in Charlotte's affair. Then follows a series of observations concluding in the exclamation that she is sick of all men, that she is thankful to be visiting the home of Mr. Collins in Kent, because he has not one agreeable quality, because stupid men are the only ones worth knowing after all. Mrs. Gardiner's warning to take care, that her speech savors strongly of disappointment, is serious. The vexations and the mortifications, with their separate meanings, have all collapsed into one, into a disappointed condemnation of others for their contradictory conduct to her. Because she cannot turn them to an occasion of growth they begin to harm her.

The turning point is in her visit to Kent, not because she meets again a stupid and disagreeable man but because she meets Darcy again. She mortifies him, in what is his most valuable moment, but not hers; she does it in the blindness and prejudice of the mind she has brought to Kent. Her moment follows when she receives, in return, his letter revealing to her what she must know to convert her own badly understood mortifications into a real mortification. Her feelings are acutely painful, difficult of definition. Her first reaction is to disbelieve what he says, it must be false, it cannot be true, because if it is true it will overthrow every cherished opinion, and she puts the letter away hastily, protesting she will not regard it, never look at it again. The value of Elizabeth is that this will not do, the pain and the difficulty must be borne, and in half a minute, collecting herself as well as she could, "she again began the mortifying perusal of all that related to Wickham," commanding herself to examine the meaning of every sentence (205). It is the necessary first step in the understanding of the real character of Wickham and of herself; the result is the eye-opening moment, as she grows absolutely ashamed of herself, her actions, her pride in her own discernment and her disdain of others. "How humiliating is this discovery!— Yet, how just a humiliation!" It is the mortification of self-discovery. "Till this moment, I never knew myself." From this knowledge it follows that when she returns once more to the letter, to that part of it in which her family are mentioned "in terms of such mortifying, yet merited reproach," her sense of shame is severe, especially when she remembers the Netherfield ball. She knows now the justice of those terms (208–9).

There is a new self-knowledge in Elizabeth. It is evident, in a minor way, in her return to Hertfordshire, when she hears Lydia describe the girl to whom Wickham had transferred his admiration; such a nasty little freckled thing, Lydia calls her, and Elizabeth is shocked to think that if she is incapable of such coarseness of expression herself, the coarseness of sentiment is what her own breast had formerly harbored and fancied liberal (220). She and Darcy have given severe lessons of liberality to each other and each is in a proper course to make use of what has been learned. What is needed is an incident that will put them to the test of action. It is a sad moment for Kitty when Lydia receives her invitation to Brighton: the rapture of Lydia, the delight of Mrs. Bennet and the mortification of Kitty are scarcely to be described (230); but in that company it is obvious that the effect on Kitty is not improving, and worse must follow if any good is to result to her. It comes through the more serious mortification of others when Lydia runs off with Wickham. The incident may be of excessive length and fuss for the balance of the novel, but it is a necessary weight for the two main characters, who must now bear the effects of their past, the old self, and respond with the liberal conquest of the new self. The alteration in Darcy's and in Elizabeth's understanding, consequent upon their mutual mortifications, has been large; but it is Lydia's elopement that brings the concluding mortifications and the deserved happiness.

To Elizabeth the elopement is "humiliation" and misery (278). It justifies Darcy in the two chief causes of offense she had laid to his charge—his offenses against Wickham and against her family—and it brings those two forces together in such a way as to sink Elizabeth's power over him. She believes that he has now made a self-conquest, is no longer subject to his feelings for her, and the belief is exactly calculated to make her understand her own wishes, that she could have loved him. Later, after Lydia's marriage is assured, Elizabeth is heartily sorry that in her distress of the moment she had told Darcy of her fears for Lydia; the beginning could have been concealed from him: there was no one whose knowledge of her sister's frailty could have "mortified her so much" (311). But it is not from any hope for herself, because the gulf between her and Darcy is now impassable, both her objectionable family and Wickham. She is wrong, but now it is to her credit. She accepts her loss. Even when she has learned what Darcy has in fact done she must hide her feelings: it was necessary to laugh when she would rather have cried; her father had most cruelly mortified her by what he said of Mr. Darcy's indifference to her (364). Her father may be right.

What she did not know, and her ignorance is no fault in her, is that Darcy is stronger than she could have thought. He has made a self-conquest more difficult than the one she imagined, by taking a responsibility for Wickham's act, by exerting himself, by going to Wickham and arranging the marriage. It was "an exertion of goodness" she had thought too great to be probable, but it was not: "he had taken on himself all the trouble and mortification" of searching out and supplicating and bribing those he had most reason to abominate, despise, avoid. He had done it, though she still cannot realize that fully, because of "his affection for her" (326). When she finally has the opportunity she thanks him for the compassion that enabled him to take so much trouble and "bear so many mortifications" (366). And, rightly, it is then that she learns it was done not for her family but for her, and she knows the value of his affection. Their story comes to a happy ending earned by two properly humbled people who have learned to bear mortification and to rise under it with love.

There are deserved little rewards at the end in the removal of mortifications, when Elizabeth and Darcy can leave the mortifying society of her family (384), when even Mary Bennet is no longer mortified by comparisons between her sisters' beauty and her own (386). But it is most pleasant to hear in the last chapter that Miss Bingley was "very deeply mortified" by Darcy's marriage (387), for it is a treatment she long has been needing; but that as she thought it advisable to retain the right of visiting Pemberley she was wise enough to drop all "resentment" and pay off arrears of civility to Elizabeth. Even she has profited from the mortification, but, necessarily, only to the degree she is capable, a degree of meanness.

SUSAN MORGAN

Intelligence in Pride and Prejudice

Murphy sat out of it, as though he were free.

P*ride and Prejudice* has a charmed place as the most popular of Jane Austen's novels. Its heroine, Elizabeth Bennet, witty, self-confident, with those dancing eyes, and not quite beautiful face, depicts for us all that is flawed and irresistible about real people. Lionel Trilling has observed about *Emma* that we like Mr. Knightley "because we perceive that he cherishes Emma not merely in spite of her subversive self-assertion but because of it."[1] This applies to Mr. Darcy as well, and Elizabeth, perfectly aware of it, cannot resist inquiring when she demands an account of his having fallen in love with her: "Did you admire me for my impertinence?"[2] Her impertinence, of course, is why generations of readers have admired her and why we recognize that the major concern of the book is with the possibilities and responsibility of free and lively thought. *Pride and Prejudice* explores the special question of the meaning of freedom, given the premise which Jane Austen assumes throughout her fiction, that the relation between a character and public reality is at once problematic and necessary. We watch Elizabeth as she moves from a belief in her own logic to a more fluid interpretation of knowing and of intelligence in terms of the backgrounds, contexts, and particulars which inform truth. And we learn to acknowledge that the pressing importance of such a movement rests not in our hopes for being right but in our hopes for being free.

From *Modern Philology* 73, no. 1 (August 1975). © 1975 by The University of Chicago.

Miss Bingley describes Elizabeth's free spirit as "an abominable sort of conceited independence, a most country town indifference to decorum" (p. 36). Certainly, Elizabeth hurrying through the muddy countryside to visit Jane, springing over puddles and jumping over stiles, is not a decorous sight. And just as certainly, those muddy petticoats and glowing cheeks contribute a great deal to Mr. Darcy's falling in love. The importance of Elizabeth's sense of freedom and the necessity of relating that idea to her growth in the novel may account for the fact that so many critics have sought to discuss *Pride and Prejudice* in terms of a dichotomy (suggested by the title) in which Elizabeth's freedom constitutes one pole and some sort of social sense the other. Her progress can then be understood as a movement from polarity to a merging or harmony, represented by her marriage to Mr. Darcy. Thus Alistair Duckworth finds it generally agreed that *Pride and Prejudice* "achieves an ideal relation between the individual and society."[3] Dorothy Van Ghent sees the book as illuminating "the difficult and delicate reconciliation of the sensitively developed individual with the terms of his social existence."[4] Marvin Mudrick, then, would account for Elizabeth's wrongheadedness as a failure to acknowledge the social context, and Samuel Kliger, in variant terms, places the dichotomy as that between nature and art.[5] All would locate the embodiment of that final harmony among the stately and tasteful grounds of Pemberley.

Although most of these individual discussions, and others like them, are both valuable and persuasive, they share an assumption which in Jane Austen criticism has sunk to a truism, that her perspective is one of social and rational good. The general objection to this prevailing view is its orderliness when applied to *Pride and Prejudice*. It is hard to see where in that vision of social and emotional harmony with which so many would have the novel end there could be room for the doubts, the blindness, and the mistakes which Elizabeth still exhibits and which are a continuing part of every major character Jane Austen creates. I do not mean at all to imply that beyond the lightness there is some dark side to the novelist, some sort of regulated hatred or repression. I do mean to ask where there would be room for the life which, as Jane Austen was perfectly aware, goes on beyond all our formulations of it. Stuart Tave, in his recent study of Jane Austen's words, reminds us that "She knows, and she shows us in her novels, messy lives, and most people are leading them, even when the surface of life seems proper."[6] We have been too eager to assume that Jane Austen's was a conclusive vision, a sort of apotheosis of the optimism of premodern fiction. Yet to understand *Pride and Prejudice* in terms of some ideal blend of the individual and the social is to speak of finalities about a writer who herself chooses to speak of the possible, the continuous, the incomplete. Jane Austen's "social" concerns are with human relations, not society. Her own reference to "the little bit (two inches wide) of Ivory" can only be called unfortunate in the light of the critical weight given that suspiciously humble remark. Jane Austen offers neither Chinese miniatures nor Dutch interiors nor any surface so finished that meanings are conclusive as well. It is hardly possible to speak of her themes as social (or as rational) without involving, by implication alone, that too familiar image of her as outside her own time and belonging to an earlier and more ordered age.

A more particular objection to the prevailing view of *Pride and Prejudice* is that it does not actually work. If Mr. Darcy is to represent society and Elizabeth a rebellious individualism, how are we to account for the fact that the first major breach of society's rules is made by Mr. Darcy, when he insults Elizabeth within her hearing at the Meryton ball? It seems evasive to conclude, with Mary Lascelles, that at the moment Mr. Darcy is out of character and the remark is a technical flaw.[7] Unquestionably, Mr. Darcy is an outstanding member of society, a landowner with both power and responsibility. His position and an accompanying sense of duties and obligations do justify a proper kind of pride. Yet this should not obscure the fact that Darcy's nature, far from being social, is reserved, independent, isolated, private, and vain. And it is Elizabeth who points to this discrepancy when she remarks to Colonel Fitzwilliam on Mr. Darcy's rude conduct at the Meryton dance: "Shall we ask him why a man of sense and education, and who has lived in the world, is ill qualified to recommend himself to strangers?" (p. 175).

Elizabeth's failures in judgment, with Charlotte Lucas but primarily with Mr. Wickham and Mr. Darcy, are not adequately explained as a headstrong insistence on private judgment in the face of social values. It is inaccurate to claim that Elizabeth should have been swayed by the fact that Mr. Wickham "is a dispossessed man in an acquisitive society."[8] He has a military commission and the militia, like the navy, is an honorable and a gentlemanly occupation and a respected part of Jane Austen's social scheme. It would be just as distorting for Elizabeth to find Mr. Darcy socially acceptable because he owns Pemberley, whatever Charlotte Lucas may think. It is Charlotte, after all, who advises Elizabeth "not to be a simpleton and allow her fancy for Wickham to make her appear unpleasant in the eyes of a man of ten times his consequence" (p. 90). Charlotte chooses "not to be a simpleton" and will spend the rest of her life with Mr. Collins. To judge others in economic or social terms is the very sort of thinking Jane Austen would expose. Mr. Wickham is socially unacceptable, but for moral reasons rather than economic ones, not because he has no possessions but because he has no principles. And this is no more a question of manners than it is of position or money. Mr. Wickham can be as polite and conversant as Mr. Darcy can be reserved and rude. Elizabeth misjudges them, but not through an individualism which fails to appreciate class or social values. If that were true, *Pride and Prejudice* would be a lesser novel. Her failure is one of intelligence.

Jane Austen's major study of the links between intelligence and freedom is cast as a love story, and of a sort which she delighted in characterizing as "rather too light, and bright and sparkling."[9] Most of the action of *Pride and Prejudice* can be accounted for as a tale of love which violates the traditions of romance. The rather unromantic beginnings of Henry Tilney's affection for Catherine Morland in *Northanger Abbey* have been expanded into a prominent motif about the lovers in *Pride and Prejudice*. For much of the story Mr. Darcy cares for Elizabeth in spite of himself, and she does not care for him at all. When Elizabeth does come to have some feelings for Mr. Darcy she understands her change as above all "a motive within her of good will which could not be overlooked. It was gratitude.— Gratitude, not merely for having once loved her, but for loving her still well enough, to forgive all the petulance and acrimony of her manner in rejecting him, and all the unjust accusations accompanying her rejection" (p. 265). Such a motive for love may not be ideal, but it has the author's full approval. It is also shared by Jane Bennet, the character in *Pride and Prejudice* who comes closest to providing standards of true sensibility. Jane explains to Elizabeth her own goodwill to Mr. Darcy on the grounds that "I always had a value for him. Were it for nothing but his love of you, I must always have esteemed him" (p. 374).

The emotional appeal of someone being in love with you is a favorite theme of Jane Austen's. It draws Marianne Dashwood to Colonel Brandon as well as Henry Tilney to Catherine and even, in a more comical way, Harriet Smith to the long-suffering farmer, Martin. It may help to explain Jane Fairfax's love for Frank Churchill, and it is strong enough to begin to lure Fanny Price toward Henry Crawford and finally to win Edmund Bertram for her. Its most powerful expression is in *Persuasion*, in the intense and muted feelings of Anne Elliot and Captain Wentworth. There love reawakens love in an almost Shelleyan cycle of reciprocity. The particular significance of this theme in *Pride and Prejudice* is that Elizabeth's gratitude and increasing affection for Mr. Darcy are inseparable from her intellectual growth. Right thinking and wrong in the novel can be measured in terms of Elizabeth's changing feelings toward Mr. Darcy and Mr. Wickham. Against Mr. Wickham's empty charm Elizabeth must balance the dangers and obligations of a demanding love. Gratitude, then, is the response through which Jane

Austen seeks to define freedom and intelligence within the binding circumstances of emotions, partial understandings, and incomplete truths.[10]

The progress in *Pride and Prejudice* need not then be described as a dichotomy resolved. Elizabeth's mistakes are not based on a rejection of society even though it is quite true that they are related to her sense of personal freedom. What we are to understand by that freedom is not the right to do and say whatever she wants in defiance of social conventions. Rather, it is a freedom from becoming involved. This is why Elizabeth's education is most appropriately a love story. Lionel Trilling has said that *Pride and Prejudice* shows us that morality can be a matter of style. It also shows us that intelligence can be a matter of the heart. Elizabeth believes that understanding, intelligence, perception, depend on being independent of their objects, and she wants most powerfully to be an intelligent observer of her world. That urge explains much of her continuing appeal and is the single most important force in her story. But for Elizabeth it means to be apart from events. Her lesson is the particularly harsh one her father has imparted that people are blind and silly and only distance can save her from being blind and silly as well. The view from that distance is necessarily ironic. For Elizabeth, then, being disengaged seems the only salvation from stupidity. Elizabeth's heart is not engaged by Mr. Wickham, her understanding is. Her opinion of him is based on her belief in her own discernment and her separation through intelligence from an essentially ugly world. Elizabeth's weapon against what she sees as stupidity and ugliness is her laughter, her impertinence, and her uncommitted heart. Andrew Wright has argued with some power that "against clarity, in *Pride and Prejudice*, involvement is set," yet his position is so unfortunately similar to Mr. Bennet's that it needs modification.[11] Mr. Bennet's clarity offers the protection against the pains of misjudgment and disillusion which only a disinterested cynicism can provide. Involvement, it is true, can give no such protection. Yet the point of Elizabeth's story is surely that she is always involved, and her recognition of that brings the kind of openness which alone can make clarity possible.

In defending Elizabeth's affection for Mr. Darcy in language almost identical with that she had used in defending Henry Tilney's for Catherine, Jane Austen makes the alternative quite explicit:

> If gratitude and esteem are good foundations of affection, Elizabeth's change of sentiment will be neither improbable nor faulty. But if otherwise, if the regard springing from such sources is unreasonable or unnatural, in comparison of what is so often

described as arising on a first interview with its object, and even before two words have been exchanged, nothing can be said in her defence, except that she had given somewhat of a trial to the latter method, in her partiality for Wickham, and that its ill-success might perhaps authorize her to seek the other less interesting mode of attachment. [p. 279]

The love at first sight that Elizabeth had tried with Mr. Wickham was curiously cold, much as the flirtation between Frank Churchill and Emma was cold. This is clear when Wickham becomes "the admirer of someone else. Elizabeth was watchful enough to see it all, but she could see it and write of it without material pain. Her heart had been but slightly touched, and her vanity was satisfied with believing that *she* would have been his choice, had fortune permitted it" (p. 149). Elizabeth's attraction for Mr. Wickham cannot be accounted for as a misplaced affection. The discrepancy between how Jane Austen presents Mr. Wickham and how Elizabeth sees him leads us to an understanding of the falseness of Elizabeth's vision.

There is a similarity of temperament (if not character) between Elizabeth and Mr. Wickham, much as there is between Emma and Frank Churchill. What all these characters share is a great deal of charm, a charm which comes from a liveliness of mind which is as interested in what is entertaining as in what is good and right. Mr. Wickham's villainy must limit the comparison, for Frank Churchill is merely irresponsible. His principles are sound. Yet Mr. Wickham's black character should not be understood as a cruder and more extreme version of Frank's, in spite of Jane Austen's general commitment to mixed character as superior both in terms of realism and technique. The first comment of Mr. Wickham that Jane Austen provides us with, when that interesting stranger has appeared on the street in Meryton with Mr. Denny, and the Bennet sisters are being informed that he has accepted a commission in the corps, is that "this was exactly as it should be; for the young man wanted only regimentals to make him completely charming" (p. 72). One wonders immediately what sort of charm would best present itself in the bright red uniform of the militia. And Jane Austen goes on to say that "his appearance was greatly in his favour; he had all the best part of beauty, a fine countenance, a good figure, and very pleasing address. The introduction was followed up on his side by a happy readiness of conversation—a readiness at the same time perfectly correct and unassuming" (p. 72). This description, unlike Jane Austen's usual introductions in the novel, tells us nothing of Mr. Wickham's qualities or nature, but only of his looks and manners. His looks and manners are all that

Elizabeth has noticed. And it will turn out that they are all Mr. Wickham has to recommend him.

Mr. Wickham, as the villain that Frank Churchill could never be, is a familiar type. That Jane Austen meant the reader to be aware of Wickham's conventionality is brought out in many scenes. A late example is Jane Bennet's horrified reaction to the discovery that Mr. Wickham is "a gamester!" There is no need to explain this response, as Henrietta Ten Harmsel does, as a bit of moralizing creeping into an otherwise sophisticated structure.[12] The point Jane Austen wants us to see is not that for Jane Bennet (or her author) gambling is as bad as or worse than eloping with Lydia but that the fact of Wickham's gambling fixes his character and so leaves no doubt as to how the elopement is to be understood. After this Jane says no more of her hope that Wickham's intentions are honorable. She knows the kind of man he is and so must we. Wickham is something of a cliché, both in his false face as a charming young man and in his true face as the fortune hunter. This lack of originality in Wickham's portrait can have nothing to do with any lack of authorial skill. We need only think of Mr. Collins, who belongs in the tradition of pious Christian hypocrites but whose character has so many peculiarities that he stands unabashedly on his own. We must then ask why Jane Austen, with her explicit contempt for the stock villain, would place such a character in *Pride and Prejudice*.

Mr. Wickham is most appropriately dressed in the scarlet uniform of the militia because he is a type rather than an individual. He is one of a class of men whom Lydia and Kitty, like their mother before them, are wild about. Mr. Wickham, to be sure, is a particularly good-looking version, and this distinction is not unnoticed by another of the Bennet sisters during that first dinner: "When Mr. Wickham walked into the room, Elizabeth felt that she had neither been seeing him before, nor thinking of him since, with the smallest degree of unreasonable admiration. The officers of the ———shire were in general a very creditable, gentlemanlike set, and the best of them were of the present party; but Mr. Wickham was as far beyond them all in person, countenance, air, and walk, as *they* were superior to the broadfaced stuffy uncle Philips" (p. 76). We cannot but notice how commonplace and how coldly evaluative this response is from the girl whose judgment is supposed to be special. Near the end of *Northanger Abbey* Jane Austen, in her role as conventional novelist, reassures us that Eleanor Tilney's new husband, though he has not actually appeared in the story, is "to a precision the most charming young man in the world." She goes on to observe that "any further definition of his merits must be unnecessary; the most charming young man in the world is instantly before the imagination of us all" (*Works,*

5:251). This idea, with its overtones of literary convention, is used more critically in *Pride and Prejudice*. How closely Mr. Wickham qualifies as Elizabeth's ideal of the most charming young man in the world may be guessed from her conviction, after taking leave for Hunsford, that "he must always be her model of the amiable and pleasing" (p. 152). The airy fictional tone of their relations is established from the beginning in the account of their first conversation: "Mr. Wickham was the happy man towards whom, almost every female eye was turned, and Elizabeth was the happy woman by whom he finally seated himself; and the agreeable manner in which he immediately fell into conversation, though it was only on its being a wet night, and on the probability of a rainy season, made her feel that the commonest, dullest, most threadbare topic might be rendered interesting by the skill of the speaker" (p. 76). The feeling and behavior of the "happy" pair are obvious clichés, an effect delightfully reinforced by Jane Austen's reference to Mr. Wickham and the other officers as Mr. Collins's "rivals for the notice of the fair" (p. 76). We notice Elizabeth's self-deception, her lack of any serious feelings for this handsome young officer about whom, as she is to realize later, she knows nothing at all.

Mr. Wickham's kind of charm, one of public and superficial ease, makes him seem unreal. He is a flat character moving amongst actual people. This is achieved in part through the fact that Jane Austen has Wickham himself make up his own public role. The aesthetic and the moral responsibility for creating a typical rake must lie with Wickham rather than with his author. It is an excellent method, for Wickham, though villainous, is neither subtle nor ingenious, and the mask he creates for Meryton's benefit and his own is tellingly unoriginal. One need only notice the silliness of the sad tale he recites to Elizabeth, in its style as well as its sentiments:

> it is not for *me* to be driven away by Mr. Darcy. If *he* wishes to avoid seeing *me*, he must go ... His father, Miss Bennet, the late Mr. Darcy, was one of the best men that ever breathed, and the truest friend I ever had; and I can never be in company with this Mr. Darcy without being grieved to the soul by a thousand tender recollections. His behavior to myself has been scandalous; but I verily believe I could forgive him anything and everything, rather than his disappointing the hopes and disgracing the memory of his father. [p. 78]

He is as trite as a scoundrel as he has been when a pretended hero. His unsettled life, indifference to Lydia, his debts and applications for money through her, are all boringly predictable. We are taught by the very language of the book, by the style of Wickham's life and conversations and the style of his author's descriptions, that he is not to be taken seriously, that he is just a made-up character, only a fiction after all. But for the characters in *Pride and Prejudice* Wickham is not some conventional villain in a novel. And, of course, his villainy has real consequences. Certainly in life there are people who are stereotypes, those limited to the superficiality and the insidious simplicity of living in roles. Like Willoughby in *Sense and Sensibility*, Wickham lacks the moral imagination to develop and so defines the limits rather than the possibilities of character.

Wickham is a danger to the very innocent (Georgiana Darcy) and the very wild (Lydia Bennet). Even Mr. Darcy acknowledges at the Netherfield ball that "Mr. Wickham is blessed with such happy manners as may ensure his *making* friends—whether he may be equally capable of *retaining* them, is less certain" (p. 92). Mr. Wickham does succeed in being universally liked in Meryton. Yet we must ask why Elizabeth, who is neither innocent nor wild nor like everyone else in Meryton, is also completely taken in. The first we know of Elizabeth is Mr. Bennet's laconic observation that "they are all silly and ignorant like other girls; but Lizzy has something more of quickness than her sisters" (p. 5). Yet to be praised by Mr. Bennet is a questionable recommendation, since by quickness he must surely mean the discernment of other people's follies. This is the way Mr. Bennet has chosen to exercise his own faculties and the way he has taught his daughter, by example and encouragement, to apply hers. Elizabeth is quick to see and laugh at the failings of many—of the Bingley sisters, of Mr. Collins, of Mr. Bingley, of her own family, and even of Jane. Yet she chooses not to see Mr. Wickham, and this in spite of the fact that she is provided with obvious evidence of his falseness—in his absurdly sentimental choices of expressions, in the discrepancies between his assertions and his behavior, and in the very improbability of his story.

Elizabeth can be charmed by Wickham and can accept his story precisely because he and his story are such clichés. Elizabeth's self-deception does not lie, like Emma's, in being a creator of one's own interesting fictions. Nor does it, like Catherine Morland's, consist of playing a created character, except for that touch at the end of the novel when she and Mr. Darcy discuss whether the moral of their story will come out as it should. If Emma behaves like an author and Catherine like a character, then Elizabeth behaves like a reader. Another way of saying this is simply that Elizabeth neither manipulates people nor acts like a heroine herself. Instead, she understands herself as an observer, an enlightened and discerning witness to all that is ridiculous and entertaining in others. And she frequently places herself in the presumably disinterested position of someone watching yet apart. In the drawing-room at Netherfield "Elizabeth was so much caught by what passed, as to leave her very little attention for her book; and soon laying it wholly aside, she drew near the card-table" (p. 38). The next evening "Elizabeth took up some needlework, and was sufficiently amused in attending to what passed between Darcy and his companion" (p. 47). She takes up much the same positions at Hunsford and even within her own home. In Elizabeth's attitude we see the influence of Mr. Bennet's cynical credo that "for what do we live, but to make sport for our neighbors, and to laugh at them in our turn?" (p. 364).

Elizabeth's observations are far from being as irresponsible and limiting as her father's. She tells Mr. Darcy that "I hope I never ridicule what is wise or good. Follies and nonsense, whims and inconsistencies *do* divert me, I own, and I laugh at them whenever I can" (p. 57). Elizabeth can do more than laugh. She is able to credit Charlotte's sensible domestic arrangements as much as she delights in the absurdities of Mr. Collins. She can sympathize with Jane's suffering and can condemn the impropriety and the evil of her father's misused intelligence. Indeed, the variety of Elizabeth's observations and the degree to which she enjoys them are basic to her charm. Nonetheless, it is this sense of herself as standing apart and watching life which accounts for at least part of her attraction to Mr. Wickham.

Jane Austen has deliberately and obviously made Mr. Wickham a stock character in order to point to Elizabeth's central moral weakness, that she does not take life seriously. Raised by a foolish mother and a cynical father who has abdicated all responsibility, and encouraged to distinguish herself from her sisters, Elizabeth sees the world as some sort of entertaining game. She is not silly in the way that Lydia and Kitty are (though she is surprisingly close to them), but she cannot imagine that anything could be expected of her. Elizabeth is morally disengaged. What she wants is to understand what she sees and she also hopes that what she sees will be exciting, will be worth understanding. And this, of course, is just what she thinks Mr. Wickham can offer. His stereotyped charm confers no individual feelings and invokes no personal obligations. His tale is bizarre, out of the ordinary, and shocking, with the initial flattering appeal of being a privileged confidence. It is presented to Elizabeth and to the reader literally as the recounting of a story. And on Elizabeth's part the hearing is complete with the proper forms of response, with expectations ("what she chiefly wished to hear she could not hope to be told, the history of his acquaintance with Mr. Darcy" [p. 77]) and the appropriate exclamations (such as, "Indeed!" "Good heavens!" "This is quite shocking!" "How strange!" and "How abominable!").

Elizabeth chooses to believe Mr. Wickham's story, and the reason she gives Jane is that "there was truth in his looks" (p. 86). We might accept this as having the familiar meaning that Mr. Wickham has an honest face if it were not that throughout Mr. Wickham's account Jane Austen has Elizabeth think about his good looks. She responds to his declarations of honoring Mr. Darcy's father (declarations made suspect as much by the triteness of their phrasing as by the fact that Mr. Wickham is even now dishonoring the father by exposing Mr. Darcy to Elizabeth) by the remarkable thought that Mr. Wickham was "handsomer than ever as he expressed them" (p. 80). And she silently remarks that Mr. Wickham is a young man "whose very countenance may vouch for [his] being amiable" (pp. 80–81). We cannot simply explain these responses by understanding Elizabeth, as we do Lydia, as a silly and ignorant flirt without any sense. Yet for her the credibility of Mr. Wickham's story is inseparable from his handsome face. Both Mr. Wickham's story and his looks have a glamor which is exceptional and dramatic without being either unpredictable or unique. Both are a recognizable type.

Because Jane Austen depicts both Elizabeth's credence and her feelings in the familiar and suspect language of sentimental fiction we must conclude that Elizabeth no more seriously believes Mr. Wickham's tale than she seriously believes she is in love with him. We need only think of how Jane Austen depicts the classic situation of a girl looking forward to seeing a man at a dance. Elizabeth, hoping to see Mr. Wickham at the Netherfield ball, "had dressed with more than usual care, and prepared in the highest spirits for the conquest of all that remained unsubdued of his heart, trusting that it was not more than might be won in the course of the evening" (p. 89). Her own high spirits are the most dominant note, and when Mr. Wickham does not come, the extent of Elizabeth's real regret may be gauged by Jane Austen's comment that "Elizabeth was not formed for ill-humour; and though every prospect of her own was destroyed for the evening, it could not dwell long on her spirits; and having told all her griefs to Charlotte Lucas, whom she had not seen in a week, she was soon able to make a voluntary transition to the oddities of her cousin" (p. 90). And it is to be doubted whether Elizabeth would have found more pleasure in dancing with Mr. Wickham than she does in laughing at Mr. Collins, or that, indeed, there is finally much difference between the two activities. Elizabeth has allowed herself to be taken in by a style which she can recognize so clearly later as stale affectation because she views the very artificiality of her connection to Mr. Wickham as an assurance of freedom. For Jane Austen it is in that fact that the immorality of their relation lies. In the terms of *Pride and Prejudice* there can be nothing between them to be grateful for. This is not just a question of freedom from emotional involvement. Elizabeth is here violating a necessity which is as much a matter of imagination and perception as it is of feelings. Herself restricting freedom is a refusal to commit her intelligence to growth, to seriousness, to a moral life.

Pride and Prejudice is about what is a pervasive theme for Jane Austen— the charm of what is passing around us, those experiences with other people out of which sound judgment can grow. The particular difficulty preventing proper relationships which Jane Austen examines in *Pride and Prejudice* is the intellectual commitment to a presumed "objectivity," to clarity without involvement. This is the source of Elizabeth's attraction to Mr. Wickham. Her ties to him are as artificial as his character. With Wickham Elizabeth has played at romance. We see a similar objectivity in Charlotte Lucas's clear-eyed economic practicality as she reflects on her forthcoming marriage: "Mr. Collins to be sure was neither sensible nor agreeable; his society was irksome, and his attachment to her must be imaginary. But still he would be her husband.—Without thinking highly either of men or of matrimony, marriage had always been her object; it was the only honourable provision for well-educated young women of small fortune, and however uncertain of giving happiness, must be their pleasantest preservative from want" (pp. 122–23). As to any question of sensibility, Charlotte quietly tells Elizabeth that "I am not romantic you know. I never was" (p. 125). There is also the objectivity of Mr. Bennet's unbiased cynicism which does not except even his own family. His unfailing recognition of Lydia's silliness is unmarred by even a touch of sympathy or of regret that his child should have such a nature. He is just as impartial to Jane, and can be amused that she is "crossed in love." Yet these two, Charlotte and Mr. Bennet, have been the only intelligent people in Elizabeth's environment and have influenced her moral growth. *Pride and Prejudice* is the story of Elizabeth's movement away from these "sensible" and coldly self-deceptive visions, of freeing her intelligence from defensiveness and negation, and of learning to understand, as Isabel Archer would learn so much more painfully seventy years later, that freedom from significant choices is a prison, that objectivity can be blind, and that to set oneself apart is only to be cut off from the means to truth and to happiness.

Elizabeth, following the disappointments of Mr. Bingley's departure from Netherfield and Charlotte's engagement, responds by a moment of blinding cynicism: "There are few people whom I really love, and still fewer of whom I think well. The more I see of the world, the more am I dissatisfied with it; and every day confirms my belief of the inconsistency of all human characters, and of the little dependence that can be placed on the appearance of either merit or sense" (p. 135). Mr. Bennet would approve of such remarks. This closed vision is a violation of Elizabeth's intelligence and an abnegation of her humanity. Nor is it forced upon her by the vicissitudes of life, being a matter of will rather than circumstance. Her hard opinion of Mr. Bingley's departure makes that clear. That quality in him she had described at Netherfield as the merit "to yield readily—easily—to the *persuasion* of a friend" (p. 50) she now determines to see as "that easiness of temper, that want of proper resolution which now made him the slave of his designing friends" (p. 133). Nor will she mitigate her contempt by recalling Charlotte's warning that Jane's feelings for Bingley were not apparent at all. Elizabeth, seeing herself as the impartial observer, unprejudiced by any feelings toward Bingley, is in fact choosing to place his actions in as bad a light as possible. Such objectivity is nothing more than cynicism. The saving difference between Elizabeth and her father is that her motive is not cool pleasure at the follies of others but a helpless sympathy with her sister's pain.

The sense of blasted hopes which passes as a realistic intelligence with Charlotte Lucas and Mr. Bennet is not allowed to influence Elizabeth unchallenged. The cynicism of these two is opposed by a warmer vision, that of Jane Bennet. It is Jane who replies to Elizabeth's despair at human nature and at Charlotte's marriage with the comment, "Do not give way to such feelings as these. They will ruin your happiness" (p. 135). For it is Jane who understands that to view the world coldly is to be neither perceptive nor superior nor safe from wrong. It is to be irresponsible and to abandon the difficulties of trust for the finalities of easy generalization. Jane's prepossession to think well of people does not lead her to be perceptive, and she is obviously wrong about the Bingley sisters. Yet Jane's kind of misunderstanding is acceptable to her author in a way that the disposition to think ill of people is not. And her role as the opponent of negativity is central to understanding Elizabeth's mistakes, her choices, and her intellectual growth.

At the beginning of the novel we are assured of Elizabeth's intelligence and Jane's blindness, in part because Elizabeth can see immediately that Bingley's sisters are not well intentioned. And we are quick to think of Jane as sweet but a fool. Although Elizabeth asserts that Jane is so good as to be quite perfect we know this to be untrue. Jane does lack discernment, does confuse her hopes with truths. We are on Elizabeth's side, the side of clarity as against softheadedness, as she takes Jane to task with an energy and realism we can only support. We remember the fineness of her reply to Jane's excuses for Charlotte's marriage: "You shall not defend her, though it is Charlotte Lucas. You shall not, for the sake of one individual, change the meaning of principle and integrity, nor endeavour to persuade yourself or me, that selfishness is prudence, and insensibility of danger, security for happiness" (pp. 135–36). And we must be delighted by her answer to Jane's attempt to explain away Mr. Wickham's accusations: "And now, my dear Jane, what have you got to say in behalf of the interested people who have probably been concerned in the business?—Do clear *them* too, or we shall be obliged to think ill of somebody" (p. 85). Against her sister's wit Jane's generous doubts seem foolish indeed. It is in this role of countering Jane's candor that Elizabeth most convinces us of her cleverness and perspicacity.

And yet, in the midst of Elizabeth's lively banter and her quick successes in teasing Jane, there emerges the disturbing fact that her superior wit actually has little to do with truth. Elizabeth may always win the arguments, but she is often wrong. Wickham's story is farfetched, even though Jane cannot sensibly explain why. She is quite right that "one does not know what to think," although the remark does sound limp when followed by Elizabeth's firm "I beg your pardon;—one knows exactly what to think" (p. 86). Nor does Jane at all deserve to be accused of subverting principle in explaining Charlotte's marriage, for she attempts to understand Charlotte as much as to excuse her. Elizabeth will not tolerate such an attempt, though a moment before she has found the marriage unaccountable. But it will be Jane who, near the end of the story, pleads with Elizabeth to "do any thing rather than marry without affection" (p. 373). Elizabeth undoubtedly was in the right about the Bingley sisters, but it should be remembered that she had the advantage not only of "more quickness of observation and less pliancy of temper than her sister" but also of a "judgment too unassailed by any attention to herself" (p. 15). Certainly, in the beginning the sisters do treat Jane with more real politeness and kindness than they do Elizabeth.

Jane's candor, then, is not just the naive blindness Elizabeth would have us believe it to be, any more than Elizabeth's lack of candor is true perception. Indeed, Elizabeth is more than eager to discover and laugh at those faults in others which Jane finds so difficult to see. Moreover, Jane's optimism has to do with her faith that there is much in life that is beyond what she knows and that certainty as to the minds and hearts of others is rare indeed. Elizabeth does not allow for her own ignorance and prefers the certainty of deciding the worst. Her just enjoyment of the follies and nonsense of her companions sometimes goes uncomfortably close to the attitude described by Mr. Darcy as when "the wisest and the best of men, nay, the wisest and best of their actions, may be rendered ridiculous by a person whose first object in life is a joke" (p. 57). For the truth is that both sisters must often judge in ignorance, must imagine, must surmise. In such a case Elizabeth's lively doubts are no more justified than Jane's candor and gentle trust.

Although the comic side of Jane's goodwill is so delightfully brought out by Elizabeth, its serious value is central to events. On Mr. Wickham's story, "Miss Bennet was the only creature who could suppose there might be any extenuating circumstances in the case, unknown to the society of Hertfordshire; her mild and steady candour always pleaded for allowances, and urged the possibility of mistakes—but by everybody else Mr. Darcy was condemned as the worst of men" (p. 138). Jane does not see that Mr. Wickham is a liar. But neither does she allow his allegation to subsume her own view of human goodness or her sense of what is probable and likely. In part this is because Jane cannot believe that Mr. Bingley could be so wrong about his friend, Mr. Darcy, and in part because she just cannot conceive of deliberate wrongs. But primarily it is because of Jane's recognition, insisted upon in the face of all Elizabeth's powerful weapons of wit, observation, and laughter, that people and events are more complex and hidden than she can know. Jane Austen has not created Jane as a simple and good-hearted character merely to provide a balance to the complexity and intelligence of her main heroine. When we consider what Jane is doing in the novel and why her author would think her creation necessary, we must recognize that Jane is by nature neither objective nor perceptive and yet Jane Austen has made her the one character in the novel who is just to Mr. Darcy. It is by reason of the very qualities which Elizabeth (and the reader) presume to be weaknesses that Jane turns out to be right. Without any "quickness of observation" and with the "wish not to be hasty in censuring anyone" (p. 14), Jane comes closer to truth than her intelligent sister. Certainly, Jane Austen is not instructing us to think pleasant thoughts rather than to apply our powers toward a better understanding of the world. Yet Jane's candor, based on a sense of her own weaknesses, allows a flexibility that Elizabeth lacks.

The willingness to commit oneself to experience, in its unknown dangers as well as its possibilities, comes naturally to Jane, and perhaps that is why she is not the central character of *Pride and Prejudice*. She has never deliberately chosen involvement over clarity. Jane Austen's major interest is always with those whose connections to reality, in terms of knowledge and goodness, are at once more questionable and more difficult. Jane is an innocent. Yet she teaches us that involvement can lead to a kind of truth which is not accessible to those who understand clarity as a vision gained through the exclusion of being involved. Elizabeth's freedom, insofar as it leads to judgments she likes to presume are untouched by commitment or concern, does not bring understanding. In accounting to Jane for her unfairness to Mr. Darcy, Elizabeth admits that "'I meant to be so uncommonly clever in taking so decided a dislike to him, without any reason. It is such a spur to one's genius, such an opening for wit to have a dislike of that kind. One may be continually abusive without saying anything just; but one cannot be always laughing at a man without now and then stumbling on something witty'" (pp. 225–26). For we are in England, where character is mixed, and that makes it always possible for an observer to find the flaws in others. As Elizabeth acknowledges, such ways of looking are selfish and distorting, and cut oneself off from one's kind. Between candor and cynicism there can be a way of understanding which presupposes neither human evil nor human good yet allows for both by the very suspension of any fixed view.

One of the most powerful facts in *Pride and Prejudice* is that after Elizabeth has her moment of shame and revelation at Hunsford so many of her perceptions continue to be quite wrong. She does see through Wickham, but she can learn to detect his artificiality only because she knows the truth. Her judgment not to reveal him turns out to be almost disastrous to her own family. And she is still virtually always wrong about Mr. Darcy. She interprets his silence at Lambton on learning of Lydia's elopement with complete assurance: "Her power was sinking; every thing crust sink under such proof of family weakness, such an assurance of the deepest disgrace. She could neither wonder nor condemn ..." (p. 278). After Lady Catherine's visit Elizabeth speculates that if his aunt appeals to Mr. Darcy to give her up, "with his notions of dignity, he would probably feel that the arguments, which to Elizabeth had appeared weak and ridiculous, contained much good sense and solid reasoning" (p. 361). Even when all these confusions are resolved by Darcy's second proposal, the two must still spend much of their courtship in the charming yet quite necessary explanations of all those motives and actions so misunderstood. Jane Austen, who did not compose love scenes for their emotional appeal, reminds the reader that in human relations, even of the kind reputed to provide immediate understanding, there is a great deal that intuition and surmise do not reveal.

We must ask what, after all, Elizabeth has learned and what her story is about if after the acknowledgment of prejudice and vanity in the lane at Hunsford her judgment seems hardly more accurate than before. Jane Austen has so arranged the plot that her heroine's moment of revelation and chagrin comes nearly in the middle of the story. After Hunsford there are few scenes of Elizabeth's quickness and wit, and much of the action seems not to depend on her at all. The Gardiners' delayed vacation and wish to visit Pemberley, the combination of Mrs. Forster's invitation, Wickham's mounting debts and Lydia's recklessness which precipitate the elopement, and Mr. Darcy's arrival at the Lambton inn at the moment of Elizabeth's receiving the news, all remind us that Elizabeth can have little control over people or events, while both may be crucial to her. The second half of *Pride and Prejudice* may be less sparkling than the first, but the quieter pleasure it offers is an extended view of Elizabeth's fate entwined with the lives of those around her.

What Elizabeth is doing in these later scenes, with a directness and care which were absent from her earlier casual wit, is seriously trying to understand the particular situations she finds herself in and the people she cares about. Whether she is trying to control her feelings enough at the Lambton inn in order to receive Georgiana Darcy and her brother, or paying a morning visit to the ladies at Pemberley, or accepting what she believes to be Darcy's giving her up after the elopement, or speculating (with the Gardiners and Jane) on Mr. Wickham's intentions, or surmising Mr. Darcy's reaction to his aunt's interference, Elizabeth is constantly engaged in trying to see and respond to other points of view. She is often wrong—and for quite the same reasons that she was wrong in the beginning, that her partialities and ignorance must limit her. The difference is that Elizabeth no longer sees her world as a place of easily discovered folly from which, in self-defense as much as in amusement, she must stand apart if she is to see the truth. She has come to value the connections and partialities which inform truth, to understand that a lively intelligence is personal and engaged, and to use that quick mind to reach for hopes and suggestive meanings rather than killing finalities. The former view had placed Elizabeth, along with her father, among those who understand human nature in crude categories of behavior and motivation. Against this reductive view Jane Austen places a vision of people as palpable yet flexible and elusive beyond our predictions for them. Even Jane's candor is not so conclusively defined as to be unchanged by Miss Bingley's unkindness. Neither Jane nor her creator can teach Elizabeth to be right. They do teach her that she has constructed protective fictions as a substitute for the pitfalls and delights of free thought.

As Elizabeth learns to suspend judgment and examine her experience she also becomes aware of her own affections. She had known by the Hunsford visit that her opinion of Mr. Darcy had been wrong. Yet her most important lesson about him is not that he is good but that he loves her in ways that can overcome the failings in his character. Lydia Bennet's elopement with Mr. Wickham is a curiously obtrusive event in a novel of Jane Austen's. Yet it is through this terrible deed that Elizabeth comes to realize her obligation to Mr. Darcy, an obligation which, as he makes clear, could only have come about because he loves her. All was done for Elizabeth's sake. And it is a romantic moment for these most unromantic lovers when Elizabeth finally expresses her obligation and finds herself being proposed to. Elizabeth's gratitude—gratitude in the sense in which Jane Austen means it—is not for a favor done, not for an act of socially right behavior. It is a gratitude that, despite all the obstacles which realism can provide, despite time, conventions, and misunderstandings, despite her wrongs and his own limitations, Mr. Darcy can see Elizabeth honestly and love her as well. Between them there are no longer any of the conventional dangers of social slips or sudden reversals of opinion, as there always were in Elizabeth's relations with Wickham. That is why Mr. Darcy's proposal would have come without Elizabeth's offered thanks. Their feelings are past being subject to the accidents of circumstance. Fate is an empty convention of romance. Instead, Mr. Darcy offers Elizabeth an understanding of herself, one that is moral and affectionate and sound. It is a vision of clarity because of his involvement, a vision from a generous heart. To recognize that and to appreciate it is a reciprocal feeling which will unite Elizabeth with Mr. Darcy. For gratitude is an act of self love which carries with it an act of love.

Near the end of the novel Mr. Bingley returns to Hertfordshire and rides into the paddock at Longbourn. Mrs. Bennet, seeing him from her window, calls to her daughters to come as well. "Jane resolutely kept her place at the table; but Elizabeth, to satisfy her mother, went to the window— she looked,—she saw Mr. Darcy with him, and sat down again by her sister" (p. 333). With this image of the two sisters, and Elizabeth's gesture of looking changed to shared embarrassment and retreat, Jane Austen captures her heroine's transformation from a detached vision to an engaged one. Elizabeth, as she joins Jane at the table, accepts her new freedom, its boundaries, its uncertainties, and its hope.

NOTES

1. Lionel Trilling, *Sincerity and Authenticity* (Cambridge, Mass., 1972), p. 77.

2. *The Novels of Jane Austen*, ed. R. W. Chapman (Oxford, 1932), 2:380. All further references to the novels are from this edition.

3. Alistair Duckworth, *The Improvement of the Estate* (Baltimore, 1971), p. 118, n.

4. Dorothy Van Ghent, *The English Novel: Form and Function* (1953; reprint ed., New York, 1961), p. 100.

5. Marvin Mudrick, *Jane Austen: Irony as Defense and Discovery* (1952; reprint ed., Berkeley, 1968); Samuel Kliger, "Jane Austen's *Pride and Prejudice* in the Eighteenth-Century Mode," *University of Toronto Quarterly* 16 (July 1947): 357–70.

6. Stuart Tave, *Some Words of Jane Austen* (Chicago, 1973), p. 33.

7. Mary Lascelles, *Jane Austen and Her Art* (Oxford, 1939), p. 160.

8. Mudrick, p. 110.

9. *Jane Austen's Letters*, ed. R. w. Chapman, 2d ed. (1952; reprint ed., London, 1969), no. 77, Thursday, February 4, 1813, p. 299.

10. Stuart Tave offers a helpful definition of gratitude as "the response to the feeling of another, the natural obligation in return for having been thought worthy of being loved" (p. 140).

11. Andrew Wright, *Jane Austen's Novels: A Study in Structure* (London, 1953), pp. 117–18.

12. Henrietta Ten Harmsel, *Jane Austen: A Study in Fictional Conventions* (The Hague, 1964), p. 68.

BERNARD J. PARIS

Pride and Prejudice

If asked to name the most attractive heroine in nineteenth century fiction, and the sanest, a great many readers would probably nominate Elizabeth Bennet. I would do so myself. For a long time I felt that Elizabeth was not a suitable subject for psychological analysis. It is customary to see her primarily as an aesthetic and an illustrative character; and her problems are considerably less severe (and hence less evident) than are those of Fanny and Emma. Her wit, charm, vitality, and intelligence also tend to obscure her defensive strategies. By calling attention to these strategies I shall obscure, I fear, the many positive aspects of her personality. This is not my intention, but it is one of the unavoidable dangers of psychological analysis. It does not do justice to a whole range of human qualities which make people with similar defenses very different from each other and quite variable in their attractiveness and humanity. Let me caution the reader, then, not to mistake Elizabeth's defenses for the whole of her being. My object, moreover, is not to prove that she has psychological problems but to gain a fuller understanding of why she acts and feels as she does. When we understand Elizabeth as a person, a creation inside a creation, we shall have reason once again to marvel at Jane Austen's psychological intuition and to admire her genius in characterization.

Elizabeth suffers, as do all of the Bennet girls, from the unhappy

From *Character and Conflict in Jane Austen's Novels: A Psychological Approach.* © 1978 by Bernard J. Paris.

marriage of her parents, from their personal defects, and from their failure to provide a well-ordered and respectable family life. Mrs. Bennet supplies little in the way of mothering and offers no model of mature womanliness. Elizabeth grows up wanting to be as unlike her mother as possible. She suffers not only from her mother's deficiencies, but also from her lack of affection; Elizabeth is "the least dear" of all her children (I, xviii). Elizabeth defends herself against the pain of having such a mother, and such a family, by detaching herself and being amused by what would otherwise hurt or embarrass her. She holds herself inwardly aloof and refuses to identify with most of her family.

Elizabeth is, in many respects, her father's daughter. She appreciates his abilities, adopts his defenses, and is grateful for his approval. Like him, she is a "'studier of character'" (I, ix) who prides herself on her self-knowledge and her ability to see through others. She "love[s] absurdities" (II, xix): "'Follies and nonsense, whims and inconsistencies *do* divert me, I own, and I laugh at them whenever I can'" (I, xi). She is able to remain detached even in rather difficult situations. When Mr. Collins proposes, she tries "to conceal by incessant employment the feelings which were divided between distress and diversion" (I, xix).

She is considerably less detached, however, than her father. Being younger and less frustrated than he, she is more hopeful, more idealistic, and more concerned about life generally. Being essentially undefeated (as opposed to her father, who has given up), Elizabeth takes herself, her values, and a chosen few of her relationships quite seriously. This makes her vulnerable in ways in which her father is not. She is deeply disturbed by Bingley's abandonment of Jane and by Charlotte's acceptance of Collins. There quickly emerges the dark view of the world against which her detachment has been a defense:

> There are few people whom I really love, and still fewer of whom I think well. The more I see of the world, the more am I dissatisfied with it; and every day confirms my belief of the inconsistency of all human characters, and of the little dependence that can be placed on the appearance of either merit or sense. (II, i)

Her reaction to Charlotte's behavior is especially intense. Apart from her father, Charlotte is the person in her world who is closest to her in temperament and intelligence. Isolated as she is, Elizabeth values the relationship greatly. She imagines Charlotte to be more like herself than she really is. When Charlotte expresses her cynical attitude toward the importance of selectivity in choosing a mate, Elizabeth cannot believe that she is serious: "'You make me laugh, Charlotte; but it is not sound. You know it is not sound, and that you would never act in this way yourself'" (I, vi). When Charlotte does behave in this way, Elizabeth's belief in human nature, already guarded, is badly shaken. Her estimate of her own judgment, moreover, receives a blow—the first of several. She defends herself against future disappointments by lowering her expectations of people still farther and by turning "with fonder regard" to Jane, "of whose rectitude and delicacy she was sure her opinion would never be shaken" (I, xxiii). She dissociates herself from Charlotte and withdraws to a safer distance.

Elizabeth's pain in this situation is the result partly of hurt pride, partly of a sense of loss, and partly of her feeling of identification with Charlotte. She is threatened by Charlotte's fate, which violates her sense of personal dignity and shows a person like herself betraying herself and being trapped by life. Elizabeth needs to criticize her friend severely in order to reaffirm her own values and expectations.

When we compare Elizabeth with her father and her friend, we can see that, while she shares many of their characteristics, she is not basically detached. They have no hopes of mastering life and have resigned themselves to a reduced lot. Elizabeth, however, is expansive. She thinks well of herself, has high expectations, and will not settle for a position which is beneath her sense of her own deserts. Her expansiveness, like her detachment, derives in large measure from her father. He looks down upon almost everyone else, but Elizabeth is clearly his favorite and the object of his admiration. This recognition from the most important person in her world, a man whose abilities even Mr. Darcy must respect, feeds her pride and helps to compensate for her shame at her family and lack of approval from her mother. Her elevated conception of herself is reinforced by her superior abilities and the absence of any real competition in her family or social circles. Like her father, she finds that one of the compensations of living among fools is the pleasure of despising them. When she decides not to reveal what she has learned about Wickham, she observes to Jane that "'sometime hence it will be all found out, and then we may laugh at their stupidity for not knowing it before'" (II, xviii).

Elizabeth's aggressiveness is most clearly visible when her pride is being threatened. She has a fear of being looked down upon and a need to show others that she cannot be laughed at, manipulated, or treated with condescension. In the defense of her pride, she becomes saucy, combative, and, sometimes, brutally frank. Some of this behavior seems like healthy self-assertion, as when she defies Lady Catherine near the end; but much of it is clearly defensive. When she first visits Lady Catherine at Rosings, she seems determined not to be overawed. As they ascend "the steps to the hall, Maria's alarm [is] every moment increasing, and even Sir William [does] not look perfectly calm," but "Elizabeth's courage [does] not fail her" (II, vi). The suggestion is that she is afraid that it would. Once inside, Sir William is "so completely awed, by the grandeur surrounding him, that he [has] but just courage enough to make a very low bow"; and Maria is "frightened almost out of her senses"; but Elizabeth finds "herself quite equal to the scene, and [can] observe the three ladies before her composedly." One senses that Elizabeth has steeled herself to this situation so as to maintain her sense of equality with Lady Catherine and superiority to Sir William Lucas. Her composure is a form of triumph. When she discovers that Lady Catherine is a fool, she becomes completely at her ease and even toys with her adversary by refusing immediately to disclose her age. Lady Catherine is not only a great lady, of course, but also a very manipulative one; and Elizabeth's satisfaction in trifling with her is evident.

We are now in a position to understand Elizabeth's reactions to Darcy. When Bingley urges Darcy to seek an introduction to Elizabeth, Darcy looks at her for a moment and then coldly replies, "'She is tolerable; but not handsome enough to tempt *me*; and I am in no humour at present to give consequence to young ladies who are slighted by other men'" (I, iii). Elizabeth overhears this remark and is deeply offended. Being an expansive person herself, she can forgive Darcy's pride, which, as Charlotte observes, has some justification:

> "One cannot wonder that so very fine a young man, with family, fortune, every thing in his favour, should think highly of himself. If I may so express it, he has a *right* to be proud."
> "That is very true," replied Elizabeth, "and I could easily forgive *his* pride, if he had not mortified *mine*." (I, iii)

Elizabeth is mortified partly because of the nature of her claims and partly because she has been rejected by a man of such importance, a man of her own type whom she cannot easily dismiss. She is accustomed to think highly of *herself*, and one might guess that she had been hoping for some form of recognition from the Netherfield party. Instead Darcy places himself well above her and interprets her not dancing as a sign of her unattractiveness to other men.

For someone like Elizabeth, this is a severe blow; and she works hard from this point on to soften the pain, to restore her pride, and to protect herself against further injury. Her immediate reaction is to make a joke of what has happened: "She told the story ... with great spirit among her friends; for she had a lively, playful disposition, which delighted in anything ridiculous" (I, iii). The implied author's analysis is rather misleading here. Elizabeth's telling the story is not the manifestation of a lively disposition. It is a defensive technique which serves several purposes. It distances her from her hurt feelings, it denies the significance of the event by turning it into an object of laughter, and it gains an immediate revenge on Darcy by making him ridiculous in the eyes of others. Jane Austen at once creates and is taken in by Elizabeth's facade.

In almost every encounter that she has with Darcy between the initial insult and the receipt of his letter Elizabeth is highly defensive; and, as a result, she misperceives him constantly. As he becomes more and more attracted to her, she continues to assume his ill will; and she interprets his various displays of interest as forms of aggression. In order to know more of her, he listens to her conversation with Colonel Forster. Elizabeth is afraid that he is observing her in order to find grounds for ridicule: "'He has a very satirical eye, and if I do not begin by being impertinent myself, I shall soon grow afraid of him'" (I, vi). She is projecting her own attitudes onto Darcy; and she fears that he is regarding her as she regards those to whom she feels superior.

While she is at Netherfield, caring for Jane, Elizabeth cannot help noticing how frequently Darcy's eyes are fixed upon her.

> She hardly knew how to suppose that she could be an object of admiration to so great a man; and yet that he should look at her because he disliked her, was still more strange. She could only imagine however at last, that she drew his notice because there was something about her more wrong and reprehensible, according to his ideas of right, than in any other person present. The supposition did not pain her. She liked him too little to care for his approbation. (I, x)

She will not allow herself to suppose that she might be an object of Darcy's admiration because to do so would make her vulnerable if she should be wrong. Darcy has hurt her once, badly; and she is going to make sure that it does not happen again. It is much safer to suppose that he is antagonistic and to attribute this to his arrogance and snobbish values. She fortifies herself against his presumed criticism by holding onto a fixed dislike. She disapproves of him so much that his attitude toward her is of no importance.

When Miss Bingley plays a lively Scotch air and Darcy asks her to dance, Elizabeth's response is highly defensive.

She smiled, but made no answer. He repeated the question, with some surprise at her silence.

"Oh!" said she, "I heard you before, but I could not immediately determine what to say in reply. You wanted me, I know, to say 'Yes,' that you might have the pleasure of despising my taste; but I always delight in overthrowing those kind of schemes, and cheating a person of their premeditated contempt. I have therefore made up my mind to tell you, that I do not want to dance a reel at all—and now despise me if you dare."

"Indeed I do not dare." (I, x)

Elizabeth makes no answer at first because she cannot analyze immediately the motive behind Darcy's invitation, but she is certain that it is insulting and that he is setting a trap. She is especially sensitive on the subject of dancing since Darcy's refusal to dance with her was the initial offense. When, during a gathering at Longbourn, Sir William Lucas had attempted to pair them off in a dance, Darcy was not unwilling, but Elizabeth drew back immediately. One way to avoid being injured again by Darcy is to reject him as a partner before he has a chance to reject her. This shows him that his initial slight does not matter, since she does not want to dance with him anyway; and it has the additional satisfaction of being a retaliation, of doing to him what he has done to her.

Elizabeth's manner in the Netherfield episode is a mixture of "sweetness and archness" (I, x). She has enough control of her feelings to conceal her sense of being threatened (any revelation of which would be a defeat) and to express her defensiveness in the form of raillery. Knowing her own feelings and having a distorted picture of Darcy, she expects Darcy to be affronted. But the disguise of wit, combined with Darcy's enjoyment of her aggressiveness, produces the opposite effect, and he is charmed.

Elizabeth misperceives Darcy again at Rosings when he stations himself near the piano "so as to command a full view of the fair performer's countenance" (II, viii):

"You mean to frighten me, Mr. Darcy, by coming in all this state to hear me? But I will not be alarmed though your sister *does* play so well. There is a stubbornness about me that never can bear to be frightened at the will of others. My courage always rises with every attempt to intimidate me."

Elizabeth *is* alarmed, of course. She is insecure about her own playing, and she fears Darcy's judgment. Her aggressiveness is designed to assure herself that she is living up to her expansive shoulds ("I should not be afraid of anyone") and to show Darcy that he has no power over her. Her reactions are so entirely inappropriate that Darcy cannot take them seriously: "'I shall not say that you are mistaken,' he replied, 'because you could not really believe me to entertain any design of alarming you.'"

Elizabeth's receptiveness to Wickham's slanders is yet another manifestation of her defensiveness. Darcy is one of the few people in her experience to whom she has not been able to feel easily superior. This is why his insulting behavior rankles her so. Had she been less deeply hurt, she might have been able to observe his interest and attraction. As it is, she interprets his behavior as consistently threatening and defends her pride by finding him haughty and disagreeable. She is comforted by the fact that "'he is not at all liked in Hertfordshire,'" that "'every body is disgusted with his pride'" (I, xvi). She has a need to tear him down, to think the worst. The more deficient he is, the less weight she must give to his judgment of her. She is at once outraged and gratified by Wickham's account of his behavior: "'This is quite shocking!—He deserves to be publicly disgraced'" (I, xvi). She can express on Wickham's behalf all of the anger which she has been feeling toward Darcy on her own account. Wickham's tale justifies her judgment and shows Darcy to be even worse than she had thought. She is now clearly superior to the man whose rejection has pained her so much.

Her receptiveness has something to do also with her feelings toward Wickham. Had her critical faculties been awake, she would have noted the impropriety of his disclosures; and she might have been less credulous. But she is blinded, as she herself comes to see, by the gratification of her pride which his attentions afford. Wickham is an attractive man, a general favorite, and therefore a prize. Unlike Darcy, he singles Elizabeth out immediately for special attention and makes her his confidant. He is not a suitable match, and Elizabeth is no more in love with him than Emma is in love with Frank Churchill; but, like Emma, she wishes to make a conquest. She dresses for the Netherfield ball with "more than usual care, and prepare[s] in the highest spirits for the conquest of all that remained unsubdued of his heart" (I, xviii). She receives Mrs. Gardiner's cautions rationally, however, because she does not really want to make a disadvantageous marriage; and she is content when Wickham shifts his attentions to Miss King: "Her heart had been but slightly touched, and her vanity was satisfied with believing that *she* would have been his only choice, had fortune permitted it" (II, iii). Wickham gives Elizabeth the recognition, the affirmation of special worth, for which she hungers and which Darcy had denied. Her strong prepossession against the one and in favor of the other, from the very beginning of their acquaintance, suggests her vulnerability and the strength of her needs.

Elizabeth's anger toward Darcy is fed by her discovery of his role in separating Jane and Bingley, and it is released by his insulting behavior during his proposal. Darcy once again injures her pride. He admires her personally, but he is deeply troubled by her family connections; and he speaks, rather compulsively, "of his sense of her inferiority ... of the family obstacles which judgment had always opposed to inclination" (II, xi). Elizabeth is especially vulnerable on this point. She has been herself deeply ashamed of her family, and she has defended herself by detachment and a sense of superiority. What Darcy is saying is that her family's inferiority is also her own, and that because of her connections, she is beneath him. By letting him know that she has "'never desired [his] good opinion,'" she nullifies his objections and restores her pride. It is he, not she, who is undesirable.

When Darcy wishes to know "'why, with so little *endeavour* at civility, [he] is thus rejected,'" Elizabeth defends her behavior by attacking his violation of decorum in expressing his reservations. She proceeds to levy her complaints on behalf of Jane and of Wickham, both of whom, as she sees it, have had their happiness destroyed by Darcy. Darcy is disturbed by her low opinion of him; but, since he feels that it is undeserved, he reacts not by meeting her charges, but by defending his "'honest confession of ... scruples,'" which he feels less comfortable about, and which he believes to be the basis of her rejection:

> "Disguise of every sort is my abhorrence. Nor am I ashamed of the feelings I related. They were natural and just. Could you expect me to rejoice in the inferiority of your connections? To congratulate myself on the hope of relations. whose condition in life is so decidedly beneath my own?"

This, of course, repeats the offense, and Elizabeth feels "herself growing more angry every moment." She retaliates in a devastating way by recounting the history of her dislike and affirming her "'fullest belief in [his] arrogance, [his] conceit, and [his] selfish disdain of the feelings of others.'" Darcy replies with dignity, but he leaves hastily in a state of evident humiliation.

Painful as it is, the proposal scene is, on the whole, a great triumph for Elizabeth. Her pride is gratified in a variety of ways. She retaliates for all past and present injuries and has, at the same time, the immense satisfaction of having received an offer of marriage from the great Mr. Darcy. In the contest of personalities, it is decidedly she who is the winner. Darcy can say nothing for which she has not an overwhelming reply. He insults her by speaking of her family's inferiority; but she mortifies him by denouncing his character, attacking his manners and morals, and declaring that he is "'the last man in the world whom [she] could ever be prevailed on to marry.'" Once he leaves, she is free to appreciate the significance of his proposal:

> That she should receive an offer of marriage from Mr. Darcy! that he should have been in love with her for so many months! so much in love as to wish to marry her in spite of all the objections which had made him prevent his friend's marrying her sister, and which must appear at least with equal force in his own case, was almost incredible! it was gratifying to have inspired unconsciously so strong an affection.

Given Elizabeth's craving for recognition, and her earlier feelings of rejection, this is a triumph indeed, one which she cannot help dwelling upon with great satisfaction. She can hardly wait till they arrive at the privacy of Longbourn in order to tell the story that "would so exceedingly astonish Jane, and must at the same time, so highly gratify whatever of her own vanity she had not yet been able to reason away" (II, xv).

In order to restore his pride, which has been deeply hurt, Darcy writes a letter in his own defense. Its contents are so threatening that Elizabeth reacts initially with anger and denial. Then her resistance collapses, and she is flooded with self-hate and depression. The significance of the letter from a psychological point of view is that it penetrates her defenses and makes it more difficult for her thereafter to maintain her feelings of superiority and detachment. The self-knowledge which she gains does not, of course, rid her of her faults, as the implied author would have us believe; but it does contribute to the changes in her defense system which prepare her for marriage to Darcy.

Elizabeth's self-hate arises largely from the discovery of her errors, which are particularly humiliating to someone who prides herself, as she does, upon her superior penetration. She is also disturbed by her recognition of the justice of Darcy's objections to her family: "'The situation of your mother's family, though objectionable, was nothing in comparison of that total want of propriety so frequently, so almost uniformly betrayed by herself, by your three younger sisters, and occasionally even by your father'" (II, xii). When she first reads this passage, she is "too angry to have any wish of doing him justice", but when she returns to it later, "her sense of shame [is] severe." When she realizes "how materially the credit of both [herself and Jane] must be hurt by such impropriety of conduct, she [feels] depressed beyond anything she had ever known" (II, xiii).

Elizabeth is so depressed because her detachment from her family has been broken down, and she is being forced to feel the painfulness of her situation. What has happened to Jane may well happen to her; and, in any event, she seems fated to share in the discredit which her family brings upon itself. She begins to dwell, as never before, upon the seriousness of her plight and upon the deficiencies of her father. She has "never been blind" to her father's failings, "but respecting his abilities, and grateful for his affectionate treatment of herself, she [has] endeavored to forget what she could not overlook, and to banish from her thoughts [his continual] breach of conjugal obligation and decorum." Elizabeth has repressed her criticism partly because she has tried to detach herself generally from the family's problems, and partly because her father's support has been so important to tier. She could not afford to be in conflict with him or to have his status, and therefore the value of his praise, diminished in her own eyes. Her critical attitudes emerge now because she feels personally threatened by his irresponsibility. Her criticism of him constitutes, however, an additional blow to her pride.

Elizabeth's depression has another important source which we have not yet examined. It is the response of an expansive person who wishes to control his own fate to feelings of helplessness. She has always felt that her value was independent of her connections and has insisted upon being treated in accordance with her own high self-estimate. She sees now, however, that her image in the eyes of others is not something which she can completely determine and that she will always be saddled with her family's shame. She feels trapped in a situation which she is powerless to change. The "unhappy defects of her family" are "hopeless of remedy. Her father, contented with laughing at them, would never exert himself to restrain the wild giddiness of his youngest daughters; and her mother, with manners so far from right herself, was entirely insensible of the evil" (II, xiv). In the face of this, there is little that she and Jane can do.

Elizabeth is deeply depressed for only a short time. Her defenses are shaken, but they are by no means shattered. She has at her command, moreover, various pride-restoring devices. She is humbled by her discoveries about herself, but proud of her self-knowledge. The thought of Darcy's offer is a great consolation, and she amuses herself the next morning by wondering what Lady Catherine's reactions would have been had she accepted. She tells Jane that her behavior toward Darcy has been "'very weak and vain and nonsensical'" (II, xvii); but a few moments later she is her arrogant self once more, as she looks forward to laughing at everyone's stupidity when the truth about Wickham is known. She can no longer be detached about her family. She tries to be "diverted" by the Brighton affair, "but all sense of pleasure [is] lost in shame" (II, xviii). She handles her discomfort by trying to do something about it, despite her feeling that nothing will ever change. She points out to her father "'the very great disadvantages to us all, which must arise from the public notice of Lydia's unguarded and imprudent manner,'" and urges him to exercise his authority. But Mr. Bennet refuses; and Elizabeth, though she is "disappointed and sorry," suffers no return of her own earlier despair. She consoles herself with a sense of her own rectitude and derives some satisfaction, no doubt, from being more perceptive than her father.

By the time she leaves on her trip with the Gardiners, Elizabeth is outwardly as buoyant as ever. But inwardly, she has been somewhat subdued. As a result of her errors and of her stronger identification with her family, she no longer thinks quite so highly of herself or of her claims upon the world. Her need for recognition and preeminence is unabated, however. Indeed, it is intensified by frustration, by the diminution of her self-esteem and of the value of her father's admiration. Her pride is suffering. This makes her extremely receptive to Pemberley and to the renewed attentions of Darcy.

Darcy's letter clears away many of Elizabeth's objections to his character. It does not arouse, however, a desire for his attentions or regret for her decision. Within an hour of her first sight of Pemberley, however, Elizabeth does experience "something like regret" (III, i). When Jane asks her later how long she has loved Darcy, Elizabeth replies, "'I believe I must date it from my first seeing his beautiful grounds at Pemberley'" (III, xvii). Jane dismisses this as a joke (with the seeming concurrence of the implied author), and most critics have done likewise. But things said in jest often reveal the deepest truths; and our understanding of Elizabeth's character gives us good reason to take her answer seriously.

The magnificence of Pemberley not only wins Elizabeth's admiration, it also feeds her pride: "She had never seen a place for which nature had done more, or where natural beauty had been so little counteracted by an awkward taste.... and at that moment she felt, that to be mistress of Pemberley might be something!" (III, i). It may or may not be the case that the grounds of Pemberley are intended as a reflection of Darcy the man—he has only been in possession, after all, for five years; but it is most certainly true that their beauty and the grandeur of the house bring home to Elizabeth the magnitude of Darcy's proposal and the elevation which it might have bestowed upon her. She has never seen a more beautiful place, and the admiration of the Gardiners feeds her sense of triumph. Her reactions to the furnishings bring out more clearly the competitive element in her response. She not only admires Darcy's taste, but she also compares Pemberley with Rosings and triumphs thereby over Lady Catherine. She is caught up for a moment or two in a fantasy of possession:

"And of this place," thought she, "I might have been mistress! With these rooms I might now have been familiarly acquainted! Instead of viewing them as a stranger, I might have rejoiced in them as my own, and welcomed to them as visitors my uncle and aunt."

The thought that she would not have been allowed to invite the Gardiners is "a lucky recollection—it save[s] her from something like regret." Her imagined joy in the rooms is not so much pleasure in their beauty as glory in their possession. The fantasy of welcoming her uncle and aunt is also one of personal grandeur. Being mistress of Pemberley would be like having a dream come true. Her desires for power, recognition, and ascendancy would be gratified beyond all reasonable expectation.

If, before, Elizabeth was disposed to think ill of Darcy because he had hurt her pride, she is now disposed to think well of him because he has fed it. The more admirable he is, the more gratifying is his proposal and the greater is its tribute to herself. She defends herself against regret by remembering Darcy's haughtiness, but she is extraordinarily receptive to Mrs. Reynolds' praise of him and is as ready now to credit an account in his favor as she had been before to believe Wickham's slanders. When Mrs. Reynolds speaks of Darcy's good temper, "her keenest attention" is awakened and she longs "to hear more." When she praises his affability to the poor, Elizabeth "listen[s], wonder[s], doubt[s], and [is] impatient for more." "'He is the best landlord, and the best master,'" declares Mrs. Reynolds, "'that ever lived.'"

As Elizabeth contemplates his portrait, her changed feelings toward Darcy begin to crystallize:

> The commendation bestowed on him by Mrs. Reynolds was of no trifling nature. What praise is more valuable than the praise of an intelligent servant? As a brother, a landlord, a master, she considered how many people's happiness were in his guardianship!—How much of pleasure or pain it was in his power to bestow!—How much of good or evil must be done by him! ... as she stood before the canvas, on which he was represented, and fixed his eyes upon herself, she thought of his regard with a deeper sentiment of gratitude than it had ever raised before; she remembered its warmth, and softened its impropriety of expression. (III, i)

Elizabeth dwells here not only on Darcy's goodness, his sense of responsibility, but also upon his power, upon the number of people who are dependent upon him. Her deeper sentiment of gratitude derives from her more vivid perception of his greatness as well as from her new appreciation of his character. Her gratitude springs to a large extent from gratified pride. It is appreciation for having been loved by so great a man, for having been done such an honor.

Since Darcy's exaltation is now her own, Elizabeth has a vested interest in believing the best of him and in suppressing awareness of his faults. Mrs. Reynolds' testimony is valid as far as Darcy's relation to his dependents is concerned, but this does not change the fact that he is stiff and haughty with members of his own social class who are strangers or whom he believes to be beneath him in wealth or status. As Colonel Fitzwilliam observed, he is a man who likes to have his own way and who is ill qualified to recommend himself to strangers "'because he will not give himself the trouble'" (II, viii). According to Darcy's own account, he was "'spoilt'" by his parents, who "'allowed, encouraged, almost taught [him] to be selfish and overbearing, to care for none beyond [his] own family circle, to think meanly of the rest of the world'" (III, xvi). This seems to be an accurate self-characterization. Elizabeth was highly conscious of Darcy's "'arrogance, ... conceit, and ... selfish disdain of the feelings of others'" (II, xi) when his pride was in conflict with her own. As she transfers her pride to him, she becomes increasingly blind to his faults, until she announces to her father, after the second proposal, that "'he has no improper pride. He is perfectly amiable'" (III, xvii). She sees him in this way partly because he has been so courteous to her and to the Gardiners and partly because she cannot see as improper a pride which is identical with her own.

It is evident that as she stands before Darcy's portrait, Elizabeth is already disposed to want him in marriage. Within a few minutes of his appearance, she is actively hoping that he still loves her. The marriage of Elizabeth and Darcy is supposed to illustrate the balancing of social and personal values, but Elizabeth's change of feeling is produced almost entirely by Darcy's wealth and grandeur. It is facilitated by the clearing away of objections to his character; but it has little to do with such positive values as temperamental compatibility, mutuality of interests and attitudes, strong personal liking, or respect based upon intimate knowledge. Both the novelist and her heroine are at pains to justify Elizabeth's desire for Darcy in terms of consciously acceptable values and to obscure its real psychological basis. Jane Austen contrasts Elizabeth's regard for Darcy, which is based on "gratitude and esteem," with her partiality for Wickham, which was based upon love at first sight (III, iv); but the comparison is misleading and will not hold. Elizabeth is attracted to both men because they feed her pride. She wants Darcy because such a marriage would satisfy her expansive needs for glory, for competitive triumph, and for recognition of her worth. She wants him because to be mistress of Pemberley would be something!

Elizabeth is attracted to Darcy, also, of course, because she is immensely flattered by his continuing affection for her. When she first encounters him at Pemberley, she reacts in a typically defensive way: "She was overpowered by shame and vexation. Her coming there was the most unfortunate, the most ill judged thing in the world! How strange it must appear to him! In what a disgraceful light might it not strike so vain a man! It might seem as if she had purposely thrown herself in his way again!" (III, ii). Elizabeth feels threatened once again by Darcy's pride. She is afraid of seeming to want him (which she does) while he no longer wants her. His gentleness and civility quiet her fears; and his attentions to the Gardiners, in whose refinement she glories, "gratif[y] her exceedingly; the compliment must be all for herself." She guesses immediately that he has changed because of her, but she is afraid to believe this lest her hopes rise too high and expose her to a humiliating disappointment. His invitation to meet his sister and his continued courtesy to the Gardiners are unmistakable signs of his interest, however; and Elizabeth becomes fairly confident of her "power" to bring on "the renewal of his addresses." Her desire to do so, which is growing steadily stronger, is motivated in large part by gratitude. "Such a change in a man of so much pride, excited not only astonishment but gratitude—for to love, ardent love, it must be attributed" (III, ii).

There is no indication that Elizabeth's feelings for Darcy ever approach a state of "ardent love." She regards him on his later visit to Longbourn "with an interest, if not quite so tender, at least as reasonable and just, as what Jane felt for Bingley" (III, xi). Darcy, however, is "a man violently in love" (III, xvi); and Elizabeth, during her visit to Pemberley, is deeply moved by the tribute of his affection. She is fully alive now, as she had not been at Hunsford, to family obstacles and to the injustice of her accusations. Darcy's greatness and pride no longer make her feel inferior but rather fill her with a sense of triumph, for they have yielded to love for her—that is, to her value and attractiveness as a person. From Jane Austen's point of view, Elizabeth's gratitude is an admirable feminine emotion; but it comes, as I have said before, from the gratification of expansive claims, from gratified pride. Darcy endears himself to Elizabeth by saving her from the lowered self-esteem into which she had fallen and confirming her idealized image. This is a potent attraction. Now that she respects him, Darcy's love means that she is, after all, a superior being, an appropriate mate for "one of the most illustrious personages" in England (III, xv), a woman whose personal worth is so great as to compensate for the undesirability of her connections.

Elizabeth's hopes are dealt a severe blow by the arrival of Jane's letters announcing Lydia's elopement with Wickham: "Her power was sinking; everything must sink under such a proof of family weakness, such an assurance of the deepest disgrace" (III, iv). Darcy is not deterred, as we learn later; but this turn of events has an important impact upon Elizabeth's feelings, both toward herself and toward Darcy. It damages her pride further, making her need Darcy the more. It gives Darcy an opportunity to behave gallantly, thus enhancing her esteem for him. And it decreases her social prestige still farther, making Darcy's continued interest all the more evidence of his ardent love and her surpassing value.

The disgrace of her sister is a serious threat to Elizabeth's self-esteem. She reproaches herself severely for not having warned everyone of Wickham's character, she feels humiliated at the thought of the neighbors' triumph, and she is convinced that the family's taint must extend to herself and destroy her chances of marrying Darcy. Her self-effacing trends, which were most evident before in her admiration for Jane, emerge now rather powerfully. They result in self-abasement, irrational feelings of guilt, and the transfer of her pride to Darcy:

> She was humbled, she was grieved; she repented, though she hardly knew of what. She became jealous of his esteem, when she could no longer hope to be benefited by it.... What a triumph for him, as she often thought, could he know that the proposals which she had proudly spurned only four months ago, would now have been gladly and gratefully received! ... It was a union that must have been to the advantage of both; by her ease and liveliness, his mind might have been softened, his manner improved, and from his judgment, information, and knowledge of the world, she must have received benefit of greater importance. (III, viii)

Her repentance is a self-effacing response to misfortune; she must be somehow to blame. After having overestimated herself and undervalued Darcy, she swings now to the opposite pole. Her ease and liveliness can give something of value to him; but it is trivial compared with the benefits which his judgment and knowledge can bestow upon her. The crushing of her pride brings out her feelings of dependency. She gives up her struggle to assert her equality, recognizes how grateful she would be if Darcy would only ask her

again, and experiences her pride in a self-effacing way by exalting him. She
has a similar response when she hears of his role in promoting Lydia's
marriage: "For herself she was humbled; but she was proud of him" (III, x).

The pattern of Elizabeth's development is familiar, of course, from our
study of *Emma*. There are important differences, however. Elizabeth's
humility and self-abasement reflect a relatively minor phase in her
psychological evolution. She is suffering more from other people's faults than
from her own; and, like Fanny Price, she is vindicated rather than chastened
by the unfolding of the action. The events which threaten her pride have the
final effect of reinforcing it. The elopement of her sister leads to a far greater
triumph than she would have had before by leading Darcy to demonstrate
her supreme importance to him. Once Elizabeth's pride is restored—indeed,
inflated—by Darcy's second proposal, she is her expansive self again. After
she marries, she revenges herself upon her mother by keeping her away; and
she seems no less disposed than Darcy to maintain a clannish exclusivity. She
is surrounded, as we have seen, by those who are respectful, deferential, or
warmly appreciative of her merit. As we close the book, she is once again
showing Darcy by her "lively and sportive manner" that she does not fear
him and that she is, at least, his equal. The thematic pattern of *Pride and
Prejudice* is one in which the protagonists are both flawed by pride and are
prejudiced as a result—Elizabeth toward Darcy and Darcy toward people of
lower status who are outside of his immediate circle. Each has his pride
chastened by the other and is awakened to realities about himself and others
to which he has hitherto been blind. Elizabeth comes to question her
superior perception, to recognize Darcy's merits, and to accept the
implications of her social identity. Darcy, likewise, is "'properly humbled'":

> "I have been a selfish being all my life, in practice, though not in
> principle.... I was given good principles, but left to follow them in
> pride and conceit ... Such I was, from eight to eight and twenty;
> and such I might still have been but for you, dearest, loveliest
> Elizabeth! What do I not owe to you! You taught me a lesson,
> hard indeed at first, but most advantageous.... You showed me
> how insufficient were all my pretensions to please a woman
> worthy of being pleased." (III, xvi)

His humiliation produces the self-insight which he displays in this passage,
the remarkable change in manners which Elizabeth observes at Pemberley,
and a transcendence of his former prejudices in his determination to ally
himself with Elizabeth despite the increased undesirability of her family.

When we understand Elizabeth and Darcy as people, the implied author's interpretation is rather difficult to accept. They both achieve some genuine insight into themselves, but the experiences which they undergo are hardly enough to produce major changes in their personalities. If Darcy's description of himself is correct, being chastened by Elizabeth could not have purged him of all that "pride and conceit," though it is understandable that he should think so. Though he is less fully developed as a character, Darcy is, like Elizabeth, a creation inside a creation. His development is psychologically comprehensible, but it does not illustrate what it is supposed to. What happens between Darcy and Elizabeth is that they first hurt and then restore each other's pride. We have examined this pattern in Elizabeth. Darcy's development is not exactly parallel, but it is in many respects similar.

Darcy is an arrogant man who feels contempt for most of his fellows, as his opening remarks reveal. He enjoys manipulating compliant people like Bingley, but he despises them in his heart. He must wonder, like Mrs. Reynolds, when he will ever marry. Who is good enough for him? It would not feed his pride to connect himself with a sycophant like Miss Bingley. He needs a woman whom he can respect and whose appreciation of him will mean something. He is attracted to Elizabeth by her intelligence and her aggressiveness. Elizabeth's analysis is, as far as it goes, quite accurate. He admired her for her "impertinence": "'The fact is, that you were sick of civility, of deference, of officious attention. You were disgusted with women who were always speaking and looking, and thinking for *your* approbation alone. I roused and interested you, because I was so unlike *them*'" (III, xviii). Elizabeth has pride; she is a challenge, another strong personality, a mental equal. It does not occur to Darcy, however, that he must win her. He assumes, in his conceit, that she would be overjoyed by an offer from *him*. His mental energy is taken up, rather, by his inner conflict, by the struggles which he describes to her in the course of his proposal. He *must* tell her about his reservations in order to assuage his feelings of humiliation. Describing his sense of degradation has the effect of restoring, in some measure at least, the pride which he is offending.

He reacts to Elizabeth's denunciations in several ways. His letter clears him of the charges concerning Jane and Wickham. What hurts him the most is her attack on his ungentlemanlike behavior and his "selfish disdain for the feelings of others" (II, xi). He is vulnerable to these criticisms for two reasons: (1) he cannot discredit their source, since he has allowed himself to feel respect for Elizabeth, and (2) he has prided himself on behaving in an exemplary manner, on being a true gentleman. He was given high standards by his parents, and he has identified himself with them. Until Elizabeth tells him otherwise, he has always felt himself to be living up to his shoulds. The collapse of this illusion damages his pride, and he is flooded with self-hate. The recollection of his behavior, he tells Elizabeth later,

> "is now, and has been many months, inexpressibly painful to me. Your reproof, so well applied, I shall never forget: 'had you behaved in a more gentleman-like manner.' Those were your words. You know not, you can scarcely conceive, how they have tortured me;—though it was some time, I confess, before I was reasonable enough to allow their justice." (III, xvi)

We may summarize Darcy's development in the following way. His parents provided him with both high standards and unqualified approval. As a result, he identifies himself with his idealized image in a narcissistic manner and feels very proud of himself. His pride is shaky, however, since it is not solidly founded on performance; and he develops a need to reinforce it by scorning others. This behavior is in conflict with his standards; but his defensive needs, combined with a continuous supply of praise and deference, keep him from being aware of the disparity between his principles and his practice. He places his pride at risk by allowing himself to admire Elizabeth so much that he would make a social sacrifice in order to gain her. This makes her opinion quite important to him. He assumes that she will both want and admire him, as everyone else always has. His narcissism and his perfectionism receive severe blows from Elizabeth's assault. He experiences intense self-hate, and as a defense he blames his parents and replaces them with Elizabeth as his primary moral guide.

As a result of Elizabeth's rejection, Darcy develops, for the first time in his life, a profound and agonizing dependency. What Elizabeth has told him, in effect, is that he is not his idealized, but rather his despised self: "'You thought me then devoid of every proper feeling, I am sure you did'" (III, xvi). Elizabeth becomes the central figure in his psychic life. His overwhelming need is to repair his pride, and this can be done only through her. He must change his image in her eyes; he must win her approbation: His behavior at Pemberley and in the Lydia–Wickham affair is a direct reply to her charges. Only if she accepts him in marriage can he be completely vindicated and his self-esteem repaired. With Elizabeth's acceptance, Darcy's pride is restored, though he is less narcissistic than he was before. The major change in him is that he tries harder to live up to his principles and that he is dependent upon Elizabeth's approval for his sense of worth.

The marriage of Elizabeth and Darcy is offered as a model of "connubial felicity" (III, ix). As marriages in Jane Austen go, it is relatively attractive; but it is not as well founded as the implied author believes it to be. Elizabeth and Darcy are bound together by the complex interdependency of their pride systems. The marriage itself fulfills some important needs; it provides recognition and status for Elizabeth, vindication and approval for Darcy. But each remains wary of the other's susceptibilities and dependent on the other for the confirmation of his idealized image. Darcy's fear and dependency are greater than Elizabeth's, making him more overtly acquiescent; but Elizabeth is careful not to push him too far. His need to win her approval is matched by her need to think well of him, to share in his grandeur, and to repress her reservations. They are happy at the end because they have a vested interest in exalting each other. This makes for a rewarding, though, I should think, a somewhat tense relationship. They will get along well as long as each continues to feed the other's pride.

SUSAN FRAIMAN

The Humiliation of Elizabeth Bennet

I belong to a generation of American feminist critics taught to read by Sandra Gilbert and Susan Gubar. *The Madwoman in the Attic* (1979) both focused our regard on women writers of the nineteenth century and formed in us invaluable habits of attention. It alerted us to eccentric characters, figures off to the side, to the lunatic fringe. We learned to see certain transients—required by the plot to move on before things can work out—as feminist doubles for the author as well as heroine. Bertha Mason in *Jane Eyre* and Lade Catherine de Bourgh in *Pride and Prejudice*, unexemplary as they are expendable, register nonetheless the screams and tantrums of Charlotte Brontë's and Jane Austen's own rage. These marginal women voice anger and defiance that split open ostensibly decorous texts.

I want, in keeping with this tradition, to stress the accents of defiance in *Pride and Prejudice*, but I locate these less at the edges than at the very center of the book; my argument concerns the much-admired Elizabeth Bennet and the two major men in her life, Mr. Bennet and Mr. Darcy. I read *Pride and Prejudice* as the ceding of Mr. Bennet's paternity to Mr. Darcy, with a consequent loss of clout for Elizabeth. Austen's novel documents the collapse of an initially enabling father into a father figure who, in keeping with his excessive social authority, tends to be rather disabling. As Elizabeth passes from Bennet to Darcy, her authorial powers wane: she goes from

From *Refiguring the Father: New Feminist Readings of Patriarchy*, edited by Patricia Yaeger and Beth Kowaleski-Wallace. ©1989 by the Board of Trustees, Southern Illinois University.

shaping judgments to being shaped by them. I want to look at Elizabeth's gradual devaluation, her humiliation, in terms of this double father.[1] Austen, I believe, stands back from her decline, ironizing both the onset of marriage and the father–daughter relation. She shows us a form of violence against women that is not hidden away in the attic, displaced onto some secondary figure, but downstairs in the drawing room involving the heroine herself.

Elizabeth's first father is a reclusive man and seemingly ineffectual; beside the rigid figure of *Northanger Abbey*'s General Tilney, Mr. Bennet may well appear flimsy. But the general (his love of new gadgets notwithstanding) is an old-fashioned father whose authoritarian style was all but outmoded by the end of the eighteenth century.[2] Mr. Bennet is not really a bad father— just a modern one, in the manner of Locke's influential text on education. Smooth-browed advocate of instruction over discipline and reason over force, he typifies the Lockean father. As Jay Fliegelman points out, however, Locke's concern "is not with circumscribing paternal authority, but with rendering it more effective by making it noncoercive."[3] Mr. Bennet, apparently benign to the point of irresponsibility, may seem to wield nothing sharper than his sarcasm. But what he actually wields is the covert power of the Lockean patriarch, all the more effective for its subtlety.

This aloof, unseen power of Mr. Bennet's suggests to me, for several reasons, the peculiar power of an author. His disposition is emphatically literary. Taking refuge from the world in his library, Mr. Bennet prefers the inner to the outer life, books to people. He asks two things only: the free use of his understanding and his room—precisely those things Virginia Woolf associates with the privilege of the male writer, the privation of the female. Most important, among women whose solace is news, he keeps the upper hand by withholding information. Mr. Bennet is a creator of suspense. In the opening scene, for example, he refuses to visit the new bachelor in town, deliberately frustrating Mrs. Bennet's expectation and desire. Actually, "he had always intended to visit him, though to the last always assuring his wife that he should not go; and till the evening after the visit was paid, she had no knowledge of it."[4] Mr. Bennet relishes the power to contain her pleasure and finally, with his denouement, to relieve and enrapture her.

But the suspense is not over. Elizabeth's father is, even then, as stingy with physical description as some fathers are with pocket money. He controls his family by being not tight-fisted but tight-lipped, and in this he resembles Austen herself. George Lewes first noted the remarkable paucity of concrete details in Austen, her reluctance to tell us what people, their clothes, their houses or gardens look like.[5] If female readers flocked to Richardson for Pamela's meticulous descriptions of what she packed in her trunk, they must surely have been frustrated by Austen's reticence here.[6] So Mr. Bennet only follows Austen when, secretive about Bingley's person and estate, he keeps the ladies in the dark. Their curiosity is finally gratified by another, less plain-styled father, Sir William Lucas, whose report they receive "second-hand" from Lady Lucas. Much as women talk in this novel, the flow of important words (of "intelligence") is regulated largely by men. In this verbal economy, women get the trickle-down of news.

When Mr. Collins proposes to Elizabeth, Mr. Bennet again contrives to keep his audience hanging. Pretending to support his wife, he hides until the last moment his real intention of contradicting her. After a stern prologue he continues: "An unhappy alternative is before you, Elizabeth. From this day you must be a stranger to one of your parents.—Your mother will never see you again if you do not marry Mr. Collins, and I will never see you again if you *do*" (112). Not only this particular manipulation but indeed the entire scene goes to show the efficacy of paternal words. Throughout his proposal, to Elizabeth's distress and our amusement, Mr. Collins completely ignores her many impassioned refusals. He discounts what she says as "merely words of course" (108); even his dim, self-mired mind perceives that a lady's word carries no definitive weight. Mr. Collins accuses Elizabeth of wishing to increase his love "by suspense, according to the usual practice of elegant females" (108). Yet creating suspense is exactly what Elizabeth, rhetorically unreliable, cannot do. She has no choice but "to apply to her father, whose negative might be uttered in such a manner as must be decisive" (109). Mr. Bennet's power resides, as I say, in his authorial prerogative: his right to have the last word.

Though Mr. Bennet uses this right to disparage and disappoint his wife, regarding his daughter he uses it rather to praise, protect, apparently to enable her. Like many heroines in women's fiction (think of Emma Woodhouse or Maggie Tulliver) Elizabeth has a special relationship to her father. She is immediately distinguished as a family member and as a character by his preference for her and hers for him. The entail notwithstanding, she is in many respects his heir. To her he bequeaths his ironic distance from the world, the habit of studying and appraising those around him, the role of social critic. In this role, father and daughter together scan Mr. Collins's letter, dismissing man and letter with a few, skeptical words. Mr. Bennet enables Elizabeth by sharing with her his authorial mandate, which is Austen's own: to frame a moral discourse and judge characters accordingly. Through her father, Elizabeth gains provisional access to certain authorial powers.

But Mr. Bennet also shares with her, illogically enough, his disdain for women; he respects Elizabeth only because she is unlike other girls. This puts his exceptional daughter in an awkward position—bonding with her father means breaking with her mother, even reneging on femaleness altogether. Elizabeth is less a daughter than a surrogate son. Like a son, by giving up the mother and giving in to the father, she reaps the spoils of maleness. We can understand her, alternatively, in terms of Freud's scheme for girls. Freud contends that girls first turn to the father because they want a penis like his. They envy, as Karen Horney explained, the social power this organ signifies under patriarchy.[7] To complete their oedipal task, however, girls must shift from wanting a penis for themselves to wanting a man who has one; ceasing to identify with the powerful father, they must accept instead their own "castration."[8] In these terms the cocky Elizabeth we first encounter is charmingly arrested in the early phase of male-identification. We can see her, then, in one of two ways: as an honorary boy who has completed his oedipal task, or as a backward, wayward girl who refuses to complete hers. The point is, first, that whatever discursive acuity Elizabeth has derives from an alliance and identification with her father. As the Mr. Collins scene demonstrates, the force of her words is highly contingent. Elizabeth's authority is vicarious, second-hand; like a woman writing under a male pseudonym, her credibility depends on the father's signature. In addition, however enabling, Mr. Bennet is essentially ambivalent toward Elizabeth. "They have none of them much to recommend them," he says of his daughters in chapter 1. "They are all silly and ignorant like other girls; but Lizzy has something more of quickness than her sisters" (5). Insisting that all of his daughters are silly and ignorant, that none of them have much to recommend them, Mr. Bennet blithely classes Elizabeth with "other girls," even as he appears to distinguish her from them. So we find, already in the opening scene, a tension between Elizabeth's "masculine" alacrity and the slow-witted "femininity" threatening to claim her. Mr. Bennet's double vision of her suggests right away the basic ambiguity of Austen's father–daughter relationship, coded not only diachronically in the Mr. Bennet–Mr. Darcy sequence, but also synchronically in Mr. Bennet's duplicity regarding Elizabeth.

For in Austen the male-bonding between father and daughter is set up to collapse. Eventually the economic reality asserts itself, the axiom of the famous first line held up to a mirror and read backward: a single woman not in possession of a good fortune must be in want of a husband. Sooner or later what Adrienne Rich calls "compulsory heterosexuality" (conspiracy of economic need and the ideology of romance) forces Elizabeth out of the library, into the ballroom, and finally up to the altar.[9] The father's business in this ritual is to give the daughter away. If Mr. Bennet is enabling up to a point, the marriage ceremony requires him to objectify his daughter and hand her over. He not only withdraws his protection and empowerment, but also gives away (reveals) her true "castrated" gender, her incapacity for action in a phallocentric society. This ceremony—posing father as giver, daughter as gift—underlies and ultimately belies the father–daughter relationship in *Pride and Prejudice*.

So Elizabeth's gradual falling out with her father, which means forfeiting her authorial status, is built into the institution of marriage. Austen makes it quite clear that Mr. Bennet neglects Lydia, failing to protect her from ruinous male designs. Yet, is not the father's letting go of the daughter precisely what the wedding ritual requires?[10] Mr. Bennet's profligacy with Lydia is simply a starker form of his cheerful readiness to give away any and all of his daughters. "I will send a few lines by you," he tells his wife, "to assure [Bingley] of my hearty consent to his marrying which ever he chuses of the girls" (4). Exposing a pattern intrinsic to the nuptial plot, Mr. Bennet's abandonment of Lydia provides a crude paradigm for Elizabeth's milder estrangement from her father and for the literal distance between father and heroine in *Northanger Abbey* and *Mansfield Park*.[11] Bennet, by retiring as Elizabeth's champion, is not ineffectual as a father, but correct.

In his discussion of marriage and the incest taboo, Lévi-Strauss proposes that the exchange of women among kin groups serves, like the exchange of money or words, to negotiate relationships among men. Women are, in effect, a kind of currency whose circulation binds and organizes male society.[12] It seems to me that *Pride and Prejudice* offers a similar anthropology. Here, too, marriage betrays the tie between father and daughter in favor of ties among men. I have the idea that Elizabeth's economic imperative is not the only motive for her marriage, that the fathers have an agenda of their own, involving considerations of class.

Mr. Bennet's class interest in a Bennet–Darcy match is fairly obvious and similar to Elizabeth's own. He may laugh at Mrs. Bennet's schemes, but the fact remains that a liaison to aristocracy will benefit him significantly. And in spite of his philosophic detachment, Mr. Bennet is not without a streak of pragmatism—after all, he has always intended to visit Mr. Bingley. Nor is he unimpressed by wealth and rank. He is frankly delighted that Darcy has used his money and influence to straighten out the Lydia–Wickham affair. "So much the better," he exults. "It will save me a world of trouble and economy" (377). Sounding even, for a moment, strangely like Mr. Collins, he consents to Elizabeth's marriage with little of his habitual irony. "I have given him my consent," he tells her. "He is the kind of man, indeed, to whom I should never dare refuse any thing, which he condescended to ask" (376).

Though Mr. Darcy's class interests may seem to rule against a connection to the Bennets, they too are subtly at work here. In her remarks on eighteenth-century marriage, Mary Poovey notes that Cinderella matches frequently allayed not only middle-class status anxiety, but also the financial anxiety increasingly rife among the well-born.[13] Cinderella's family may be obscure, but her share in merchant profits is attractive to a prince who is poor. Austen does not fully represent, until *Persuasion*'s Sir Walter Elliot, the material as well as moral impoverishment of the landed class in her day. Yet as early as *Sense and Sensibility* (1811) she gives us Willoughby who, unsure of his aristocratic heritage, leaves Marianne for a certain Miss Grey with fifty thousand pounds. Of course in *Pride and Prejudice* cash flows the other way: Darcy has it and Elizabeth needs it. But a decline in aristocratic welfare is nevertheless suggested by the sickly Miss De Bourgh. It may well be the enfeeblement of his own class that encourages Darcy to look below him for a wife with greater stamina. As a figure for the ambitious bourgeoisie, Elizabeth pumps richer, more robust blood into the collapsing veins of the nobility, even as she boosts the social standing of her relatives in trade. Most important, however—to the patriarchs of both classes—she eases tensions between them. By neutralizing class antagonism, she promotes the political stability on which industrial prosperity depends.[14]

I turn, now, to the handing of Elizabeth from Bennet to Darcy, which is prefigured by a scene on the Lucas dance floor. Here Sir William Lucas stands in for Mr. Bennet, jockeying for power with Mr. Darcy, who has the upper hand. Sir William begins to despair, when suddenly he is "struck with the notion of doing a very gallant thing" (26). Laying claim to Elizabeth, he offers her up to Darcy as "a very desirable partner." Sir William understands that gift-giving can be an "idiom of competition." As anthropologist Gayle Rubin explains, there is power in creating indebtedness.[15] We imagine the three of them: Elizabeth between the two men, her hand held aloft by Lucas, Lucas eager to deposit it, Darcy "not unwilling to receive it" (26). The fathers' device here is synecdoche. Elizabeth is reduced to a *hand*, extended in friendship or hostility, the means of fraternal intercourse. Suddenly, however, Elizabeth pulls back. With startling resolution she withdraws herself from the debt nexus. Indeed, throughout much of the novel Elizabeth resists the conventional grammar of exchange. She would not only extract herself as object but, contesting the fathers' right to control the action, insert herself as subject. Saboteur, Elizabeth threatens to wreck the marriage syntax. Needless to say, this makes for one of the stormier courtships in nineteenth-century fiction.

It was, as I have noted, Lévi-Strauss who first saw marriage as a triangulated moment, a woman exchanged between two (groups of) men. Gayle Rubin went on to identify this kind of traffic, its organization of a sex-gender system, as the basis for female subordination. But the immediate model for my placing such an exchange at the heart of *Pride and Prejudice* is provided by Eve Sedgwick; her recent book, *Between Men*, examines the way men bond across the bodies of women in a range of English texts.[16] Her mapping of "male homosocial desire" posits, however, an essentially passive female term. It imagines a triangle that is stable and uncontested; even women who begin active and ambitious, once drawn into the space between two men, fall automatically still. What I have tried to suggest above is that Elizabeth does not readily accept a merely pivotal role. The book stretches out because she puts up a fight before acceding (and never entirely) to the fathers' homosocial plot. The site of her resistance, as well as her compromise, is language.

This brings us to Mr. Darcy—a father by virtue of his age, class, and a paternalism extending to friends and dependents alike. A man given to long letters and polysyllables, a man with an excellent library and even hand, Darcy may also be seen as an aspiring authorial figure. If Bennet sets out to create suspense, Darcy hankers to resolve it. Their relation is one of literary rivals, with Elizabeth the prize. The complication is Elizabeth's own formidable way with words. As surrogate son, father's heir, Elizabeth is herself a contender for the authorial position. Instead of rewarding Darcy for his accession, she competes with him for it. In these terms, Elizabeth's and Darcy's matching of wits is more than flirtation—it is a struggle for control of the text. There are two heated and definitive moments in this struggle: Elizabeth's refusal of Darcy's first proposal and the day after, when he delivers his letter.

Chapter 11 of the second volume finds Elizabeth alone at the Collins's house in Kent. Concerned sister and conscientious reader, she is studying Jane's letters. Suddenly Darcy bursts in and blurts out a proposal, more an admission of weakness than a confession of love. The chapter closes by resuming Elizabeth's internal dialogue, "the tumult of her mind" (193) after Darcy's departure. But have we, throughout this chapter, been anywhere but in Elizabeth's mind? By all rights this should be Darcy's scene, his say. In fact, we get relatively few of his actual words. His amatory discourse is quickly taken over by a narrator who represents the scene, renders Darcy's language, from Elizabeth's point of view: "His sense of her inferiority ... [was] dwelt on with a warmth which ... was very unlikely to recommend his suit" (189). The text of Darcy's proposal is completely glossed, and glossed over, by her interpretation of it. Of Elizabeth's refusal, by contrast, Austen gives us every unmediated word, a direct quotation four times as long as that permitted Darcy. This sets the pattern for what follows. Every time Darcy opens his mouth, he is superseded by a speech of greater length and vehemence. She answers his question—Why is he so rudely rejected?—with a tougher question of her own: "I might as well enquire ... why with so evident a design of offending and insulting me, you chose to tell me that you liked me against your will, against your reason, and even against your character? Was not this some excuse for incivility, if I was uncivil?" (190). Conceding nothing, she accuses him at some length of everything: of breaking Jane's heart and unmaking Wickham's fortune, of earning and continually confirming her own dislike. She betters his scorn for her family by scorning him. "I have every reason in the world to think ill of you" (191), she asserts. Her language, her feelings, her judgments overwhelm his and put them to shame. They drive him to platitude, apology, and hasty retreat. This rhetorical round leaves Elizabeth clear victor.

The following day, however, she is obsessed by Darcy: "It was impossible to think of any thing else" (195). She receives his letter. As the man has crowded out all other thoughts, so now his letter crowds out all other words, monopolizing the narrative for the next seven pages. Longer than the entire preceding chapter, it completely dispels Elizabeth's inspired performance of the day before. If Darcy was not "master enough" of himself then, he regains his mastery now. He takes back his story and, in a play for literary hegemony (to be author and critic both), tells us how to read him. The letter is a defense of his judgment, its impartiality and authority. About Jane he insists: "My investigations and decisions are not usually influenced by my hopes or fears.—I did not believe her to be indifferent because I wished it;—I believed it on impartial conviction" (197). As for Wickham, the letter documents Darcy's early suspicions and the events that proved him right. It further demonstrates the power of Darcy's moral discourse over others. Bingley has "a stronger dependence on [Darcy's] judgment than on his own" (199). Georgiana, fearing her brother's disapproval, decides not to elope after all.[17]

Only after Darcy's unabridged epistle do we get Elizabeth's response to it. She reads "with an eagerness which hardly left her power of comprehension, and from impatience of knowing what the next sentence might bring, was incapable of attending to the sense of the one before her eyes" (204). Darcy's letter saps her power to comprehend, disables her attention. It addresses her as reader only to indispose her as reader. At first Elizabeth protests: "This must be false! This cannot be! This must be the grossest falsehood!" (204). She rushes through the letter and puts it away forever. But the text, unrelenting, demands to be taken out, read and reread. Against the broad chest of Darcy's logic, Elizabeth beats the ineffectual fists of her own. Putting down the paper, she "weighed every circumstance with what she meant to be impartiality ... but with little success" (205). Her interruptions, procrastinations, do nothing to stop the inexorable drive of

Darcy's narrative to its foregone conclusion. In what Roland Barthes might call its "processive haste," it sweeps away Elizabeth's objections and has its way with her.[18]

In its second sentence, the letter disclaims "any intention of paining" (196). It apologizes for wounding, yet proceeds all too knowingly to wound. There is indeed a disturbing insistence on its hurtfulness, a certain pleasurable recurrence to the violence of its effect. "Here again I shall give you pain" (200), the writer unhesitatingly announces. But now Darcy's determination to inflict seems matched by Elizabeth's to be afflicted. They coincide in their enthusiasm for her humiliation: "'How despicably have I acted!' she cried.—'I, who have prided myself on my discernment!—I, who have valued myself on my abilities! who have often disdained the generous candour of my sister, and gratified my vanity, in useless or blameable distrust.—How humiliating is this discovery!—Yet, how just a humiliation!'" (208). Vindicating Darcy's judgment and debasing Elizabeth's, disqualifying her interpretation of things in favor of his, the letter leaves her "depressed beyond any thing she had ever known before" (209).

This is the point, the dead center, on which the whole book turns. Darcy's botched proposal marks the nadir of his career, after which, launched by his letter, he rises up from infamy in an arc that approaches apotheosis. In the ensuing chapters he turns deus ex machina, exerting an implausible power to set everything straight—a power Mr. Bennet conspicuously lacks. It is Darcy who arranges for three lucky couples to be, each, the happiest couple in the world. Like the authorial persona of *Northanger Abbey*, Darcy herds us all to "perfect felicity." The nature of his unseen influence is precisely authorial. Darcy's letter proves his textual prowess. At this point he succeeds Mr. Bennet as controlling literary figure and displaces Elizabeth as her father's scion. From now on the pen, as *Persuasion*'s Anne Elliot might say, is in his hands.

Soon after receiving Darcy's letter, Elizabeth meets up with Kitty and Lydia. Officer-crazy as ever, Lydia gushes on about Brighton and her plans to join the regiment there for its summer encampment. This first reference to Brighton unfolds into an unexpectedly earnest seduction plot that might seem more at home in a novel by Richardson or Burney. It is latent, however, in Lydia's very character, throwback to those too sentimental heroines so mercilessly parodied by Austen's juvenilia. That such a plot should surface now, seize center page and, brash as its heroine, hold the spotlight for more than seven chapters, is by no means accidental. The Lydia–Wickham imbroglio creates, for one thing, a situation before which Mr. Bennet will prove inadequate, Mr. Darcy heroic. Elizabeth first doubts her father regarding his decision to let Lydia go to Brighton, and she blames her father bitterly for the subsequent scandal. For Mr. Darcy, by contrast, the calamity is a chance to prove his nobility both of heart and of purse, his desire to rectify and his power to do so. The Lydia plot therefore accomplishes Elizabeth's separation from her father and her reattachment to another. It works a changing of the paternal guard.

By showcasing Darcy, the upstart plot that seems to delay and even briefly to replace Elizabeth's and Darcy's courtship serves actually to advance it. Yet there is another reason that Lydia's story, a classic case of seduction, moves into the foreground at this moment. It fills the curious gap between Elizabeth's first, private softening and her final, public surrender. I would argue that, at this juncture, Elizabeth's narrative is displaced onto that of her sister. Lydia's seduction registers an emotional drama—of coercion, capitulation, and lamentation—missing from but underlying Elizabeth's story proper. Of course Elizabeth is a foil for Lydia, one sister's wisdom held up to the other's folly. Yet there remains a sense in which their positions are scandalously similar. At one point, in response to Lydia's rudeness, Elizabeth admits, "However incapable of such coarseness of *expression* herself, the coarseness of the *sentiment* was little other than her own breast had formerly harbored" (220). And perhaps this is more generally the case: that Elizabeth and Lydia differ more in style than in substance. In other words, far from being an alternative plot, Lydia's is, albeit in cruder terms, a parallel one. Like the interpolated tales in that protonovel *Don Quixote*, Lydia's tale works less to distract from the central narrative than to distill its meaning. It does not defer Elizabeth's progress toward marriage so much as code the seduction and surrender on which her marriage relies.

We leave Elizabeth at the end of volume 2, chapter 13, completely, under Darcy's influence. "She could think only of her letter" (209). As the next chapter explains, "Mr. Darcy's letter, she was in a fair way of soon knowing by heart" (212). The unusual syntax here is succinct indication of the new order—Mr. Darcy and his text come pointedly before Elizabeth, would-be subject. The narrator continues, "When she remembered the style of his address, she was still full of indignation; but when she considered how unjustly she had condemned and upbraided him, her anger was turned against herself" (212). Elizabeth's reversal here, the introversion of her anger, is again revealing. Her initial judgment of Darcy is now recanted as unjust, its accusation redirected against herself.

When we first meet Elizabeth, daughter of a social critic resembling Austen herself, she is proud of her ability to know things deeply and to judge them knowingly. Yet by the end of the novel she claims only to be high-spirited. Sorry to have refused Darcy, she longs to be schooled by his better judgment: "By her ease and liveliness, his mind might have been softened, his manners improved, and from his judgment, information, and knowledge of the world, she must have received benefit of greater importance" (312). It should not surprise us to find, in an Austen novel, that judgment, information, and knowledge rate higher than ease and liveliness. While these are all Austen's professional virtues, the former are fundamental to her moral lexicon.[19] (Thus her impatience with Jane's dumb neutrality.) What may surprise and sadden us, however, is that a heroine who began so competent to judge should end up so critically disabled, so reliant for judgment on somebody else. Not that Elizabeth lapses into sheer Lydiacy. Just that by the closing chapters her eye is less bold, her tongue less sharp, the angularity— distinguishing her from the rest of her more comfortably curvaceous sex— less acute.

According to one critical truism, *Pride and Prejudice* achieves a kind of bilateral disarmament: Elizabeth gives up her prejudice, while Darcy relinquishes his pride.[20] I am arguing, however, that Darcy woos away not Elizabeth's "prejudice," but her judgment entire. While Darcy defends the impartiality of his opinion, Elizabeth confesses the partiality and thus worthlessness of hers. His representation of the world is taken to be objective, raised to the level of universality; hers is taken to be subjective— *prejudiced*—and dismissed. True, Elizabeth was wrong about Wickham. But was she really that wrong about Darcy? He may warm up a bit, and his integrity is rightly affirmed, yet the fact remains that he is hardly less arrogant than Elizabeth at first supposed. Her comment to Fitzwilliam can stand: "I do not know any body who seems more to enjoy the power of doing what he likes than Mr. Darcy" (183).

And is Darcy's own record of accuracy much better? His judgment of Jane is just as mistaken, and as partial, as Elizabeth's of Wickham. Yet his credibility remains intact. Finally admitting to having misinterpreted Jane, Darcy explains that he was corrected not by Elizabeth, but by his own subsequent observations (371). On the basis of his new appraisal he readvises the ever-pliant Bingley. His error, far from disqualifying him to judge, only qualifies him to judge again. Elizabeth's error, on the other hand, is irreparably discrediting. What happens in *Pride and Prejudice* is not that an essentially prejudiced character finally sees the error of her ways. Rather, a character initially presented as reliable, who gains our and Austen's respect precisely for her clear-sightedness, is ultimately represented as prejudiced. The real drama lies not in the heroine's "awakening" to her true identity, but in the text's reidentification of her.

If Elizabeth does not overcome her "prejudice," neither does Darcy abandon his pride. Early in the book Elizabeth declares, "I could easily forgive *his* pride, if he had not mortified *mine*" (20). Yet by the last volume her feelings have changed considerably: "They owed the restoration of Lydia, her character, every thing to him. Oh! how heartily did she grieve over every ungracious sensation she had ever encouraged, every saucy speech she had ever directed towards him. For herself she was humbled; but she was proud of him" (326–27). Elizabeth and Darcy begin skeptical of each other, proud of themselves, and they reach a connubial consensus that is altogether different: at last both are skeptical of her, both proud of him.

But wait. Does not Darcy make a pretty speech to his bride confessing, "By you, I was properly humbled" (369)? Here it is useful to see how the text itself defines "pride," and how this definition relates to Mr. Darcy. The bookish Mary—another figure for Austen, if a self-mocking one—distinguishes "pride" from "vanity": "Pride relates more to our opinion of ourselves, vanity to what we would have others think of us" (20). As for Darcy, Charlotte Lucas suggests that his pride is excusable: "One cannot wonder that so very fine a young man, with family, fortune, every thing in his favor, should think highly of himself. If I may so express it, he has a *right* to be proud" (20). A younger Lucas puts it more bluntly: "If I were as rich as Mr. Darcy ... I should not care how proud I was. I would keep a pack of foxhounds, and drink a bottle of wine every day" (20). The practical Lucases have a point. Darcy's richness gives him if not a "right," then a careless readiness to be proud. A man in his social position need not consider any opinion but his own. Darcy is proud because he does not have to be vain—others' opinions do not affect him. His pride, we might say, comes with the territory. It is less a psychological attribute than a social one, and as such it is only heightened by Darcy's enhanced status—as husband, hero, and authorial figure—in *Pride and Prejudice's* last act.

Of course we continue to admire Elizabeth. She may care for Darcy's regard, but she is not so utterly enslaved by it as Miss Bingley. She may hesitate to laugh at Darcy, but she does show Georgiana that a wife may take (some) liberties. We admire her because she is not Charlotte, because she is not Lydia. I am insisting, however, that Elizabeth is a better friend to Charlotte, a closer sister to Lydia—that her story runs more parallel to theirs—than previous readings have indicated. The three women live in the same town, share the same gossip, attend the same balls—why, as some critics have claimed, should Elizabeth alone be above the social decree?[21] There are, in Elizabeth's marriage, elements both of crass practicality and of coercion. Elizabeth is appalled by Charlotte's pragmatism, and yet, choosing Darcy over Wickham, she is herself beguiled by the entrepreneurial marriage plot.[22] If she is embarrassed by her personal connection to Lydia, she is also implicated by the formal intersection of their plots: in the course of the novel she loses not her virginity but her authority.

Elizabeth marries a decent man and a large estate, but at a certain cost. Though she may stretch the marriage contract, it binds her nonetheless to a paternalistic noble whose extensive power is explicitly ambiguous: "How much of pleasure *or* pain it was in his power to bestow!—How much of good *or evil* must be done by him!" (250–51, emphasis added). If Mr. Bennet embodies the post-Enlightenment, modified patriarch, Mr. Darcy harks back to an earlier type—before fathers were curbed by Lockean principles, before aristocrats began to feel the crunch. Darcy disempowers Elizabeth if only because of the positions they each occupy in the social schema: because he is a Darcy and she is a Bennet, because he is a man and she is his wife. If Mr. Bennet permits Elizabeth to fill the role of "son," she marries another father figure only to revert, in terms of privilege, to "daughter."

In *Pride and Prejudice*, Austen shows us an intelligent girl largely in the grasp of a complex mechanism whose interests are not hers. She does this, I think, less in resignation than in protest; here, as in *Northanger Abbey*, Austen is concerned to ironize girls and novels that hasten to the altar for conclusive happiness.[23] I should stress, however, that my purpose in outlining a trajectory of humiliation has been not to displace but to complexify the reading that takes for granted connubial bliss. We can experience the ending as euphoric (most readers do) and still recognize those aspects of the novel working strenuously against this. I want, as Gilbert and Gubar suggest, to appreciate the doubleness that characterizes the work of nineteenth-century women writers, the tension between conventionality and subversion. This tension is, on the one hand, produced by an author who knows what she is doing, whose art is a deliberate shaping, whose ironic tendencies were manifest at fifteen. To ignore any such intentionality is to slight Austen's mastery. But the ideological slipperiness of *Pride and Prejudice* is, on the other hand, finally a matter of the text's own logic, its own legibility. Beyond any fully conscious intention on Austen's part, a pattern of duplicity is at work in the narrative itself, with a consistency amounting to design.

As I have argued, part of this novel's design is to reveal a system of homosocial relations underlying the institution of heterosexuality. Anticipating Claude Lévi-Strauss, Gayle Rubin, and Eve Sedgwick, it recognizes in marriage a displacement of the father–daughter bond by a bond between fathers. Elizabeth's humiliation has everything to do with transactions between various fathers that take place behind her back, over her head, and apart from, if not against, her will. I want to close by offering some further support for this view.

By the end of the book, Mr. Bennet's paternal role has been assumed by his brother-in-law, Mr. Gardiner. Mr. Gardiner, though "gentleman*like*," is not technically a gentleman. Living by trade "and within view of his own warehouses" (139), he represents, more than Mr. Bennet, the rising middle class. No wonder Elizabeth fears that Darcy will rebuff him, unkind as Darcy has been toward her bourgeois relations. She is quite unprepared for Darcy's civility to Gardiner, and for the apparent power of fishing to overcome class differences. Perhaps their shared fondness for Elizabeth, their lengthy haggle over Lydia, as well as their equal passion for trout, serve to reinforce the social/economic advantages of a Darcy–Gardiner alliance. They become, in any case, suggestively close. The very last paragraph of the novel informs us that: "With the Gardiners, they were always on the most intimate terms. Darcy, as well as Elizabeth, really loved them; and they were both ever sensible of the warmest gratitude towards the persons who, by bringing her into Derbyshire, had been the means of uniting them" (388).

At first this seems a peculiarly insignificant note on which to end. On second glance it appears to confirm the notion I have had: that just as the Gardiners have been the means of uniting Darcy and Elizabeth, so Elizabeth has been the means of uniting Mr. Darcy and Mr. Gardiner. *Pride and Prejudice* attains a satisfying unity not only between a man and a woman, but also between two men. Austen's novel accomplishes an intercourse not merely personal, but social—as much a marriage of two classes as a marriage of true minds.

NOTES

1. My title and my argument area turn on Mark Schorer's "The Humiliation of Emma Woodhouse" (1959), in *Jane Austen: A Collection of Critical Essays*, ed. Ian Watt (Englewood Cliffs, N.J.: Prentice-Hall, 1963), 98–111. Here he remarks: "The diminution of Emma in the social scene, her reduction to her proper place ... is very beautiful" (102).

2. See Lawrence Stone, *The Family, Sex and Marriage in England: 1500–1800* (New York: Harper and Row, 1977), 239–58.

3. Jay Fliegelman, *Prodigals and Pilgrims: The American Revolution Against Patriarchal Authority* (Cambridge: Cambridge University Press, 1982), 13. See Beth Kowaleski-Wallace's discussion of the Lockean father in "Milton's Daughters: The Education of Eighteenth-Century Women Writers," *Feminist Studies* 12, no. 2 (1986): 275–95.

4. Jane Austen, *Pride and Prejudice* (1813), ed. R. W. Chapman, 3rd edition (Oxford: Oxford University Press, 1932), 6. Future references are to this edition.

5. Lewes's observation is cited by Judith O'Neill in her introduction to *Critics on Jane Austen: Readings in Literary Criticism*, ed. Judith O'Neill (London: George Allen, 1970), 8.

6. See Ian Watt, *The Rise of the Novel* (Berkeley: University of California Press, 1957), 153.

7. Karen Horney, "The Flight from Womanhood: The Masculinity Complex in Women as Viewed by Men and by Women" (1926), in *Psychoanalysis and Women*, ed. Jean Baker Miller (New York: Penguin Books, 1973), 19.

8. For a useful recapitulation of Freud on fathers and daughters, see Nancy Chodorow, *The Reproduction of Mothering: Psychoanalysis and the Sociology of Gender* (Berkeley: University of California Press, 1978), 94, 114–16.

9. Adrienne Rich, "Compulsory Heterosexuality and Lesbian Existence" (1980), in

Powers of Desire: The Politics of Sexuality, eds. Ann Snitow, Christine Stansell, and Sharon Thompson (New York: Monthly Review, 1983), 177–205.

10. See, for example, Lynda E. Boose, "The Father and the Bride in Shakespeare," *PMLA* 97, no. 3 (1982): 325–47. According to Boose, King Lear's faux pas is his unwillingness to release Cordelia—he "casts her away not to let her go but to prevent her from going" (333)—thereby obstructing the ritual process of her marriage to France.

11. In these terms, Emma's conclusion may have certain advantages for its heroine. It is true that Emma defers to Knightley's worldview much as Elizabeth does to Darcy's. But remaining under her father's roof may preserve some of the authority she has had, in his household and the community, as Mr. Woodhouse's daughter.

12. Claude Lévi-Strauss, *The Elementary Structures of Kinship* (1949) (Boston: Beacon, 1969), 61.

13. Mary Poovey, *The Proper Lady and the Woman Writer: Ideology as Style in the Works of Mary Wollstonecraft, Mary Shelley, and Jane Austen* (Chicago: University of Chicago Press, 1984), 11.

14. See Terry Eagleton, *The Rape of Clarissa: Writing, Sexuality and Class Struggle in Samuel Richardson* (Minneapolis: University of Minnesota Press, 1982), 15.

15. Gayle Rubin, "The Traffic in Women: Notes on the 'Political Economy' of Sex," in *Toward an Anthropology of Women*, ed. Rayna R. Reiter (New York: Monthly Review, 1975), 172.

16. Eve Kosofsky Sedgwick, *Between Men: English Literature and Male Homosocial Desire* (New York: Columbia University Press, 1985).

17. Georgiana's position as "daughter" in relation to Darcy contributes to our sense of him as "paternal," as does his fatherly advice to Bingley.

18. Roland Barthes, *The Pleasure of the Text*, trans. Richard Miller (New York: Hill and Wang, 1975), 12.

19. See Austen's famous defense of the novel as a "work in which the greatest powers of the mind are displayed ... the most thorough knowledge of human nature ... the liveliest effusions of wit and humour" (*Northanger Abbey*, 1818, ed. R. W. Chapman, 3rd edition [Oxford: Oxford University Press, 1933], 38).

20. John Halperin's recent biography, *The Life of Jane Austen* (Baltimore: Johns Hopkins University Press, 1984) is notably complacent toward this formulation: "It is unnecessary to rehearse again the process by which Darcy's pride is humbled and Elizabeth's prejudice exposed—'your defect is a propensity to hate every body,' she tells him early in the novel; 'And yours ... is wilfully to misunderstand them,' he replies" (70).

21. I have in mind D. W. Harding and Marvin Mudrick, old guard of Austen criticism's "subversive school" (as opposed to Alistair Duckworth, Marilyn Butler, et al., who see Austen as a social conservative): D. W. Harding, "Regulated Hatred: An Aspect of the Work of Jane Austen," *Scrutiny* 8 (1940): 346–62; Marvin Mudrick, *Jane Austen: Irony as Defense and Discovery* (Princeton: Princeton University Press, 1952); Alistair M. Duckworth, *The Improvement of the Estate: A Study of Jane Austen's Novels* (Baltimore: Johns Hopkins University Press, 1971); Marilyn Butler, *Jane Austen and the War of Ideas* (Oxford: Clarendon Press, 1975). While I am taking Harding's and Mudrick's side, I disagree with their view that Austen challenges her society by allowing Elizabeth somehow to transcend it, that Elizabeth represents the "free individual." *Pride and Prejudice* is not, in my opinion, about the heroine's independence of the social context; it is about her inextricability from it.

22. See Karen Newman, "Can This Marriage Be Saved: Jane Austen Makes Sense of an Ending," *ELH* 50, no. 4 (1983): 693–710. Newman points out that critics as early as Sir Walter Scott have noticed Elizabeth's fascination with Pemberley: "Austen is at pains from early in the novel to show us Elizabeth's response to Darcy's wealth" (698). It is interesting

that Hollywood, of venal habits and puritanical tastes, should recognize and be uneasy with Elizabeth's suspicious position as Austen wrote it. In the 1940 film version of *Pride and Prejudice*, Lady Catherine threatens to cut Darcy out of her will if he goes ahead and marries a Bennet. Elizabeth proves her romantic integrity by vowing to marry him anyway. Needless to say, Austen conspicuously chose not to test Elizabeth in such a manner.

23. In *The Madwoman in the Attic: The Woman Writer and the Nineteenth-Century Literary Imagination* (New Haven: Yale University Press, 1979), Gilbert and Gubar refer us to Lloyd W. Brown (*Bits of Ivory: Narrative Techniques in Jane Austen's Fiction* [Baton Rouge: Louisiana State Press, 1973]) for "the most sustained discussion of Austen's ironic undercutting of her own endings" (667). Karen Newman also sees the happy ending in Austen as parodic: despite its comic effect, there remain "unresolved contradictions between romantic and materialistic notions of marriage" (695). The idea of a fairy-tale union is falsified by Austen's clairvoyance about why women need to marry. My reading accords a good deal with Newman's, though I am less confident than she that Austen's heroines manage nevertheless to "live powerfully within the limits imposed by ideology" (705).

DONALD A. BLOOM

Dwindling into Wifehood:
The Romantic Power of the Witty Heroine in
Shakespeare, Dryden, Congreve, and Austen

T he relationship of wit, power, gender, romance, and comedy may seem hopelessly obscure, a mere piling up of complex terms until they become conflicting. But actually I have a rather simple point to make: a witty heroine can give added pleasure and depth to a comedy through expanding our sense of the romance, the added depth and pleasure deriving from the sense of power that wit brings to a character, and particularly to a heroine. To illustrate this, I propose to look at the witty dialogue of five comic heroines: Rosalind from *As You Like It*, Florimell from Dryden's *Secret Love* and Doralice from his *Marriage a la Mode*, Millamant from *The Way of the World*, and Elizabeth Bennet from *Pride and Prejudice* (which is not, of course, a drama but includes many scenes that are superb comic drama, and is written by a woman). In each case, the witty heroine plays a dual part, both fulfilling an archetypal role necessary to romance, and establishing her independence (which I will subsequently refer to as Love) bears a certain kinship to other kinds of affectionate attachment (love) that we may feel towards our parents, siblings, children, friends, and pets, not to mention religions, countries, causes and so forth, because they all bring together affection, a sense of belonging, and a desire to help and even to sacrifice ourselves for them. Likewise, Love shares with erotic desire a need for closeness and touching of a sexually stimulating sort, yet the two are easier to tell apart than is

From *Look Who's Laughing: Gender and Comedy*, edited by Gail Finney. ©1994 by OPA (Amsterdam) B.V. Published under license by Gordon and Breach Science Publishers S.A.

commonly credited. One of the strongest stimulants to desire, unfortunately, is the desire to dominate the other, which can become an urge to harm. Not only is harm to the Other incompatible with any kind of love, but domination absolutely negates Love.

This point has great relevance to a discussion of the witty, independent heroine of romantic comedy. In the first place, just as you cannot dominate your unconscious, so you cannot dominate its archetypal figure, the object of your Love, for Love simply does not exist where it is not freely given. In this sense, Love cannot be seized, forced, bought or attained by any process except wooing, the process by which you offer yourself as an archetypal pattern to the Other, dressing yourself attractively, speaking whatever you think is loving, bringing presents, performing deeds, hoping to generate in the Other what already exists in the Self. But the Other's choice remains unconstrained—*truly* unconstrained because the choice ultimately lies outside the control of the Other's consciousness.

Wooing, however, has a great deal in common with seducing, an aspect of erotic dominance, and they cannot easily be told apart even by the wooer or seducer, because the wooer, being a sexual animal stirred by the passion of Love, desires much that the seducer also wants. The wooer differs because sexual congress is not an end in itself but merely physical expression of the total spiritual union of the two Lovers. Although neither wooing nor seducing would appear to have anything innately gender-specific about them, these activities have been commonly associated with men. At the same time, because throughout history females have generally faced much greater risks, socially and biologically, from seduction, they have needed to tell the difference and avoid a disastrous mistake. But marriage customs, especially arranged marriages enforced by law or custom, may take any choice in that matter out of the hands of either or both parties of the courting couple. Where choice exists, however, or is imagined to exist, an Other (whichever gender) must decide whether the suitor is a wooer, a seducer, or merely some irrelevancy. To Elizabeth Bennet, for example, Darcy is a wooer, Wickham a seducer and Collins an irrelevancy. Mirabell, a notorious seducer, has to persuade Millamant of his seriousness as a wooer, while Witwoud, Petulant and Sir Wilful all belong to the irrelevant group. Orlando is no seducer, but he could be an irrelevance to Rosalind if his love should prove inadequate— and marrying an irrelevance could generate as much misery as succumbing to a seducer. Doralice and Florimell face still more complex situations, living in a time when ambiguous attitudes toward marriage make the difference between wooer and seducer almost disappear.

In every case, however, the witty heroine provides an amazing complex of literary attractions: from a masculine standpoint, her intelligence and insight allow her to establish her autonomy, thereby making her that much more attractive, if sometimes more threatening to vulnerable male egos; from a feminine standpoint, she provides a powerful ego identification figure for a feminine romance; at the same time she supplies a solid partner for the comic resolution in marriage, a satirist of the masculine power structure, and a commentator on the realities of woman's existence. Not every man will be attracted to such a woman, but a man who appreciates her insight and humor will be naturally drawn to such a woman, and find immense satisfaction in being loved by her, since her wittiness derives from her intelligence and her independence of mind. If she, who can see so much and judge so acutely, loves you, then there must be something to you. From her own standpoint, the witty female will often find that her wit frightens away many suitors, so that she has to hide it, or else, if she is not left alone, be faced with the fact that it is only her looks (or worse, her fortune) that are gaining attention. A man, however, who loved her for her wit, that is, for the person she truly is, would be a man after her own heart, a man likely to fit the archetypal matrix of her own unconscious. The potential of such heroines in a romantic comedy, though immense, is infrequently realized, so that when we do find them, we find not only wonderfully rewarding literature, but some very interesting insights into the possibilities of human relationships.

2

Of the witty heroines of Shakespeare's three comic masterpieces—Beatrice, Viola, and Rosalind—the last best serves my purposes, for the first has little serious problem with Benedick once their love for each other is discovered, and the second has no fulfilling love relationship until the very end of the play. Although Rosalind, like Viola, changes her garb in order to change her sex role, she uses her changed role to explore the possibilities of Love and marriage with Orlando. Like much of Shakespeare—like much of literature—this play can be confused by excessively subtle readings, which, fascinating though they may be, lose track of its fundamental simplicity. In it, a young man, victimized by his older brother, and a young woman, victimized by her uncle, meet briefly and fall in love. Escaping separately from danger, they fetch up in the same forest where the young woman, disguised as a boy, agrees to instruct him in what Love, courtship, and women are like. In doing so, she exercises her wit at the expense of both sexes and leads him through a maze of possibilities, which, I feel, lay the groundwork for a lasting relationship. Rosalind's effervescent wit explores the meaning of Love, not just as an ideal or fantasy but as a practical possibility.

Love, we should note here, has only obliquely to do with any feminist issues. Male chauvinism or patriarchalism can interfere with its personal realization, as can any other imposition of tyranny or injustice, but it can do nothing about its existence or its etiology. Thus, responses to the play like Clara Claiborne Park's "As We Like It: How a Girl Can be Smart and Still Popular" and Peter Erickson's (in his *Patriarchal Structures in Shakespeare's Drama*), though useful for many insights, strike me as mostly beside the point. If she is in Love, Rosalind would have no desire to dominate or humiliate Orlando in any substantive way, as that negates Love no matter which gender is doing the dominating. On the contrary, what is most important about Rosalind is that, as C. L. Barber put it, "[r]omantic participation in love and humorous detachment from it ... meet and are reconciled in Rosalind's personality" (233). Most especially, "Shakespeare keeps that part of the romantic tradition which makes love an experience of the whole personality" (238). Ruth Nevo has also noted the importance of wholeness of personality and self-exploration in her remarks on the play. I agree with her that the role of "Ganymede releases in Rosalind her best powers of improvisation, intuition, and witty intelligence" (190), and that, as a result, she "can discover not only what he is like, but what she is like; test his feelings, test her own" (191). Alexander Leggatt also points out how liberating the Ganymede role is for her (202), but that she must balance it with a return to her "self' (203), and he compares her to Millamant (206). Robert Ornstein emphasizes her "schooling" of Orlando that is also "playfully extracurricular" (147), and demonstrates that "she can dissect the artificialities of the romantic convention at the same time that she ardently affirms the meaning of romantic commitment" (149). None of these, however, reaches quite the point about Rosalind that I am seeking to make.

We already see the greater depth of Rosalind in her first conversation with Celia, for although the latter offers a well-phrased but fairly stock idea (that they "sit and mock the good housewife Fortune from her wheel, that her gifts may henceforth be bestowed equally" (1.2.30–2)), the former makes us think ("I would we could do so; for her benefits are mightily misplaced, and the bountiful blind woman doth most mistake in her gifts to women" (33–5)). Not only do we sense her wistfulness about her own hapless state, but we glimpse how different, when we think about it, is Fortune for a man and a woman, for it frequently refers not to luck, but to the results of public actions—just the sort of actions which women were largely excluded from. We know she is thinking of her father, displaced by the machinations of his younger brother, a fall of Fortune having nothing to do with luck. Similarly, when Celia tries to top Rosalind she can only resort to a nice phrasing of a rather hackneyed—and anti-feminist—linking of beauty with unchastity:

"'Tis true; for those that she makes fair she scarce makes honest, and those that she makes honest she makes very ill-favouredly" (36–8). Hamlet may have reason for such a remark, but Celia has none—as her cousin and herself stand in proof of. Rosalind, however, is wiser for she answers, "Nay, now thou goest from Fortune's office to Nature's: Fortune reigns in gifts of the world, not in the lineaments of Nature" (49–41). That is, beauty is a gift of Nature not Fortune, and while it might appear to be a great good fortune to its possessor, actual experience proves otherwise. Moreover, the religious undertone of the key phrase, "reigns in the gifts of the world," should remind us how little we should trust it.

If Rosalind has the superior wit, that wit is nonetheless grounded on a kind of sympathetic wisdom that has long been associated with the feminine. She immediately sympathizes with both the old man, grieving for his three sons, all terribly injured in wrestling against Charles, and with Orlando, who is to try his skill next. Yet she falls for Orlando not (it seems) for his strength, skill and looks, but for his courage, natural good manners, and pride in his father. She has already stated that she was thinking of love, and her match with Orlando has all the logic of both comic myth and human nature behind it. Orlando is courageous and heroic, yet also pitiable—and so is Rosalind. Orlando, sensing the burgeoning love of Rosalind, as she gives him the chain, in turn falls in love with her. They have, for the moment, matched: the romance is complete. Sort of.

Reality requires a bit more than a look, a few kind words, and a gift to make a marriage of true minds last, and for all its fantastic trappings, the play is very strongly rooted in the realities of human relationships. There remains, in fact, the rest of the process of self-exploration, for Rosalind possesses wit and independence, and the two must come to terms with the full range of their personalities. Though Rosalind says, "He calls us back: my pride fell with my fortunes" (1.2.225), the point is neatly ironic, both true and untrue. Yes, she must sacrifice some of the beautiful lady's tyrannous vanity when falling in love, and even some of her social independence, but she gains something far more valuable and liberating—her inmost self. She will experience the exact opposite of a fall of fortune, and nearly the opposite of a fallen pride—provided Orlando should love her as much as she loves him. And therein lies the tale: having intelligence and independence of mind, she will explore and test this Love thoroughly, using her talent for wit to make the exploration both funny and satiric, both delightful and instructive, as well as romantically satisfying.

When the two meet again, Rosalind is already disguised and now adopts her role of "saucy lackey" (3.2.292), putting Orlando through the catechism on Time to establish her own wit credentials and making up a story about being raised in the forest by an "old religious uncle." who not only taught her to speak correctly, but "read [her] many lectures against" love, courtship and women. As many commentators have said, she is clearly luring him into this discussion in order to test his love and her own, and to teach him about the conflicts of human relationships. Orlando, who knows nothing of women, takes the bait and asks about the "principal evils ... laid to [their] charge," but Rosalind refuses on the grounds that she "will not cast away [her] physic but on those that are sick," the logical patient being "that fancy-monger" who "haunts the forest ... abuses our young plants with carving Rosalind on their barks; hangs odes upon hawthorns and elegies upon brambles." Orlando claims to be the young man, but she assures him that he cannot truly be a lover for he lacks the "marks": "a lean cheek ... a blue eye and sunken ... an unquestionable spirit ... a beard neglected ... hose ... ungartered ... bonnet unbanded ... sleeve unbuttoned ... shoe untied ... and everything about [him] demonstrating a careless desolation" (350–9).

This catalogue of the lover's marks, though traditional and subject to a good deal of scoffing, has a logic of its own. As Rosalind says, at the end of that speech, Orlando's being well-groomed ("point-device") is suggestive of his "loving himself than seeming the lover of any other." The absurdity of the tradition aside, the point is well taken: the attention of the seducer (whether outright rake or not) is on himself and his own pleasures; the attention of the Lover is on the Other. The catalogue represents the extremist view, that all moderation is tepidity or even falseness, so that the more the Lover loses any sense of himself the more truly he is a Lover. If the Lover is to woo the Other by showing the intensity and thus authenticity of his Love, he must (in this view) show a complete loss of Self. Or, as Rosalind puts it a few lines later, "Love is merely madness, and, I tell you, deserves as well a dark house and a whip as madmen do" (391–3).

But this is one of Shakespeare's favorites jokes, even though—as the sonnets indicate—told on himself. In the world of wit, in which Rosalind is one of the reigning queens, you must have judgment, which requires not only the reason that madmen have lost, but a strong, though ironical, sense of self. Rosalind is as foolishly in love, as "fond," in the old sense, as Orlando, but she does not lose her wit as a result. Thus, she does not simply borrow a dress and make herself known to Orlando as "his Rosalind" immediately. Romance or no, two people do not stop being two people just because they have fallen in love, and Rosalind, needing to find out just how true this Love is, embarks on the more dangerous ground of the list of women's "giddy offenses" and "principal evils"—

I being but a mooning youth will grieve, be effeminate, changeable, longing and liking, proud, fantastical, apish, shallow, inconstant, full of tears, full of smiles; for every passion something and for no passion truly anything, as boys and women are for the most part cattle of this colour; would now like him, now loathe him; then entertain him, then spit at him. (379–86)

These constitute, of course, a traditional catalogue of such offenses and evils, and can be looked at superficially as just another annoying example of gender-prejudice. Looked at again, however, they take on a rather more ambiguous cast. To call a woman effeminate, for example, is hardly insulting, being essentially tautological. Other terms, taken out of context, reveal their uncertainty: would any man want his Beloved to be unsmiling and ungrieving, never "longing and liking" at all? Finally, the remainder (changeable, proud, fantastical, apish, shallow, inconstant) have as much application to one gender as the other, but may indeed be applicable to "his Rosalind." In the long run, as Rosalind is a human being she will display all these foibles at times. So will he. Once the initial infatuation wears off, the Lover must still desire to *be* with the Other, despite her humanity. Will he?

Rosalind herself then brings up the question of his being "cured," although Orlando (fortunately) does not want any such cure. She needs, however, to explore and test Orlando's feelings for her still further, by regaling him with more horrifying possibilities. Thus, at their next meeting, when Orlando fails to arrive on time, we find her calling him a snail both for his tardiness and the fact that, as a snail, "he brings his destiny [horns] with him" (4.1.49). Orlando takes (or pretends to take) this possibility seriously, and asserts that Rosalind, being virtuous, would not do such a thing. Satisfied with this, she urges him to press his opportunity, as she is in a "holiday humour and like enough to consent" (58–9). But when Orlando tries to play the role of courtly lover, she constantly interrupts him to correct or tease. When he puts forth the standard idea that rejection will cause his death, she responds with her most famous line, "Men have died from time to time, and worms have eaten them, but not for love" (91–2). When he asks for her love, she assents, but when he asks her to have him, she assents too much—"Ay, and twenty such"—for if Orlando is good, "can one desire too much of a good thing?" (105) Before he can respond to this possibility she shifts into the mock-wedding. Once that is completed she asks him how long he will "have her after [he has] possess'd her." Once more his response (the cliché, "forever and a day") causes her to pounce: "Say 'a day' without the 'ever.' ...

Men are April when they woo, December when they wed. Maids are May when they are maids, but the sky changes when they are wives" (125–8). She goes on to warn him to expect Rosalind to be jealous, clamorous, newfangled, giddy, and prone to inappropriate tears or laughter.

Near the end of this scene Celia remarks that Rosalind deserves to be stripped and exposed for her abuse to her own sex, but Rosalind has more going on than the intelligent but unimaginative Celia suspects. In the first place, the accusation of change from courtship to post-marital tedium or dismay is applied first to men. In the second place, he needs no warning against the moodiness of men since he does not propose marrying one. Third, all these are merely wifely versions of the "giddy offenses" iterated in the previous scene. Fourth, however much these may be slanders against the gender as a whole, they may be at any time true of any individual woman— some of them for very good reasons—which is what he proposes to marry, not the Anima archetype which she represents. He would thus be wise to determine what this woman is like, and whether he can enjoy or at least put up with her human foibles.

Orlando, we see, is still much too naive. When he is told that Rosalind will do as Ganymede is doing, he responds: "O, but she is wise!" He is correct that she is wise, or wiser than most young people, and probably wiser than he—wise enough, at any rate, to make as sure as she can of her husband, the way he ought to of his wife. Still, his point is correct: the key is wisdom, that is, good judgment. But where before he was counting on *her* virtue, so now he is counting on *her* wisdom—an unwise method that, in this case, will work for him, but might lead to disaster with another woman (as it does with Elizabeth Bennet's father). Still, he is learning. When she expatiates on the impossibility of stopping up a witty woman's wit, he responds with the pun, "Wit, whither wilt?" Once more she threatens cuckolding ("Nay, you might keep that check for it till you met your wife's wit going to your neighbour's bed"), and when he asks how that could be justified ("And what wit could wit have to excuse that?"), she responds with an answer worthy of the Wife of Bath ("Marry, to say she came to seek you there. You shall never take her without her answer unless you take her without her tongue."). But Rosalind is no Wife, nor is Orlando a Jankyn. These are tests, puzzles, challenges. Rosalind can use them to explore the kind of man Orlando really is. Clearly, he is no cynical seducer, and he does not seem to have the kind of arrogance that would make him an unpleasant partner to a woman of independence and spirit. But he might be little better than a fool. If he should prove such, Rosalind would face another kind of challenge.

Here, however, the author brings this game to an end. Rosalind is trapped. She would like to keep playing, but she cannot expect him to take

Ganymede very seriously. Nor would she want him to. If Orlando is naive enough to need the instruction Ganymede can offer into the realities of human interaction at its most intimate (including its possible horrors), and witty enough to enjoy the word-play of a master-wit, he is wise enough to remember that his responsibility to the duke, his new master, outweighs any game-playing. The play concludes, therefore, with the ritualized game that Rosalind plays in sorting out the couples, winding up her role as the mediator between Orlando and his own Love, which he so poorly understood, as well as between herself and hers, which she explored along with his. By the end she is ready to *be* that Love, and he as ready to be hers, the archetypal conclusion we are surely supposed to derive from the appearance of Hymen to confirm all engagements. Rosalind's efforts have not been merely for fun, but to match the archetypal fulfillment of romance with the reality of human foibles.

3

If in Shakespeare's time the fulfillment of romance through marriage was only occasionally managed, and thus remained largely in the realm of the fantastic, by Dryden's time it had become much more common, though arranged and compelled marriage also remained common enough. In the meantime, however, the whole institution, as John Harrington Smith shows in *The Gay Couple in Restoration Comedy*, had taken on a rather bad odor. Although in an arranged marriage the couple had almost no hope of romantic fulfillment, marrying to please themselves left them stuck for life with someone they might as easily fall *out* of Love with as they did *in*. Thus, the cynicism about Love that characterizes Suckling's cavalier poetry also permeates the drama, or at least the comic side of it. The heroic and tragic drama still followed the idealized love-and-honor themes of the Caroline court, and can be seen in the companion plots of both plays: the hopeless love of the Queen for the courtier Philocles, himself in love with someone else, in *Secret Love*; the dilemma, in *Marriage*, of Leonidas and Palmyra, as first one and then the other is identified as the long-lost child of the usurper, Polydamas, and each is ordered to reject the True Love they feel for each other to marry someone else. But these idealized plots are as unreal as the characters who enact them. In the comic plots the characters represent more or less accurate versions of contemporary courtiers, who view love as primarily lust, and courtship as a self-serving game. Thus, in the one type, romantic fulfillment by Love and marriage turns out a lifeless charade, and in the other a self-deception fit only for fools. Nevertheless, like other playwrights of the time, Dryden had a strong romantic streak, which he could not suppress even in the subplots, and they reveal a longing after romantic fulfillment even as they are built on the countervailing cynicism. This internal contradiction, however, leaves us wondering just what these characters want, or hope to achieve.

Smith shows how, in *Secret Love*, Dryden reworked the witty heroines of earlier playwrights (especially Fletcher), changing them from widows to girls (Florimell), approximately the equivalent to the rakish hero (Celadon) in wit and wildness—approximately, because although she talks gaily enough about having many lovers or servants, she is also militantly virginal. Though they eventually marry after several wit-duels and comic "situations," through most of play Florimell finds herself in a tricky position—wanting something that perhaps cannot exist. She has no interest, she says, in "one of those solemn Fops; they are good for nothing but to make Cuckolds: Give me a servant who is an high Flier at all games, that is bounteous of himself to many women; and yet whenever I pleas'd to throw out the lure of Matrimony, should come down with a swing, and fly the better at his own quarry" (3.1.296–302). We may take it as a rule that at least some women are attracted to men who are great womanizers, because they are elusive, or because they make themselves interesting, or because they radiate a kind of sadism that attracts a corresponding masochism. But what Florimell wants may be impossible to *have*: wildness and yet reliability. Her use of the image from falconry is significant, but ambiguous. If successful, she would reach the seductively powerful position of dominating the Other as the human does the trained animal, doubly ego-gratifying where the animal has a powerful and fiercely independent personality. But this is not, of course, Love. If she does not care about Love, it doesn't matter, for if she is only interested in affection, passion or sexual pleasure, they can love or not, marry or not, have sex or not, and the question of "with whom" never means much.

The issue comes up only because Celadon holds to the standard contempt for marriage—"Marriage is poor folk's pleasure that cannot go the cost of variety" (1.1.29–30)—yet unexpectedly falls in love with Florimell. When she queries him about this ("But, without raillery, are you in Love?"), he responds frankly, "So horribly much, that contrary to my own Maxims, I think in my conscience I could marry you" (2.1.57–9). Florimell thus faces a dual dilemma: is he really in Love? and does she want to marry him, whether he is or not? The advantages, we remember, are all on his side; if they marry, but become estranged or even just bored, he can return to his old life with comparative ease, but she cannot. And, of course, he may not really be in Love with Florimell, but just subject to a transitory infatuation, for he doesn't stop being attracted to other women, in particular, the two sisters, Sabina and Olinda, whom he was courting before he met Florimell.

She tests him by proposing that he act the part of the True Lover, willing to kill himself out of despair, or at least developing the "pale, and lean, and melancholick" air, but he brushes these aside as unreasonable. She then proposes "a whole year of probation ... to grow reserv'd, discreet, sober and faithful, and to pay [her] all the services of a Lover" (2.1.89, 107–9). He accepts on the condition that if he does well the time will be reduced, and she allows the condition, though noting that if he "prove unfaithful" the time will be extended. Sure enough, when Florimell makes a wager with her friend Flavia as to Florimell's power over Celadon, he promptly fails. In the midst of excusing himself for recent attentions to Sabina and Olinda, he receives a bogus invitation from the sisters, actually from Flavia, and accepts. But Florimell finds herself more jealous than angry, and vows to win him over yet. Catching him in the midst of his attentions to the others, she jeers the other two out of countenance, and rails about taking a "Wencher's word," but through the use of wit in her power games with the romantic hero. It is the union of these two factors that makes these heroines so memorable.

Before going into specific characters, I must clarify some terms. By wit, first, I mean statements that in general or in context show significant insight, and are phrased in a particularly apt and vivid way, generally involving either the surprise of humor or the irony of satire, or both. The witty heroine, then, displays a talent for these well-turned and amusing insights, and in doing so, shows both her wisdom and the power of her personality. By power I mean not dominance or authority over another, but freedom from such dominance over oneself—that is, independence—remembering that established legal and customary authority does not necessarily reflect the practical and psychological dominance of a given relationship. We find this especially in the case of women, who have, in most times and places, found themselves subordinated to the men of the same rank to whom they are legally attached, such as their husbands, fathers, or brothers. Thus, the gender (both her chromosomal sex and the mythology attached to it) of the witty heroine plays a central part not only in the romance, but in the comedy, for the wit and independence of such a heroine tends to undermine or overturn the expected hierarchical order. Yet, as we shall see, she fulfills the romantic myth more completely than other heroines.

Most complicated is the idea of romance. By this I mean either or both of two related literary phenomena: a story that depicts the search for and discovery of the inner or true or total Self, what Jung calls the process of Individuation; or a story that deals with falling in love. These I take to be almost, but not completely, overlapping, for I assume that what we call "falling in love" occurs when we find someone who exactly matches the matrix we have built up in our unconscious, which Jung associates with the archetypal figure of the Animus/Anima, and which is the ultimate goal of the search. In a pure romance the search for self (the quest) may sprawl over many hundreds of pages and involve the ego figure in dozens of adventures with a variety of archetypal figures (including the Shadow, the dark Self, often a rival for the Animus/Anima). In a romantic comedy, however, this quest is commonly compressed into a very small number of adventures, but all pointing toward the culminating event of romance and comedy—the marriage of hero and heroine. For, as Northrop Frye has shown, the comic resolution of a restored society centering on the youthful hero and his bride blends naturally with the romantic resolution of a hero culminating his (or her) archetypal quest of self-discovery with marriage.

In this sense, romance is not only a literary form but an aspect of human development, a process of self-exploration and self-realization that all undergo, including finding the archetypal matrix of the Other in our deep unconscious. In order to do this we project the archetype onto some real human being who closely matches it—that is, we fall in love. This kind of love he escapes again through appeal to the cynical standard of the day: "Why should you speak so contemptibly of the better half of Mankind. I'le stand up for the honour of my Vocation" (4.1.194–6).

Florimell has her greatest success in pretending to be a young fop, cutting the two sisters away from Celadon before her disguise is broken. He makes the best of his embarrassment, but she is now in the driver's seat. When he attempts to swear "by these Breeches," which we assume are hers, since it would be odd to swear by his own, she retorts, "Which if I marry you I am resolv'd to wear" (5.1.171). She succeeds not only in driving away the two girls he is dallying with, but in exposing, through parody, the whole shallow business. If she can seduce girls as well as he can, without the slightest real interest in them, how much point is there to it? If he wants sex, wouldn't a prostitute be more straightforward? If he wants merely the satisfaction to his vanity that these games afford, what kind of flimsy person is he? If he wants more, that is, the fulfillment of himself through Love, why can't he pay the necessary price in fidelity?

These questions are never fully answered. At the end of the play, after an early contest of wills, they resolve to wed if they can only, as Florimell says, "invent but any way to make it easie" (5.1.531–2). As Celadon sees it, the problem is that "[s]ome foolish people have made it uneasie by drawing the knot faster than they need" (533–4), to which she agrees and they make up a list of provisos so that the idea of marriage will be tolerable: giving up jealousy and pretense, not inquiring about gambling losses or excursions. Most important, they agree that "the names of Husband and Wife hold forth nothing, but clashing and cloying, and dulness and faintness in their signification," so that "they shall be abolish'd for ever betwixt" them, and instead they "will be married by the more agreeable names of Mistress and Gallant" (571–6). The goal clearly is still romance, and for the moment we might imagine we are back in the Middle Ages where it must be divorced from marriage. But this is no love out of the courtly love cycles, passionate but eternal. They have no faith in the continued need for that particular Other, but rather assume that this Love will wear out as all loves do, only lasting some months longer.

The play thus ends as *Marriage a la Mode* begins: it is impossible for Love to last through the eternity of marriage. Doralice's song, "Why should a foolish marriage vow," which begins *Marriage*, reiterates how love wears out, making the married state a waste. A few lines later, Rhodophil describes to his friend, soon to be rival, Palamede, what has happened to his relationship with Doralice. Though once he "lov'd her passionately," now "those golden days are gone" and all he knows of "her perfections ... is only by memory." Again we find the mixture of cynicism and regret. He claims to have "lov'd her a whole half year, double the natural term of any Mistress," and admits that he "could have held out another quarter; but then the World began to laugh at" him, and he was shamed by fashion into giving up so soon. Love did not last, he says, because there was "nothing left in us to make us new to one another," now they pace like "lions in a room" and lying as far apart as their fashionable "great Bed" will allow (1.1.162–77).

Both say much the same thing: love is something vitally important but transitory; if marriage must be permanent, then everyone must accept the fact that people will continue to pursue love outside it. The song, indeed, is much more sinister, for marriage is associated with an array of negative terms (foolish, decay'd, dead, madness and pain), and set in opposition to passion, pleasure and joy, defining the anti-marital, anti-romantic code of the time. But it is only a song, and not necessarily to be regarded as the opinion of the singer. Indeed, when Doralice is approached by Palamede, she keeps him at some distance, agreeing only to listen to his suit, and then only for the three days before his marriage. Moreover, Rhodophil's statement includes two mitigations: one, the admission that he was partly motivated by a sense of being out of fashion; the second, the observation that their passion for each other lasted twice as long as the normal affair—or more, since they were first in love two years ago and it is only now that he is seriously pursuing an affair.

As he says, however, they are now as friendly as caged cats. For example, once pretence is unnecessary, they begin to bicker like a sitcom couple, with Doralice generally winning the duels. When Rhodophil wonders about his sins that led him into this marriage, Doralice asserts, "Whatever your sins, mine's the punishment" (3.1.57); when he contemplates his "Holy-day" at her death, she agrees that he has surely made her a martyr; when he says he will swear over her corpse never to marry again, she resolves "to marry the very same day" he dies, "if it be but to show how little" she is concerned for him (70–2). Having lost these rounds, he asks what she would suggest to end their "heathenish life," offering any "reasonable atonement" before they sleep. But she demolishes him: "What should you talk of peace abed, when you can give no security for performance of Articles?" (80–1).

At first this appears to be merely a cutting, even slightly cruel joke, with a double entendre attached—a sure-fire laugh line in the long tradition of the bickering couple, provided the audience is sufficiently sophisticated. But Rhodophil's subsequent defensiveness indicates that it is true. He complains that it is too "easy" to have her, and insufficiently "unlawful" (84). He has, in fact, exercised his erotic imagination to "enjoy" her, "fancied [her] all the fine women in the town to help [himself] out," but failed. Thus, he says, "Thou art a wife, and thou wilt be a wife," as harsh a condemnation as imaginable under the circumstances. In some ways, we feel sorry for Rhodophil, since it is easy enough to imagine the falling off of his performance as a sexual athlete, and his subsequent attempt to protect his self-esteem by blaming his wife. But he does not seem to understand or care about how his coldness undercuts *her* self-esteem. Moreover, the immediate advantages lie with him: he can return to his earlier womanizing, gain prestige and risk nothing except a tongue-lashing from his wife. She cannot follow his lead without gaining the brand of whore and facing the possibility of a major scandal, even a duel (as nearly happens in the play).

Justice, in fact, lies with her, since she is approximately as vulnerable as he in the area of self-esteem, and at a serious disadvantage in the game of sexual self-indulgence. After her husband's departure, Doralice reiterates the wife's lament: "'Tis a pretty time we Women have on't, to be made Widows, while we are marry'd." Their husbands complain that they are the same, when they "have more reason to complain, that [the husbands] are not the same." And she concludes with a surprisingly raunchy conceit on marital sex as a kind of *table d'hote* meal ("'Tis enough that they have a sufficient Ordinary, and a Table ready spread for 'em: if they cannot fall to and eat heartily, the fault is theirs"). But her most telling remark comes at the beginning of her complaint, when she turns his insulting term back on him: "Well, since thou art a Husband, and wilt be a Husband, I'll try if I can find out another!" But *husband* means not only dull drudge as wife does; it means cuckold. There lies her greatest power and the key to restoring their relationship, though she does not realize it yet.

In the first of her efforts to gain revenge, the grotto scene, she goes to keep a rendezvous with her suitor, Palamede, only to run into her husband trying to keep an assignation with Melantha, his prospective mistress and Palamede's wife-to-be. Each must lie barefacedly in order to avoid the difficult truth. Later, with both Melantha and herself disguised as boys, they again all meet and she has the opportunity to flirt openly with her lover in front of her husband, though he does the same to her. At the end, though, Doralice reluctantly disconnects herself from Palamede because she knows that his father has arrived to stand upon terms in the arrangement with Melantha's father and she has no interest in a married servant. Their only hope is to outlive their spouses, to which they dedicate themselves. Discovered by her husband, Doralice persuades him out of forcing Palamede into a duel, but also realizes her opportunity: "Then have I found my account in raising your jealousie: O! 'tis the most delicate sharp sawce to a cloy'd stomach; it will give you a new edge" (5.1.348–50). Moreover, when Rhodophil tries to make it conditional on his being sure she was "honest," she shrewdly refuses, "If you are wise, believe me for your own sake: Love and Religion have but one thing to trust to; that's a good sound faith" (353–55). Perpetual jealousy does not constitute much of a solution, but it is the best, perhaps, that a cynical and materialistic age has to offer. Doralice, at any rate, seems to have the skill to make the best of it.

4

By the end of the century, the cruder sort of cynicism about marriage had ebbed away again. Though we find it in the backbiting of the Fainalls in *The Way of the World*, this hardly constitutes an attack on marriage as romantic fulfillment, since the Fainalls were never in love in the first place. More telling are Millamant's remarks during the proviso scene, where she says she won't be called names after marriage:

> Aye, as wife, spouse, my dear, joy, jewel, love, sweetheart and the rest of that nauseous cant, in which men and their wives are so fulsomely familiar ... Let us never visit together, nor go to a play together. But lets us be very strange and well-bred; let us be as strange as if we had been married a great while, and as well bred as if we were not married at all (4.1.175–87).

Mirabell accepts this condition as well as the others without demur, so we can assume he feels much the same, and for a moment we might be back in the world of Doralice and Florimell. But there is more going on in Millamant's provisos than some leftover Restoration clichés on the contemptible state of marriage.

We must remember that her first demand was that she be allowed to loll in bed as late as she likes in the morning (163–9), and her third a whole series of fundamental rights guaranteeing her privacy in visits, letters, and meals, and her freedom of choice in friends, acquaintance, garb, and conversation. "These articles subscribed … [she] may by degrees dwindle into a wife" (202–3). The effect is cumulative. If in the first condition she merely demands the right to go on being a coquette, and in the second to avoid the cloying sentimentality of some couples, in the third she puts forward a feminist Bill of Rights. Even the very adaptable Mirabell finds these "something advanced," but accepts on the simple conditions that she avoid behavior that would make him a fool or damage the health of his unborn children. But if the third set of conditions is a clear statement of personal freedom, the other two have their points as well. In the class to which she belongs, this apparent laziness—her enjoyment of solitude, contemplation, morning thoughts, *douceurs, sommeils du matin* (164–7)—defines her. She will not become a busy housewife for any husband. The point, I think, is not that she will not at times be housewifely, but that she will not be forced into such a role.

Likewise, the "nauseous cant" that she refers to is not merely sentimental but frequently hypocritical, as the example of Sir Francis and Lady Fadler (178–9) makes evident. It has, moreover, an undertone of possessiveness, which, even if the terms themselves are used by both genders, almost invariably works to the disadvantage of the female. Finally, the last part takes us once more into that fascinating world of Millamant's imagination, for it suggests they act at once as if they no longer cared for each other and as if they were having an adulterous affair. I suggest that this is a tentative, if slightly fantastical solution to the dilemma posed by the Restoration critique of marriage—that it must inevitably spoil romance. Congreve uses "never" to make it a joke—surely they must sometimes visit together—but if they remain at once new and well-mannered to each other, they may avoid the over-familiarity, the bickering, the humdrum conversations that doom so many marriages. Millamant sees the danger, and this demand leads naturally into her demand for large-scale personal liberty, for as a woman she has much more to lose if the marriage should go flat. When Mirabell recognizes the rightness of her conditions, and proposes nothing that she objects to in return, then she can rest as secure in her marriage as she could ever hope to be.

Reaching this point requires a significant change in the character of

Mirabell, however, and this change has not been well understood. A number of critics (Van Voris, Roberts, Foakes, Donaldson, for instance) have exercised themselves on the general unworthiness of Mirabell, though he has been admirably defended by others (the Mueschkes, Williams). Likewise, Millamant, though appreciated for her wit, has often been thought affected and illogical, while even Virginia Birdsall, who correctly identifies her creativity, also remarks on her self-admiration—which to me is nothing more than a gambit in the game she is playing. More to the point, from my view, are several recent studies that have gone back to the question of marriage and society. Alvin Snider, for example, has shown how Congreve rejects the popular neo-Epicureanism with its antagonism to a romantic ideal of marriage, while Richard Kroll makes a strong point about the struggle of all the characters, but Millamant especially, to achieve a "contingent but real social liberty" (749). Most significant, Richard W. F. Braverman emphasizes the emerging companionate marriage, and demonstrates the way that Millamant can gain both social and political power through a "productive marriage which [combines] sentimental love and sexual satisfaction" while still legitimating the ancient dynastic function (155).

Frankly, I also find a great deal more to Millamant than whimsy, fancy and vanity, and I think Kroll and Braverman, in their different ways, are quite right to point out the tricky sociopolitical situation all the characters, especially Millamant, find themselves in. Her position as queen of coquettes, so apparently easy, has many pitfalls. Though it gives her great power for the moment, that power lasts only as long as her beauty. Like an athlete, she must win her gold medal while she can, for she cannot hope to compete in another Olympics—but what is a victory? She may have her pick of men, but after the ceremony she is stuck for life with that husband, and has little recourse if he turns out a boor or a cad. Moreover, her very beauty puts her in greater peril of an unwise choice, for many of the men flocking around her will be stimulated by a desire to possess her beauty not love her self. With more choices, she has perhaps a better chance of finding her own romantic fulfillment in one of those paying court, but she must also sift those suitors to find one that will truly Love her. Thus, she must make sure of Mirabell's intentions: a mere offer of marriage is not enough, for it may be simply a more honorable way to possess her. Toward deciding this question most of her dialogue runs.

When, on her first appearance, Witwoud remarks that she did not inquire of Mr. Fainall about the location of his wife and Mirabell, she responds, "By your leave, Mr. Witwoud, that were like asking after an old fashion, to ask a husband for his wife" (2, 1, 317–8), showing she has no delusions about the importance of many wives to their husbands: about as much as out of fashion gowns to wealthy ladies. When she sails off into the wondrous and delightfully goofy fantasy about the use of love-letters as curling papers, and the disastrous effect of prose on her hair-do, she affirms her social power as belle of belles and her intellectual power as a wit of wits—and shows in the process why Mirabell is crazy about her. When Mirabell attempts to deflect her annoyance at his jealous behavior of the previous night by suggesting that her cruelty is affected and not natural, while her "true vanity is in the power of pleasing," she retorts, "Oh, I ask your pardon for that. One's cruelty is one's power and when one parts with one's cruelty, one parts with one's power; and when one has parted with that, I fancy one's old and ugly" (347–51). Never mind the medieval tradition of the Lady's cruelty, Millamant has neatly synopsized the coquette's dilemma. While it would be handy to Mirabell, as to any other importunate male, if Millamant were to opt for the power to be had from "pleasing" her suitor by giving up her power, Millamant is too wise for any such thing, not when she holds the high trumps, and not until married to a man she can trust to Love her. To Muir the key word is "respect" (237); to Birdsall "love of freedom" (243); in either case Millamant has no desire to lose what she sometimes calls "power" and "liberty" but is, at bottom, selfhood.

When Mirabell, faced with the "challenge that Millamant flings at him" (Birdsall, 241), loses his confidence and resorts to whining that it is only in the eyes, and thus the praises, of the lover that a woman is beautiful, Millamant rightly accuses him of "vanity," and demolishes his image by reversing it. Far from the lover creating the lady's beauty, it is the beautiful lady who creates the lover "as fast as [she] pleases" (365–7). To Witwoud's complaint that this reduces the lover to a kind of homemade kitchen match, she retorts: "One no more owes one's beauty to a lover than one's wit to an echo" (370–1). The world is full of men who desire to possess the lovely Millamant—rakes, fops, humorists, bumpkins—but how many are truly interested in the person inhabiting the exquisite body and residing behind the beautiful face? Such echo-lovers do play up to one's vanity, but no more, and until she finds one who isn't, she is safer and happier treating them all as such.

As soon as they are alone, Mirabell begins crabbing at her, ostensibly giving her advice on the folly of spending time conversing with fools like Witwoud and Petulant, but actually giving vent to his own wounded vanity. Millamant dismisses this complaint first by saying simply, "I please myself" (and why shouldn't she?), before going into another of her fantasies: fools as a kind of antibiotic for the "vapors," that all-purpose term for boredom masquerading as melancholia. But when Mirabell takes her literally ("You are not in a course of fools?"), the crude suggestiveness of this offends her and she presses her advantage, offering the possibility of rejecting him absolutely. The problem, she correctly foresees, is that they "shall be sick of one another." Most especially, "I shan't endure to be reprimanded nor instructed; 'tis so dull to act always by advice, and so tedious to be told of one's faults— I can't bear it" (408–10). We must not overlook the absolute forthrightness of these remarks. Who *does* like to be reprimanded or instructed? Certainly not Mirabell. Moreover, it doesn't matter whether Mirabell is mainly a male chauvinist trying to exert control or mainly a jealous lover trying to sequester and enjoy alone the beloved, for both roles are innately egocentric and oppressive, denying the independent human subjectivity of the love object. As long as he continues in this frame of mind, Millamant has good reason for keeping him at a distance.

As Mirabell loses points in the wit duel, he becomes more self-pitying and she becomes wittier. When he grumbles about the impossibility of "win[ning] a woman with plain dealing and sincerity," she annihilates him: "Sententious Mirabell! Prithee, don't look with that violent and inflexible wise face, like Solomon at the dividing of the child in an old tapestry hanging" (420–2). She is correct: Mirabell has begun taking himself seriously, congratulating himself on his honesty, while whining to Millamant about how little she praises him for it. But a stuffed shirt can be regarded as little improvement on a rake as a bad bet for a husband. If Mirabell has reformed from rakishness, as the lines suggest, he must also be reformed from pomposity. Ignoring his plea for her "for one moment to be serious," she says, "What, with that face? No, if you keep your countenance, 'tis impossible I should hold mine. Well, after all, there is something very moving in a love-sick face. Ha! ha! ha!—Well, I won't laugh, don't be peevish—Heighho! Now I'll be melancholy, as melancholy as a watch-light. Well, Mirabell, if ever you will win me, woo me now.—Nay, if you are so tedious, fare you well" (425–431). And, leaving him sputtering, she departs.

Vanity? Affectation? Perhaps. But also great good sense to go along with her flights of wit. Mirabell, having fallen in love, still wants everything his own way. He wants Millamant to be serious, when her most lovable trait is her *joie de vivre*. And he wants her to be schooled by him when she is at least as wise as he. Thus he grumbles about women that "[t]here is no point of the compass to which they cannot turn, and by which they are not turned" (446–7). Yet there is nothing whimsical about Millamant below the surface. She needs to get along with her guardian aunt, and she does so. She wishes to have a good time in her inevitably temporary position as chief coquette: ditto. She will not allow Mirabell to spoil either of these, but cares for him enough to keep him encouraged. However flighty or foolish other women may have been, Millamant moves in a straight and predictable line: she will not jeopardize her present happiness, but she will not interfere with Mirabell's efforts to free her from Lady Wishfort's control.

This utter defeat seemingly wakes Mirabell up, for in their next encounter he is more like himself, and the easiness that marks his relationships with others now manifests itself in his dialogue with her. Yet he cannot top her. When he asks slyly if his finding her locked in a room is "a pretty artifice contrived, to signify that here the chase must end and my pursuit be crowned for you can fly no further" (4, 1, 136–8), she dismisses the idea as vanity: "No, I'll fly and be followed to the last moment. Though I am upon the very verge of matrimony, I expect you should solicit me as much as if I were wavering at the grate of a monastery, with one foot over the threshold. I'll be solicited to the very last, nay and afterwards" (139–43). This idea naturally startles Mirabell, since solicitation has a decidedly sexual undertone, and he, the ex-rake, imagining himself honorably wedded to the girl of his dreams, naturally also imagines himself exempt from the necessity of "solicitation." Not Millamant, or so she claims: "Oh, I should think I was poor and had nothing to bestow, if I were *reduced to inglorious ease and freed from the agreeable fatigues of solicitations*" (145–7, emphasis mine). The phrasing of this passage is wonderfully ironic. The idea of ease being inglorious, as if she were of that hardworking, Puritanical sort that would find loafing shameful, and of solicitation being fatiguing (a dirty job, listening to handsome men plead for your favors, but someone has to do it), throws us once more into that slightly surreal world of Millamant's imagery, but the satire is directed as much at herself as Mirabell.

When Mirabell tries to reason her out of the position, she rejects the premises of his logic ("[i]t may be in things of common application, but never sure in love"), and she also isolates the real issue: "There is not so impudent a thing in nature as the saucy look of an assured man, confident of success. The pedantic arrogance of a very husband has not so pragmatical an air" (155–7). These last two sentences need little comment. They are witty, yet very true and very much to the point. Mirabell's attitude will determine the outcome. The romantic impetus requires independence of both, and the reduction of either destroys the validity of the experience—they could have sex, of course, and even some degree of love, but they could not have Love. Thus she concludes, "Ah, I'll never marry, unless I am first made sure of my will and pleasure" (158–9).

Mirabell pretends to misunderstand, taking "pleasure" with a sexual undertone, and making it into a rather off-color joke, but she is not distracted any more than she is offended, and dismisses his remark as impertinence. There follows her disquisition on liberty, and the proviso scene considered earlier. Even with the provisos accepted on both sides, she finds herself still reluctant to take the final step until urged to by her cousin Mrs. Fainall. Even then she won't be kissed, except on the hand, until there is public recognition of all in the final scene: she will be no one's toy, not even Mirabell's, whom, she now admits, she loves violently. While it has been accurately said that the play, especially the proviso scene, brings her "from girlhood to maturity" (Holland 185), I think the phrase applies more strongly to Mirabell, for it is the rake's life that is the most thoroughly adolescent—with its antagonism to established morals, its slangy and obscene barracks wit, its preoccupation with girls as sexual objects, its endless drinking parties, brawls, and scrapes. Millamant, however, displays no girlish traits except her enjoyment of what is enjoyable in her youth, though that she enjoys to the fullest. What Millamant must make sure of is that Mirabell does not regard her as simply a new acquisition, a mistress more difficult to obtain than others. Once she's sure that *he* is grown up, then she knows that she can put away her own coquetry. This romance is complete.

5

What makes *Pride and Prejudice* perhaps the most profound of all the works we have been reviewing is the way that Austen shows the relationship of romantic love to archetypal need, accomplishing this without overburdening the manners comedy or spoiling our enjoyment of Elizabeth's (and her own) satiric wit. If we look back to *AYLI*, we see that although Shakespeare gives us many reasons to enjoy the play, he does not give us a very clear reason why Orlando and Rosalind should love each other and not someone else. Congreve goes farther: making use of the wit duels from Restoration comedy, he gives us at least an idea of Mirabell's and Millamant's need for each. To graduate from casual affairs into something profound, Mirabell has had to find a woman who can match his wit and social graces, who is romantically sensual yet not a slut. Millamant's need for him specifically is less pressing (giving her the advantage), but she too must find an archetypal mate to gain archetypal fulfillment, and only Mirabell—the changing Mirabell—fills that bill. Similarly, but even more intensely, Darcy needs Elizabeth to achieve personal wholeness: she has, or is, what he lacks most. She, more like Millamant, has not such an obvious need, but only Darcy, who also must change even as he forces her to a self-examination and change, can do for her what she most needs.

For a long time, however, criticism generally ignored this matter of mutual needs, tending to focus on the title faults, their application to the central couple, and blame—finally resolved, I believe, by Howard Babb's landmark book (see also Heilman, Craik, and Kroeber). Beginning with

Gilbert and Gubar's *The Madwoman in the Attic*, though, attention shifted to feminist issues, especially power, and Austen's alleged sell-out to patriarchal ideology, es evidenced by her romantic endings. Several feminist critics (Newton, Newman) have modified this initial harsh judgment by suggesting that Austen was instead subverting or parodying this ideology. And now at least one (Shaffer) has gone so far as to accept *Pride and Prejudice* at face value, and claim that Elizabeth is able to assert herself both before and after marriage (as the text of the book clearly suggests). Moreover, some useful new comments have been offered on the characters, including Darcy's shyness (Ewin) and Elizabeth's Spenseresque quest through the cardinal virtues (Wiesenfarth). Nevertheless, none of these quite gets at the point I am trying to make.

As we all know, the faults of Elizabeth and Darcy can be found in the title of their story. Both have both faults, but they are not so confirmed in their sinfulness as some of the more rigorous critics would suggest. On the contrary, both are decent, moral individuals whose judgments are more often right than wrong. Darcy, for example, is correct in his condemnation of Elizabeth's mother and two youngest sisters, but he is not the snob that Bingley's sisters are. He misjudges, perhaps partly because it is handy to do so, the fervor of Jane's love for his friend, and he forgets that his own connections (most obviously Lady Catherine, but also Miss Bingley) are less than perfect. But his apparent coldness we discover to be shyness, and his arrogance, though real, is not so strong as some have claimed. He has more self-confidence, and less humility, than is good for him, so that he takes himself and his judgment a bit too seriously. Which of us does not?

Elizabeth likewise rushes headlong into judgments about others, allows her prejudice to cause serious misreadings of the facts, and thus acts on her misreadings with unfortunate consequences. Although we see more intimately Elizabeth's failures in this regard, and especially her humiliating trust in the despicable Wickham, her sins are less serious than his. In fact, Elizabeth would not have been so likely to fall into her basic misjudgment of Wickham had not Darcy already antagonized her with his rude comment during his first appearance. Though it was given in a private conversation and inadvertently overheard by Elizabeth, the insult can only be regarded as the result of insufferable arrogance. Of course, it turns out to be something else, the defensive reaction of a shy man, who can be sociable only in circumstances where he feels very secure. Elizabeth, her vanity nettled, and her prejudice against him invoked first by his general coldness and then later by Wickham's crafty slanders, conceives a decided antagonism toward him. Moreover, Darcy is a very imposing figure, not only rich and well-born, tall and good-looking, but highly intelligent and well-educated. Even if he is no seducer of the Lovelace sort, nor even a Rochester, she must regard him as a dangerous and intimidating figure. She herself notes his "satirical eye," and tells Charlotte Lucas, "[I]f I do not begin by being impertinent myself, I shall soon grow afraid of him" (15).

Thus, the contest between Elizabeth and Darcy, unlike the usual battle of the sexes plot, begins with her genuine dislike of him. At their second encounter, when Sir William Lucas tries to promote a partnership between them in the dance, Elizabeth refuses, and responds to Darcy's effort to recover the situation from Sir William's ineptitude by saying, "Mr. Darcy is all politeness" (17), a piece of acidulated irony that unfortunately none but Elizabeth and the reader can enjoy. Typically, however, as Elizabeth fails to realize how Darcy's opinion of her is changing, Darcy also fails to understand how Elizabeth's ironic independence is motivated partly by antipathy.

When they are thrown together at Bingley's house by Jane's illness, we find that they are not bickering like Benedick and Beatrice, but simply working and thinking at cross-purposes, like a comic Lovelace and Clarissa. Darcy has no idea how suspicious Elizabeth is of his arrogant aloofness, while she has no idea how intrigued he is becoming by her "fine eyes." Elizabeth first enters the skirmishing to defend Bingley from the criticisms of his friend. Moreover, when Bingley remarks that she has only changed what Darcy had said about his weakness of will "into a compliment on the sweetness of [his] temper," she responds, "Would Mr. Darcy then consider the rashness of your original intention as atoned for by your obstinacy in adhering to it?" (33) Bingley himself is befuddled, and leaves it up to Darcy, who, of course, is much too intelligent to be taken in by Elizabeth's rhetorical trick of casting the argument in heavily loaded terms like "rashness" and "obstinacy." But he can only answer in a rather ponderous fashion about "propriety" and "understanding," which allows Elizabeth to point out that he has overlooked the claims of "friendship and affection." Both are right in their different ways. Bingley is both impressionable and flighty, as Darcy claims, and Darcy likewise sees through Bingley's effort to make his slovenly letter-writing into a virtue. On the other hand, as Elizabeth sees, Darcy has momentarily forgotten that there is virtue in complying with the wishes of a friend. Brought up short by her, he doubtless could, if Bingley had not interrupted, have worked out his precise claims of "friendship and affection." But even that would miss the real point, his humorless and overbearing preachiness. If Darcy has seen through Bingley, Elizabeth has at least partly seen through Darcy.

A short time later, Elizabeth notices "how frequently Mr. Darcy's eyes were fixed on her," but concludes only that he considered her somehow "reprehensible." She is thus startled (though the reader is not) when he suggests they dance a reel while Miss Bingley plays "a lively Scotch air." She refuses in terms that make clear her suspicion of his motives—"You wanted me, I know, to say 'Yes,' that you might have the pleasure of despising me" (35)—but fails to affront him because the "mixture of sweetness and archness in her manner ... made it difficult for her to affront anybody" (35). For his part, "Darcy had never been so bewitched by any woman as he was by her" (35). Though sounding enough like an ordinary romantic love story, so that the reader can now look forward to the ultimate resolution in marriage, the story really explores their mistaken judgments. Elizabeth, blinded by prejudice, misses the possibility that Darcy could have changed his mind. Fortunately, her "mixture of sweetness and archness," both facial expression and general body language, mitigate any rudeness in her response. She is, after all, neither arrogant nor vain, but rather a nice, warm-hearted, intelligent young woman, who wants to be loved and appreciated the same as any other human being—on the right terms. But she is really as lost as Darcy, or more so. He knows, or is coming to know, what he wants. Still far from such knowledge, Elizabeth pushes ahead, daring him to try and get the better of her in a battle of wits, and thereby following by accident the design most likely to win his heart.

Their next verbal encounter illustrates this unknowing and accidental strategy even more vividly. Darcy has suggested that Miss Bingley and Elizabeth are walking about the room mainly to show off their figures, but when Elizabeth suggests they tease him back and Miss Bingley refuses, she protests that being exempt from teasing is an "uncommon advantage" which she hopes remains uncommon. Darcy responds, from the height of his superiority, that "the wisest and best of men ... may be rendered ridiculous by a person whose first object in life is a joke." Elizabeth is not awed by this sentence: "I hope I never ridicule what is wise or good. Follies and nonsense, whims and inconsistencies *do* divert me, I own, and I laugh at them whenever I can.—But these, I suppose, are precisely what you are without" (50–1).

Darcy has tried to do back to her what she has done to him, put the opponents on the defensive, make them explain, backtrack, bluster, excuse themselves. But she is too fast for him. When he tries to recast the argument in terms of the frivolous and the wise, she readily explains the seriousness, and thus wisdom, of being satirical at the expense of folly and nonsense, and then once more puts him on the defensive by assuming that he has thus characterized himself as altogether wise and good. His response is significant for what it reveals about him and his need for Elizabeth: "Perhaps that is not possible for any one. But it has been the study of my life to avoid those weaknesses which often expose a strong understanding to ridicule" (51). While wishing not to go overboard—that is, into Darcyism—one can see the problem of the man very clearly. No one would dispute the worthiness of a program of avoiding blamable weaknesses, but Darcy has adopted a rather skewed value system in pursuit of it. Rather than avoiding doing harm to others or to his own moral standing, he merely wishes to avoid ridicule for looking foolish. That is manifestly impossible. We are all fools, and wise only to the degree that we recognize our folly. But Darcy is so full of his self-conceit as a man of stature and wisdom that he has forgotten it.

Elizabeth, who has the same problem, overconfidence in her judgments, immediately seizes on the key point: Darcy's self-satisfaction about avoiding weaknesses. She responds, "Such as vanity and pride." Once more he is forced to justify himself, and the justification he offers is still more telling: "Yes, vanity is a weakness of mind indeed. But pride—where there is real superiority of mind, pride will always be under good regulation." To this Elizabeth responds by hiding a smile. If her mind is not superior to Darcy's, her insight certainly is. Thus, when Miss Bingley re-enters the conversation to ask the result of Elizabeth's "examination of Mr. Darcy," she can offer one of the perfect touches in all of literature: "I am perfectly convinced by it that Mr. Darcy has no defect. He owns it himself without disguise" (51).

Darcy, of course, has not said exactly that, but has come close enough to it to make the exaggeration very just. If you do not want to be accused of thinking yourself faultless, you must go much farther than Darcy has into the depressing swamp of self-inspection, where no gentleman wishes to go. Half of Elizabeth's success, however, lies in the way she phrases her insight. If she only pounced on his remarks and accused him of conceit, he could ignore her as merely rude, and dispose of her remarks with the self-assured logic he generally displays. By agreeing with his "claim" of faultlessness she attributes the insight to him-yet with an irony that is expertly phrased. To a humorless arguer of Darcy's sort, this attack can scarcely be met, for the second sentence is an irony worthy of Swift, pretending to praise him for courage and forthrightness when it actually refers to his smugness and vanity.

As Darcy tries to reassert his mastery of the situation, he reveals more of his patronizing attitude toward mere mortals, and falls into another trap by concluding: "My good opinion once lost is lost for ever." Elizabeth promptly seizes this point, identifies it as "implacable resentment," and admits that she cannot possibility laugh at such a failing (51). Elizabeth's responses, generated partly by self-defense and partly by antipathy, constitute precisely the right strategy to win his heart. Caroline Bingley has no clue as to how to deal with him, and her efforts to be ingratiating annoy him, while those to be fashionable and witty merely expose her limitations. Attacked for his smug vanity, Darcy is left astonished. A man in Darcy's position can hardly be too careful: short of murder or abject flight, he has few options in regard to a woman like Elizabeth except marriage. He cannot hope to shut her up, of course, but at least he could make her his ally.

And this he eventually does, though not before he offers his condescending proposal, is bitterly refused, and justifies himself by revealing the humiliating (to her) truth about Wickham. Over the variety of episodes that follow we see Elizabeth blaming herself for her pride and prejudice, but late discover that Darcy has also reevaluated his own attitudes and behavior, and now can perform an appropriately heroic deed in finding and buying off Wickham. As a result, when they do at last achieve that "understanding" for which the reader becomes so impatient, Elizabeth's joy causes the normal bubbliness of her temper to turn almost into giddiness. She begins an inquisition on how he came to love her, and supplies most of the answers herself, correcting his "liveliness of ... mind" to "impertinence" (319). Nevertheless, her view is typically accurate: "The fact is you were sick of civility, of deference, of officious attention. You were disgusted with the women who were always speaking and looking and thinking for your approbation alone. I roused, and interested you, because I was so unlike *them*" (319–20). Darcy is wise enough to realize that he needs Elizabeth to make him what he wishes to be, that she represents the other half of himself—demonstrably affectionate where he is cool and distant, effervescent where he is serious, yet his match in intelligence—his Anima, but the key to his completion as a human being. But she can only do this by being as complete, and intellectually powerful, a person as himself. She must find her own completion in him, a little more judgment and restraint, and, more than anything, a sober and intelligent appreciation for the woman she can be.

With the marriage of Elizabeth and Darcy we reach the end of our investigation of the witty heroine in romantic comedy. No author has, I believe, ever explored the psychological and literary potential of this figure as profoundly as Austen. Even Millamant, even Rosalind, wonderful as they are, pale in comparison. Moreover, we can also see why the character is not attempted more often—not, I believe, because of antagonism to her on the part of some male power structure, but simply because she is very difficult to bring off well. For the romance to work she must have a powerful character, an inner self that is worth exploring, that we can view in heroic terms, and that can make the idea of Love profound instead pedestrian. For the comedy" to work, she must be lighthearted yet true, able to provide a point of stability in the conflict of societies or ideals that interferes with the marriages that will form the new society. But at the same time, she must be a wit, an intelligent, insightful, and verbally skillful person who can express truths vividly. It is a rare author (male or female) who can bring off such a character (male or female). But when we find one, we should enjoy her to the fullest, just as the authors clearly did.

WORKS CITED

Auburn, Mark S. "Introduction" to John Dryden, *Marriage a la Mode*. Regents Restoration Drama Series. Lincoln: University of Nebraska Press, 1981.

Austen, Jane. *Pride and Prejudice*. New York: New American Library, 1961.

Babb, Howard S. *Jane Austen's Novels: The Fabric of Their Dialogue*. Columbus: Ohio State University Press, 1962; reptd. New York: Archon, 1967.

Barber, C. L. *Shakespeare's Festive Comedy*. Princeton: Princeton University Press, 1959.

Beaurline, L. A. "General Introduction" and "Introductions" to *Secret Love* and *Marriage a la Mode*, in John Dryden, *Four Comedies*, eds. L. A. Beaurline and Fredson Bowers, Curtain Playwrights Series. Chicago: University of Chicago Press, 1967.

Birdsall, Virginia Ogden. *Wild Civility: The English Comic Spirit on the Restoration Stage*. Bloomington: Indiana University Press, 1970.

Braverman. Richard. "Capital Relations and *The Way of the World*." *ELH* 52 (Spring 1985) 133–158.

Bruce, Donald. *Topics of Restoration Comedy*. New York: St. Martin's, 1974.

Congreve, William. *The Way of the World*, ed. Kathleen M. Lynch. Regents Restoration Drama Series. Lincoln: University of Nebraska Press, 1965.

Craik, W. A. *Jane Austen: the Six Novels*. London: Methuen, 1965.

Donaldson, Ian. *The World Upside Down*. Oxford: Clarendon, 1970.

Dryden. John. *Four Comedies*, eds. L. A. Beaurline and Fredson Bowers. Curtain Playwrights Series. Chicago: University of Chicago Press, 1967.

Erickson, Peter. *Patriarchal Structures in Shakespeare's Drama*. Berkeley: University of California Press, 1985.

Ewin, R. E. "Pride, Prejudice and Shyness." *Philosophy*. 65 (April 90): 137–54.

Foakes, R. A. "Wit and Convention in Congreve" in Bernard Morns, ed., *William Congreve*. Totowa, NJ: Rowan & Littlefield, 1974.

Frye, Northrop. *Anatomy of Criticism*. Princeton: Princeton University Press, 1957.

Gilbert, Sandra M., and Susan Gubar, eds. *The Madwoman in the Attic*. New Haven: Yale University Press, 1979.

Heilman, Robert B. "Parts and Whole in *Pride and Prejudice*," in *Jane Austen: Bicentenary Essays*, ed. John Halperin. Cambridge: Cambridge University Press, 1975, 123–43.

Holland, Norman N. *The First Modern Comedies*. Cambridge: Harvard University Press, 1959.

Jung, C. G., and M.-L. von Franz, eds. *Man and His Symbols*. New York: Dell, 1964.

Kroeber, Karl. "*Pride and Prejudice*: Fiction's Lasting Novelty," in *Jane Austen: Bicentenary Essays*, ed. John Halperin. Cambridge: Cambridge University Press, 1975, 144–55

Kroll, Richard W. F. "Discourse and Power in *The Way of the World*." *ELH* 53 (Winter 1986) 727–58.

Leggatt, Alexander. *Shakespeare's Comedy of Love*. London: Methuen, 1973.

MacCary, W. Thomas. *Friends and Lovers: The Phenomenology of Desire in Shakespearean Comedy*. New York: Columbia University Press, 1985

Muir, Kenneth. *The Comedy of Manners*. London: Hutchinson, 1970.

———. "The Comedies of William Congreve," in *Restoration Theatre*, eds. John Russell Brown and Bernard Harris. New York: Capricorn, 1967, 221–237.

Mueschke, Paul, and Miriam. *A New View of Congreve*. Ann Arbor: University of Michigan Press, 1958.

Nevo, Ruth. *Comic Transformations in Shakespeare*. London: Methuen, 1980.

Newman, Karen. "Can This Marriage be Saved: Jane Austen Makes Sense of an Ending." *ELH* 50 (Winter 1983): 693–70.

Newton, Judith Lowder. *Women, Power and Subversion*. Athens: University of Georgia Press, 1985.

Ornstein, Robert. *Shakespeare's Comedies*. Newark: University of Delaware Press, 1986.

Park, Clara Claiborne. "As We Like It: How a Girl Can be Smart and Still Popular." *The American Scholar* 42 (Spring 1973): 262–78; rev. and rptd. in Carolyn Ruth Swift Lenz, Gayle Green, and Carol Thomas Neely, eds., *The Woman's Part: A Feminist Criticism of Shakespeare*. Urbana: University of Illinois Press, 1980, 100–116.

Roberts, Phillip. "Mirabell and Restoration Comedy," in *William Congreve*, ed. Bernard Morris. Totowa, NJ: Rowan & Littlefield, 1974.

Shaffer, Julie. "Not Subordinate: Empowering Women in the Marriage Plot—the Novels of Frances Burney, Maria Edgeworth, and Jane Austen." *Criticism* 34 (Winter 1992): 51–73.

Shakespeare, William. *As You Like It*, rev. ed., eds. Irving Ribner and George Lyman Kittredge. Waltham, MA: Ginn, 1941, 1971.

Smith, John Harrington. *The Gay Couple in Restoration Comedy*. Cambridge: Harvard University Press, 1948; rptd. New York: Octagon, 1971.

Snider, Alvin. "Professing a Libertine in *The Way of the World*." *Papers on Language and Literature* 25 (Fall 1989): 376–97.

Van Voris, W. H. *The Cultivated Stance*. Dublin: Dolmen, 1970.

Williams, Aubrey L. *An Approach to Congreve*. New Haven: Yale University Press, 1979.

Wiesenfarth, Joseph. "The Case of Pride and Prejudice." *Studies in the Novel*, 16 (Fall 1984): 261–73.

GLORIA SYBIL GROSS

Wit With a Vengeance:
Pride and Prejudice

T he sublime artistry and psychological acuity of *Pride and Prejudice*, a project first begun in 1796 and revised several times before its publication in 1813,[1] resonates with Johnsonian accents. Austen's famous first line, which introduces the theme of the marriage-go-round and whets the bite of wit, leaps straight from the pages of Mr. Rambler's files on marriage and courtship. In *Rambler* 115, Hymenaeus, an aggrieved young bachelor, who becomes a featured correspondent, frets and complains:

> I was known to possess a fortune, and to want a wife; and therefore was frequently attended by these hymeneal solicitors, with whose importunity I was sometimes diverted, and sometimes perplexed; for they contended for me as vulturs for a carcase; each employed all his eloquence, and all his artifices, to enforce and promote his own scheme, from the success of which he was to receive no other advantage than the pleasure of defeating others equally eager, and equally industrious. (Yale *Works*, IV, 248)

Hymenaeus relates a series of blistering entanglements with unabashed gold diggers, whose sole object was to snare him and his money. To play fair,

From *In a Fast Coach with a Pretty Woman: Jane Austen and Samuel Johnson.* ©2002 by AMS Press.

Mr. Rambler offers the misadventures of wealthy Tranquilla, a female counterpart, likewise hounded by panting young louts. Austen opens *Pride and Prejudice* in tribute to Johnson's raucous satire on matchmaking and the dogged-minded, money-grubbing bourgeoisie:

> It is a truth universally acknowledged, that a single man in possession of a good fortune, must be in want of a wife.
>
> However little known the feelings or views of such a man may be on his first entering a neighbourhood, this truth is so well fixed in the minds of the surrounding families, that he is considered as the rightful property of some one or other of their daughters. (*PP*, vol. 1, chap. 1; Austen *Works*, II, 3)

Hailing directly from Johnson, the satire scintillates with the debacle of civilized aggressiveness. Its savagery and rapid-fire repartee set the parameters for this, Austen's most celebrated work of fiction, from narrative to characterization to social commentary.

If in *Pride and Prejudice*, Austen first pays homage to Johnson, her ideal heroine, Elizabeth Bennet, has a notable precursor in a story written by Johnson honoring Mrs. Thrale. "The Fountains: A Fairy Tale" originally appeared in Anna Williams's *Miscellanies in Prose and Verse* (1766) and, between 1766 and 1791, was reprinted in eight popular periodicals.[2] Its heroine, Floretta, represents the young Mrs. Thrale, whom Johnson compliments at the beginning of their long-abiding friendship.[3] As reward for a kindness, Floretta is bestowed magical powers and shown two fountains, one of joy, the other of sorrow: to drink from the first grants her fondest desire; to drink from the second retracts it. Wishing, by turns, for drop-dead gorgeousness, a perfect lover, empowerment, riches, wit, and longevity, Floretta tries them, but unhappily revokes them, hopes dashed and disillusioned. All except for wit, which proves a hazardous bonus. A "wit for life," she cannot restrain a fierce and lively imagination: "She felt new successions of imagery rise in her mind.... She now saw that almost every thing was wrong, without often seeing how it could be better; and frequently imputed to the imperfection of art these failures which were caused by the limitation of nature" (Yale *Works*, XVI, 244). She launches a one-woman crusade to expose vice and folly, becoming a formidable *persona non grata*: "As every deformity of character made a strong impression upon her, she could not always forbear to transmit it to others; as she hated false appearances, she thought it her duty to detect them, till, between wantonness and virtue, scarce any that she knew escaped without some wounds by the shafts of ridicule" (XVI, 245–46). Johnson stresses that Floretta's character is generous and good, that she "honoured virtue where she laughed at affectation," but she brandishes a scourge to polite society. Defying social convention, talking boldly to men, pillorying knaves and fools, she is both an object and a reckonable force of belligerence.

For a heart of gold welded to an incorrigibly satiric disposition, Austen's Elizabeth Bennet bears a striking resemblance to Johnson's Floretta, undaunted humorist and truth-teller. In her beloved character, the author captures the combative spirits of "my dear Mrs. Piozzi" and Johnson,[4] as well as her own temperamental affinity to them. Writing to Cassandra at the novel's publication, she anxiously awaits the verdict on Elizabeth: "I must confess that I think her as delightful a creature as ever appeared in print, and how I shall be able to tolerate those who do not like *her* at least I do not know" (Austen *Letters*, 29 January 1813, 297, no. 76). Doubtless her unease grew from the streak of aggressiveness that might be construed as ill-tempered and shrewish (Miss Bingley's opinion), in short, unladylike. To a culture shaped by male supremacy, an outspoken woman poses an alarming, troublesome prospect. Resoluteness of thought, and a powerful ratiocinative intellect, capped by a mastery of the pugilistic arts of satire, are farthest from a woman's province. But not for Johnson. Championing the independent ambition of many, supporting and advancing their writing careers, he clearly respected educated women and their deliberate variation from the mold. On Johnson's authority, Austen draws an unforgettable portrait, sanctioned and sustained by his unorthodox backing of spirited femininity. In Elizabeth, she fuses an almost warlike, retaliatory wit, a taste for verbal assault, with an unslakable appetite for laughter and amusement.

As we have seen, Austen found abundant accounts of Johnson's pure zest for fun. Recalls Mrs. Thrale: "He used to say, 'that the size of a man's understanding might always be justly measured by his mirth,' and his own was never contemptible. He would laugh at a stroke of genuine humour, or sudden sally of odd absurdity, as heartily and freely as I ever yet saw any man; and though the jest was often such as few felt besides himself, yet his laugh was irresistible."[5] That he saluted wit and wit-makers and strove himself for accolades was frequently witnessed in company. Boswell observes a favorite pastime, that "he talked for victory": "One of Johnson's principal talents ... was shewn in maintaining the wrong side of an argument, and in splendid perversion of the truth.... He had ... all his life habituated himself to consider conversation as a trial of intellectual vigour and skill; and to this, I think, we may venture to ascribe that unexampled richness and brilliancy which appeared in his own."[6] And, summing up the best recollections of his traveling companion at the beginning of the *Journal of a Tour to the Hebrides*: "He united a most logical head with a most fertile imagination, which gave him an extraordinary advantage in arguing; for he could reason close or wide, as he saw best for the moment. He could, when he chose it, be the greatest sophist that ever wielded a weapon in the schools of declamation."[7]

Presumably felled more than once by Johnson gone ballistic, fellow club member Oliver Goldsmith declares, "There is no arguing with Johnson; for when his pistol misses fire, he knocks you down with the butt end of it."[8] To mix it up with Johnson, one must have proceeded at his own risk. Taking on all comers, answering blow for blow, boldly on the offensive, he thrived on a hard contest. "Well," he once said after a lively dinner party, "we had a good talk." "Yes, Sir," said his companion sardonically, "you tossed and gored several persons."[9] This fighting spirit also accords with the notorious droll reflection to Mrs. Thrale that he loved a "good hater."[10] Shades of Elizabeth Bennet? Here indeed is a woman after his own heart in a story aglow with hot tempers and a heroine almost always called to arms. Elizabeth must use all her arts to outflank the enmity of fools, bald-faced insolence, even defection by reputed allies. And sometimes she argues just to argue. Her field of action is the parlor room and weapon of choice, wit with a vengeance. As she informs Mr. Darcy, "There is a stubbornness about me that never can bear to be frightened at the will of others. My courage always rises with every attempt to intimidate me." Hinting at the "talk for victory," he retorts, "You find great enjoyment in occasionally professing opinions which in fact are not your own" (vol. 2, chap. 8; Austen *Works*, II,174). A veritable slug-fest, *Pride and Prejudice* creates an arena for Austen to draw strategic battlelines reminiscent of Johnson's, in the very sort of competition they both relished.

That Elizabeth is a good hater informs her every instinct. In a world rife with bluff and bluster and withering presumption, wit is almost a condition of survival. Royally snubbed from the start by the superbly arrogant Mr. Darcy, she dodges the insult adroitly. At the assembly ball, others would have perished by the tall, handsome, rich stranger's rude rebuff: "he looked for a moment at Elizabeth, till catching her eye, he withdrew his own and coldly said, 'She is tolerable; but not handsome enough to tempt *me*; and I am in no humour at present to give consequence to young ladies who are slighted by other men'" (vol. 1, chap. 3; II, 12). But Elizabeth knows a horse's ass when she sees one and immediately rallies. Summoned to the fore, she begins telling the story "with great spirit among her friends; for she had a lively, playful disposition, which delighted in any thing ridiculous" (II, 12). From this moment, she launches a robust, relentless campaign, spurred on by renewed anger and provocation. At every opportunity, she mocks, taunts, and belittles the man unmercifully. Pressing forward a longstanding acrimonious engagement, she settles only at last for a wedding engagement. Mr. Darcy's magical transformation from horse's ass to Sir Galahad enables another heroine's negotiated truce: letting go her rage, she acquires prodigious wealth and status. Moreover, Austen draws the tantalizing interplay between aggression and sexuality, how one impulse may gain, then lose, ascendancy over the other. But first, to Elizabeth's glorious rage.

Determined on visiting sister Jane, confined with a cold at Mr. Bingley's estate, Elizabeth endures many a round in bouts with awesome stupidity. Mrs. Bennet's hairbrained scheme to send Jane in the rain on horseback, obliging an overnight stay, nearly backfires when Jane takes ill. Braving bad weather, let alone the anticipated snootiness of her hosts, Elizabeth walks three miles one morning to create a sensation in the breakfast parlor. Ushered through the door with dirty stockings and a red face, she is greeted with stares aghast, as Mrs. Hurst is so good as to observe, "She really looked almost wild" (vol. 1, chap. 8; II, 35). Her mother's subsequent visit makes things go from bad to worse. Checking her daughter's friendly banter with Mr. Bingley, she scolds her before *tout le monde*: "Lizzy ... remember where you are, and do not run on in the wild manner that you are suffered to do at home" (vol. 1, chap. 9; II, 42).

Performing to such a crowd, Elizabeth indeed seems wild, and her unconventional behavior causes more than a little unease and antipathy. Mrs. Bennet just does not understand, while the Hursts and Miss Bingley vaguely do, and piqued by envy and resentment, they rarely miss a grimace or a mean-spirited dig. In an altogether different vein, Mr. Darcy tackles Elizabeth apparently because he never met an unsubservient, tough-minded woman. Presumably bored at first, he baits her at Netherfield, and she, bored to distraction, rises to the occasion. Alluding doubtless to cavorting at the late assembly ball, he snickers during a pianoforte recital: "Do not you feel a great inclination, Miss Bennet, to seize, such an opportunity of dancing a reel?" Brushed off, he takes another jab, when she deftly parries: "You wanted me, I know, to say 'Yes,' that you might have the pleasure of despising my taste, but I always delight in overthrowing those kind of schemes, and cheating a person of their premeditated contempt. I have therefore made up my mind to tell you, that I do not want to dance a reel at all—and now despise me if you dare." Now startled and disarmed, he holds off, "Indeed I do not dare" (vol. 1, chap. 10; II, 52).

Here begins in earnest Elizabeth and Darcy's fire-and-ice relationship, which mingles eroticism and aggression, at once in opposition and interaction. Austen explains the play of contradictory feelings: "Elizabeth, having rather expected to affront him, was amazed at his gallantry; but there was a mixture of sweetness and archness in her manner which made it difficult for her to affront anybody; and Darcy had never been so bewitched by any woman as he was by her" (vol. 1, chap. 10; II, 52). The mutual engagement of powerful urges, love and hate, makes them irresistible to each other. Clearly projecting but hardly missing the mark, she hurls the accusation: "*Your* defect is a propensity to hate every body," and he sidesteps: "And *yours* ... is wilfully to misunderstand them" (II, 58). While Darcy gives ground much earlier, it is Elizabeth's hard and fast hostility on which Austen shrewdly zeroes in. Almost to the last, she struggles not just with Darcy, but with her own turbulent feelings. The verbal sparring, the "talk for victory," follows Johnson's uproarious tradition, boosting the odds with man and woman as equal adversaries. The ultimately civilized peace offering goes to the winner, whose identity Austen, ever coy in such matters, leaves pending.

At the Netherfield ball, Elizabeth is besieged once more by Mr. Darcy, as well as by her cousin, that stupendous stooge, Mr. Collins, and she rises bravely to the occasion. In the course of two dances, she prods Darcy to more and more ridiculous hauteur. Precisely on target, she volleys a backhanded compliment: "I have always seen a great similarity in the turn of our minds.—We are each of an unsocial, taciturn disposition, unwilling to speak, unless we expect to say something that will amaze the whole room, and be handed down to posterity with all the eclat of a proverb" (vol. 1, chap. 18; II, 91). The subject of the charming reprobate, Mr. Wickham, scores a coup de grâce, but Darcy is soon revived by the lunacies of the Bennet family in all its splendor. Mrs. Bennet's loud whispers about Bingley's fortune, Mary's deplorable singing, Mr. Collins's bowing and scraping, restore his high and mightiness and, to Elizabeth's dismay, "the expression of his face changed gradually from indignant contempt to a composed and steady gravity" (vol. 1, chap. 18; II, 100).

Subsequent events prove more unlucky. Elizabeth needs bear Mr. Collins's galling marriage proposal and her best friend Charlotte Lucas's acceptance of him, as well as the mortification of Bingley's abandoning Jane, a setback clearly instigated by Darcy. Consoling her temperamentally mild sister, she, by contrast, turns cross and bitter, scattering rage in all directions: "The more I see of the world, the more am I dissatisfied with it; and every day confirms my belief of the inconstancy of all human characters, and of the little dependence that can be placed on the appearance of either merit or sense" (vol. 2, chap. 1; II, 135). It is a low point, and she repeats the cynicism to Aunt Gardiner in London, on the way to Hunsford and the newly wed Mr. and Mrs. Collins. Brooding on her former favorite, Mr. Wickham, and his fast retreat for richer spoils, she dismisses men in general, "I am sick of them all. Thank Heaven! I am going tomorrow where I shall find a man who has not one agreeable quality, who has neither manner nor sense to recommend him. Stupid men are the only ones worth knowing, after all" (vol. 2, chap. 4; II, 154). Perceiving the "disappointment" behind her niece's raillery, good

Aunt Gardiner proposes a summer's pleasure tour. With that prospect, Elizabeth is braced with "fresh life and vigour." She will need it for what awaits at Rosings Park: another round with Darcy, seconded by his aunt, that inimitable dragonness, Lady Catherine De Bourgh.

Mr. Collins's patroness, Lady Catherine, represents a mad caricature of the nephew. An insufferable snob, she reeks money and status, issuing cranky dispensations and meddling tactlessly in other people's affairs. For Austen, Johnson's episode with Lord Chesterfield, would-be patron of the *Dictionary*, offers a wry lesson in tangling with pride of place. The story goes that Chesterfield, promising to support him through the project (which took nine years) apparently forgot or ignored his distressed protégé. At the publication of the *Dictionary* in 1755, however, Chesterfield was not remiss in taking credit, an outrage that prompted Johnson's famous letter etched in acid. In it, he mocks "favours from the great" and spurns officious overture: "Is not a patron, My Lord, one who looks with unconcern on a man struggling for life in the water and when he has reached ground encumbers him with help."[11] In "The Vanity of Human Wishes," enumerating evils that befall the aspirant to learning, he lists patronage among the worst: "There mark what ills the scholar's life assail, / Toil, envy, want, the patron, and the jail" (Yale *Works*, VI, 99, II, 159–60). Surely Lady Catherine lends new ghastliness to the meaning of patron. A burlesque of Darcy, she proves, as Elizabeth archly observes much later, "of infinite use, which ought to make her happy, for she loves to be of use" (vol. 3, chap. 18; Austen *Works*, II, 381).

Perhaps Mr. Collins's character also originates in part from Johnsonian sources, to wit, Fanny Burney's priceless takeoff on Boswell: "He had an odd mock solemnity of tone and manner, that he acquired imperceptibly from constantly thinking of and imitating Dr. Johnson."[12] In company, she relates how he hangs in rapture at the great one's every intonation:

> In truth when he met with Dr. Johnson, he commonly forbore even answering anything that was said, or attending to anything that went forward, lest he should miss the smallest sound from that voice to which he paid such exclusive, though merited homage. But the moment that voice burst forth, the attention which it excited in Mr. Boswell amounted almost to pain. His eyes goggled with eagerness; he leant his ear almost on the shoulder of the Doctor; and his mouth dropt open to catch every syllable that might be uttered: nay he seemed not only to dread losing a word, but to be anxious not to miss a breathing; as if hoping from it, latently, or mystically, some information.[13]

While such narrow scenes escape Johnson's notice, owing to nearsightedness, as Dr. Burney suspects, he frequently treats his principal hanger-on "as a schoolboy, whom, without the smallest ceremony, he pardoned or rebuked."[14]

Re-creating that hilarity, Austen skewers and roasts Mr. Collins and carves him in Boswell's image. Well-read in Burney, and surely in the diary entries touching on Johnson, she captures every fawning pose and pretention. An irrepressible toady, it is Boswell come to life: "Mr. Collins was eloquent in her [Lady Catherine's] praise. The subject elevated him to more than usual solemnity of manner, and, with a most important aspect he protested that he had never in his life witnessed such behaviour in a person of rank—such affability and condescension" (vol. 1, chap. 14; II, 66). Like the original, he is "altogether a mixture of pride and obsequiousness, self-importance and humility" (vol. 1, chap. 15; II, 70). At Rosings, he presides at the foot of the table, looking "as if he felt life could furnish nothing greater" (vol. 2, chap. 6; II, 70), while at the head, Lady Catherine barks orders and gloats. At Netherfield, he truckles to Mr. Darcy, forcing an introduction, while the latter "was eying him with unrestrained wonder" (vol. 1, chap. 18; II, 98). Like Johnson, who was "often irritated by the officious importunity of Mr. Boswell,"[15] but unlike Lady Catherine, Darcy is no glad sufferer of fools.

In an act of impulse, Mr. Darcy proposes marriage to Elizabeth, but his heart is not really in it. Wavering desperately between eros and aggression, he presses for hard mastery as well as for sexual gratification. Aping Lady Catherine, who exults in appropriating the rights of others, he makes love with an air of imperious privilege. In this, he apes another comic foil, the graceless Mr. Collins. Ludicrously out of time and place, Darcy's proposal parodies the ancient custom of the droit du seigneur, a claim by the feudal lord of the manor to have sex with the vassal's bride. (Mr. Collins, heir to Longbourn, also intends to have one of the Miss Bennets, but he is not particular). Elizabeth correctly interprets her lover's motive and reels from the insult. It takes all of her keen wit and militant rage to take him down in a high-stakes game of demolition.

At Rosings, Lady Catherine sets the stage for Elizabeth's triumph when, shamelessly bullying her guests, she pries, pontificates, and heaps abuse upon abuse. For one visitor at least, the evenings are a strenuous exercise in forbearance. Elizabeth does a slow burn at her hostess's interrogation and grandstanding beneficence. What for ever-groveling Mr. Collins is "all affability and condescension" (vol. 2, chap. 5; II, 157), for Elizabeth is sheer effrontery. Lady Catherine's bounty consists in hand-me-down concessions, like the offer of an old pianoforte temporarily for her guest's use: "I have told

Miss Bennet several times, that she will never play really well, unless she practices more; and though Mrs. Collins has no instrument, she is very welcome, as I have often told her, to come to Rosings every day, and play on the piano forte in Mrs. Jenkinson's room. She would be in nobody's way, you know, in that part of the house" (vol. 2, chap. 8; II, 173). Elizabeth is as repulsed by the aunt as she was by the nephew and, striking up a friendship with the amiable Colonel Fitzwilliam, she is relieved from harassment by the former two. It is through Colonel Fitzwilliam that she discovers Darcy's certain part in her sister's unhappy romance, how he all but vetoed the match. Ironically the Colonel, much attracted to Elizabeth and regretting an impossible attachment, speaks discreetly of deference to wealth and social position in marriage. In doing so, he unwittingly discloses cousin Darcy's interference in a friend's affair, where "there were some very strong objections against the lady" (vol. 2, chap. 10, II, 185), namely Jane. Elizabeth swells with righteous indignation. Shortly thereafter, Darcy turns up inamorato.

Like a shot out of the blue, Mr. Darcy's marriage proposal staggers its recipient. Making a rash pitch for supremacy, he alters the rules of the game. Having sported long enough, he strikes while appearing to surrender and moves in for the kill. But he has sorely underestimated his opponent. Elizabeth launches a counteroffensive that brings him to his knees (where, in the first place, a suitor ought to be!) and sinks any last remnant of his asinine self-conceit. In the arena of sexual farce, say in Shakespeare or Restoration comedy, verbal jousting plumbs deeper levels of rage, fear, and repressed sexuality, where erotic and aggressive instincts are often inseparable, at times, indistinguishable. True to form, Elizabeth and Darcy start and blush, grow pale and shaken by each new fusillade of insults and struggle to maintain composure. While his feelings are now published by his declaration and subsequent letter, hers are more hidden and complex. Though anger appears to impel her every move, Austen delves beneath the surface to find a more complicated skein of motives. Like Johnson's, her attention to an inward life is piercing and not to be deflected by the obvious.

In fiction, Johnson selectively praised those characters rendered in depth and penetrating detail. Of the two leading novelists of his generation, he preferred Samuel Richardson, as Mrs. Thrale notes, for "Richardson had picked the kernel of life (he said), while [Henry] Fielding was contented with the husk."[16] Boswell also registers the partiality: "In comparing those two writers, he used this expression; 'that there was as great a difference between them as between a man who knew how a watch was made, and a man who could tell the hour by looking on the dial-plate.'"[17] Whatever the subject, his pleasure in reading and writing, as we have seen, was enhanced by an active and vital sounding of human emotion. Invariably he sought out causes and effects not immediately apparent. When Mrs. Thrale once echoed the popular sentiment that Richardson's Clarissa was a perfect character, he disagreed, "On the contrary (said he), you may observe there is always something which she prefers to truth."[18] It was an extraordinary insight, as critics since have demonstrated: the "truth" for Clarissa is her sexual feeling for Lovelace, which she dare not own.[19] Coincidentally, Elizabeth's outrage is mixed with desire. To use Johnson's metaphor, Austen invites us to learn what makes her heroine tick.

Between Colonel Fitzwilliam's dire revelation and Darcy's amorous unmasking, Elizabeth meditates on the series of events that led to Mr. Bingley's walking. Not Jane's fault, she thinks aloud, "Neither could any thing be urged against my father, who, though with some peculiarities, has abilities which Mr. Darcy himself need not disdain, and respectability which he probably never will reach" (vol. 2, chap. 10; II, 186–87). For love of that father, she protects him from well-founded charges of neglect. Mr. Bennet's aloof and satirical disposition, a stalwart defense against disappointment in marriage and domestic life, by and large brings on the family's misfortune, including Jane's unhappiness, Lydia's disgrace, and Elizabeth's worsening alienation. Smug and superior, he meets his wife's and daughters' folly with amused indifference, affecting philosophical resignation. His comic foil is Mary, straining for distinction, who rehearses a "threadbare morality" (vol. 1, chap. 12: II, 60).[20] To Mr. Bennet, his wife's nerves are a joke, her vulgarity diverting, and his daughters' frenzied man-hunt confirms an incorrigible depreciation of women, among people in general. His raillery belies a freaky misogyny, even as he confides to the apple of his eye. Mulling over Jane's desertion, he chuckles, "So, Lizzy ... your sister is crossed in love I find. I congratulate her. Next to being married, a girl likes to be crossed in love a little now and then. It is something to think of, and gives her a sort of distinction among her companions." Then finding an opening for a merry little tussle, father and daughter trade barbed well-wishes:

> "When is your turn to come? You will hardly bear to be long outdone by Jane. Now is your time. Here are officers enough at Meryton to disappoint all the young ladies in the country. Let Wickham be *your* man. He is a pleasant fellow, and would jilt you creditably.
>
> "Thank you, Sir, but a less agreeable man would satisfy me. We must not all expect Jane's good fortune.
>
> "True ... but it is a comfort to think that, whatever of that kind may befal you, you have an affectionate mother who will always make the most of it. (vol. 2, chap. 1; II, 136–38)

The exchange is knowing and intimate, holding a secret shared by the two alone. The sallies back and forth expose the epidemic idiocy of the world, as well as a conspiratorial aversion toward almost everyone in it. Mrs. Bennet, the younger sisters, the Bingley party, Mr. Collins, Mr. Darcy—all afford the symptoms and earn the due measure of heartfelt contempt. Toward each other, the pair vie lovingly for Johnson's accolades to a "good hater." A sly, satirical bearing masks a whole lot of rage. And Elizabeth learned rage at her father's knee. Tutored by a master, she also learned how to put it to best advantage. She prevails with honors over Mr. Darcy and company, beating them at their own surly game. In retrospect, she explains, still jaunty but somewhat shamefaced, to Jane: "I meant to be uncommonly clever in taking so decided a dislike to him, without any reason. It is such a spur to one's genius, such an opening for wit to have a dislike of that kind. One may be continually abusive without saying any thing just; but one cannot be always laughing at a man without now and then stumbling on something witty" (vol. 2, chap. 16; II, 225–26). Her father's daughter, Elizabeth admirably fulfills his principal article of faith, "For what do we live, but to make sport for our neighbours, and laugh at them in our turn?" (vol. 3, chap. 15; II, 364). The occasion for this pronouncement is perhaps her lowest point. Having been chaperoned to Pemberley by fairy-godparents Aunt and Uncle Gardiner and met a late transformed Mr. Darcy, still smitten but subdued, Elizabeth is summoned home. Her family's ignominy (Lydia's elopement), Mr. Darcy's mysterious intercession, Jane and Bingley's even more mysterious reunion, leave her confused and quite alone. Presently Lady Catherine deigns to call, bent on fresh harassment and browbeating, and Mr. Collins's letter arrives to snoop into rumors of pending nuptials. Flummoxed, Mr. Bennet turns his wit in the worst possible direction. Flouting the report of an alliance with Darcy, he takes aim at his beloved daughter: "Mr. Darcy, who never looks at any woman but to see a blemish, and who probably never looked at *you* in his life!" As he waves Elizabeth to join in and gleefully takes inappropriate shot after shot, she is crestfallen: "Never had his wit been directed in a manner so little agreeable to her.... Elizabeth had never been more at a loss to make her feelings appear what they were not. It was necessary to laugh, when she would rather have cried. Her father had most cruelly mortified her, by what he said of Mr. Darcy's indifference, and she could do nothing but wonder at such a want of penetration, or fear that perhaps, instead of his seeing too *little*, she might have fancied too *much*" (II, 363–64). Her beloved father has gone too far.

But has he? If not for Mr. Bennet, Elizabeth could never have hooked and landed Mr. Darcy. Indeed, her father and lover are two of a kind, and she makes three. Standoffish, competitive, addicted to the upper hand, they pose an intriguing triangle. As the two men cross swords for Elizabeth, no wonder Mr. Bennet strikes so desperate and ferocious near the end. The showdown between Darcy and Mr. Bennet takes place, thank heavens, behind closed doors, as the older man relinquishes her to the younger. She passes from one to the other, a natural progression. But before he yields, Austen underscores Mr. Bennet's cri de coeur. Prizing his daughter's spirit, the spit and image of his own, he cautions: "Your lively talents would place you in the greatest danger in an unequal marriage. You could scarcely escape discredit and misery. My child, let me not have the grief of seeing you unable to respect your partner in life" (vol. 3, chap. 7; II, 376). Of course he alludes poignantly to his own marriage.[21]

By numerous venues, Johnson tracks the pitfalls of marriage and courtship, and the gnarly subject fills an entire section of *Rasselas*. A princess with rare perspicuity, Nekayah observes:

> I know not ... whether marriage be more than one of innumerable modes of human misery. When I see and reckon the various forms of connubial infelicity, the unexpected causes of lasting discord, the diversities of temper, the oppositions of opinion, the rude collisions of contrary desire where both are urged by violent impulses, the obstinate contests of disagreeing virtues, where both are supported by consciousness of good intention, I am sometimes disposed to think with the severer casuists of most nations that marriage is rather permitted than approved, and that none, but by the instigation of a passion too much indulged, entangle themselves with indissoluble compacts. (chap. 28, Yale *Works*, XVI, 104)

Rasselas concurs and describes how impetuous appetite leads to lifelong regret: "What can be expected but disappointment and repentance from a choice made in the immaturity of youth, in the ardour of desire, without judgment, without foresight, without enquiry after conformity of opinions, similarity of manners, rectitude of judgment, or purity of sentiment?" With a heavy dose of sarcasm mixed with reproof, not far from Austen's raking Mr. and Mrs. Bennet over the coals, Rasselas conveys Johnson's views on youthful indiscretion:

> Such is the common process of marriage. A youth and maiden, meeting by chance or brought together by artifice, exchange glances, reciprocate civilities, go home, and dream of one another. Having little to divert attention or diversify thought, they find themselves uneasy

when they are apart, and therefore conclude that they shall be happy together. They marry, and discover what nothing but voluntary blindness before had concealed; they wear out life in altercations, and charge nature with cruelty. (chap. 19, Yale *Works*, XVI, 107)

By the same token, Austen gives her heroine a glimpse into the sources of her parents' perversity:

> Had Elizabeth's opinion been all drawn from her own family, she could not have formed a very pleasing picture of conjugal felicity or domestic comfort. Her father captivated by youth and beauty, and that appearance of good humour, which youth and beauty generally give, had married a woman whose weak understanding and illiberal mind, had very early in their marriage put an end to all real affection for her. Respect, esteem, and confidence, had vanished for ever; and all his views of domestic happiness were overthrown.

Foiled by his wife, disenchanted by his household, defeated in the expectation of a son to cut off the entail of his estate, Mr. Bennet converts blighted hopes into vitriol. As the family lurches from disaster to disaster, he perches on the sidelines cheering them to new heights of stellar stupidity. Only the open scandal of Lydia and Wickham brings him forward, but saved by his future son-in-law, he retreats to the library sneering and jeering much the same. While his favorite tries to protect him, she senses the misconduct, which has injured them all:

> Elizabeth, however, had never been blind to the impropriety of her father's behavior as a husband. She had always seen it with pain; but respecting his abilities, and grateful for his affectionate treatment of herself, she endeavoured to forget what she could not overlook, and to banish from her thoughts that continual breach of conjugal obligation and decorum which, in exposing his wife to the contempt of her own children, was so highly reprehensible. But she had never felt so strongly as now, the disadvantages which must attend the children of so unsuitable a marriage, nor ever been so fully aware of the evils arising from so ill judged a direction of talents; talents which rightly used, might at least have preserved the respectability of his daughters, even if incapable of enlarging the mind of his wife. (vol. 2, chap. 19, Austen *Works*, II, 236–37)

No doubt the wretchedness of the Bennets tallies with pathologies galore of many bourgeois families, but scarcely was such wretchedness publicized or even privately owned. Flying in the face of maudlin sops to convention, Johnson's salvo helped make Austen's possible. Indeed she could have fashioned the Bennets after Nekayah's scorching rebuke: "Some husbands are imperious, and some wives perverse; and, as it is always more easy to do evil than good, though the wisdom or virtue of one can very rarely make many happy, the folly or vice of one may often make many miserable" (*Rasselas*, chap. 26; Yale *Works*, XVI, 98). Without reservation, Elizabeth would agree.

For all its celebration of Cinderella romance, *Pride and Prejudice* packs a powerful punch. The neglect, abuse, the wounding disrespect, the tribulation suffered by good characters, all leave indelible marks. (It is no coincidence that they live at *Long-bourn*). Elizabeth puts it succinctly when her mother, prompted to untapped reservoirs of bad taste, falls all over herself at Bingley and Darcy's return. As Mrs. Bennet begins to ballyhoo: "Elizabeth's misery increased, at such unnecessary, such officious attention! Were the same fair prospect to arise at present, as had flattered them a year ago, every thing, she was persuaded, would be hastening to the same vexatious conclusion. At that instant she felt, that years of happiness could not make Jane or herself amends, for moments of such painful confusion." For Jane, Bingley, Darcy, and herself, she is humiliated and has the unwonted impulse to hide: "'The first wish of my heart,' she said to herself, 'is never more to be in company with either of them. Their society can afford no pleasure, that will atone for such wretchedness as this! Let me never see either one or the other again!'" (vol. 3, chap. 11; Austen *Works*, II, 337).

Like a hobgoblin, the specter of humiliation haunts the entire narrative. Damned fools and rogues bedevil almost every honorable, decent influence. Perhaps that is why we are tickled by Mr. Collins, a world-class pain in the derriere, always apologizing. In him and Mrs. Bennet, Austen mixes low cunning with nonsense, the very formula that makes Mr. Bennet a misanthrope. In a testament to bad faith, they specialize in needling ineptitude, too brainless themselves to feel inept. By virtue of his unrivalled toadyism, he thrives at Rosings to await the inheritance of Longbourn where, until that woeful day, Mrs. Bennet does the honors. Neither are Lydia or Wickham really taken down for their selfish, scheming mendacity. Unapologetic gamesters, they make off in quest of new titillation, she à la Lady Susan or Johnson's sex-crazed vixens, he without even the erstwhile chivalry of a Willoughby. Presumably, Lady Catherine will persevere in patronizing and persecuting anyone within stalking distance. Counterfeiters all, they apparently get off scot-free to wreck future havoc. Once more urging a psychological rather than moral-punitive dispensation, Austen defies the customary standards of denouement. Backed by Johnson, she deposes poetic justice once and for all.

Rewards and punishment all the same, Austen gives Mr. Darcy to Elizabeth. No doubt he surpasses the consolation prize offered Marianne Dashwood in *Sense and Sensibility*, the humdrum Colonel Brandon. Following an evolving artistic pattern, Elizabeth too must compromise a strong-willed, passionate nature. A credit to her father, she has manned the battlements and waged the campaign, and talked the "talk for victory," by Johnson's truculent standard. But men are warriors, women keepers of the hearth. By accepting Darcy, Elizabeth yields to civilized expectations and the payoff is sumptuous. Also her mother's daughter, she reveals to Jane, not altogether in jest, the progress of her love: "It has been coming on so gradually, that I hardly know when it began. But I believe I must date it from my first seeing his beautiful grounds at Pemberley" (vol. 3, chap. 17; II, 373). There is more here than meets the eye. Elizabeth is lavishly recompensed for settling into bourgeois domesticity. From the moment she accepts Darcy, Austen promises a delirious pleasure in Mrs. Bennet's reception. Never one to forgo self-expression, the old war horse fulfills all expectation: "Oh my sweetest Lizzie! How rich and how great you will be! What pin-money, what jewels, what carriages you will have! Jane's is nothing to it—nothing at all. I am so pleased—so happy.... A house in town! Every thing that is charming! Three daughters married! Ten thousand a year! Oh Lord! What will become of me. I shall go distracted" (vol. 3, chap. 17; II, 378). Austen generates the deepest irony in that Mrs. Bennet's triumphant vulgarity is the very sort of evil Elizabeth loathes.

Elizabeth marries Darcy, the high representative of all she once detested. Having had a basin full of the Wickhams and the Collinses of this world, she chooses the man who most resembles her father. She means to coast serenely, some would say passively, into a state of wedded bliss. In the tempestuous couple, Austen plays out the clashing propulsions of eros and aggression, a drama later invoked by Freud as humanity's greatest challenge. Civilization requires the taming of brute instinct and the sacrifice of savage goals. Mr. Darcy has already capitulated twice, once reluctantly, once truly, madly, deeply. We can only wish for our fiery, passionate young heroine that she every now and then tap the mad part; though Austen necessarily consigns them to harmony and repose. But not to worry, Mr. Bennet enjoys randomly popping up and taking them by surprise: "He delighted in going to Pemberley, especially when he was least expected" (vol. 3, chap. 19; II, 385). For better or worse, he will be back.

NOTES

1. The history of the composition of *Pride and Prejudice* is still conjectural. Park Honan, *Jane Austen: Her Life* (New York: St. Martin's Press, 1987), provides the general consensus that "[having begun in 1796], we think she reworked her story in 1799 and rewrote it substantially, perhaps on 1802, and yet left something to be done in the months before she sold it to Egerton in November 1812" (308). See John Halperin, *The Life of Jane Austen* (Baltimore: Johns Hopkins University Press, 1984), 66–69, for notable disagreement.

2. See Robert D. Mayo, *The English Novel in the Magazines 1740–1815* (Evanston, IL: Northwestern University Press, 1962), 497, for an account of favorable reviews and publication history.

3. For a full account of Mrs. Thrale's identity in "The Fountains," see Gwin J. Kolb, "Mrs. (Thrale) Piozzi and Dr. Johnson's *The Fountains: A Fairy Tale*," *Novel* 13 (1977), 68–81.

4. Like her affectionate address to "my dear Dr. Johnson" Austen invokes "my dear Mrs. Piozzi" by paying her the tribute of imitation in a droll letter to Cassandra: "I had some thoughts of writing the whole of my letter in her style" (*Jane Austen's Letters to Her Sister Cassandra and Others*, ed. R.W. Chapman, 2nd ed. [London: Oxford University Press, 1952], 11 June 1799, 66, no. 21). Another time, she gaily quotes Mrs. (Thrale) Piozzi, "But all this, as my dear Mrs. Piozzi says, is flight & fancy & nonsense—for my Master has his great casks to mind, & I have my little Children" (Austen *Letters*, JA to Cassandra, 9 December 1808, 66, no. 21), referring to the family's brewing spruce beer while Cassandra is away, presumably minding children.

5. *Johnsonian Miscellanies*, ed. George Birkbeck Hill, 2 vols. (Oxford: Clarendon Press, 1897), II, 344–45.

6. James Boswell, *Life of Samuel Johnson*, ed. George Birkbeck Hill; rev. L.F. Powell, 6 vols. (Oxford: Clarendon Press, 1934–50) IV, 111–12.

7. James Boswell, *Journal of a Tour to the Hebrides, with Samuel Johnson, LL.D.* (1785), ed. R.W. Chapman (London: Oxford University Press, 1970), 170.

8. Boswell, *Life*, II, 100.

9. Ibid., 66.

10. *Johnsonian Miscellanies*, I, 204.

11. Samuel Johnson, *The Letters of Samuel Johnson*, ed. Bruce Redford, 5 vols. (Princeton: Princeton University Press, 1992–94), I, 96, SJ to Lord Chesterfield, 7 February 1755. For an account of Chesterfield's dealings with Johnson, see J.H. Sledd and G.W. Kolb, *Dr. Johnson's Dictionary* (Chicago: University of Chicago Press, 1955), 85–104. See also Paul J. Korshin, "The Johnson–Chesterfield Relationship: A New Hypothesis," *PMLA*, 85 (1970), 247–59.

12. *Dr. Johnson & Fanny Burney Being the Johnsonian Passages from the Works of Mme. D'Arblay*, ed. Chauncey Brewster Tinker (New York: Moffat, Yard & Co., 1911), 221. Tinker suggests the occasion for this diary entry took place Monday, 29 March, 1779.

13. Ibid., 224.

14. Ibid., 222.

15. Ibid., 223.

16. *Johnsonian Miscellanies*, I, 282.

17. Boswell, *Life*, II, 49. See also Johnson's comment to Boswell, "Sir, there is more knowledge of the heart in one letter of Richardson's, than in all 'Tom Jones'" (*Life*, II, 174).

18. Hill, ed. *Johnsonian Miscellanies*, I, 297.

19. See Ian Watt, *The Rise of the Novel* (1957; rpt. Berkeley and Los Angeles: University of California Press, 1971), 228.

20. See Mary's estimable ranking in Donald Greene, "Jane Austen's Monsters," in *Jane Austen: Bicentenary Essays*, ed. John Halperin (Cambridge: Cambridge University Press, 1975), 262–78.

21. For an interesting psychoanalytic view of fathers and mothers in Jane Austen, see Geoffrey Gorer, "The Myth in Jane Austen," in *Art and Psychoanalysis*, ed. William Phillips (New York: Meridian Books, 1963), 218–25.

Character Profile

One of the most famous female characters in English literature, Elizabeth Bennet of Jane Austen's *Pride and Prejudice* is smart, witty, verbally gifted, lively, caring, and moral. At the same time, she is flawed enough to make her seem thoroughly real. She is "not one and twenty" and the second oldest of the Bennet's five daughters. While not a physical beauty, she is remarkable because of her other characteristics.

There is no concrete physical description given of Elizabeth, since most of the events in *Pride and Prejudice* are related from her perspective. The small amount of information we have on Elizabeth's physical characteristics is garnered from dialogue between other characters in the novel. For example, Elizabeth's own mother describes Elizabeth in the first chapter as "not half so handsome as Jane, nor half so good humored as Lydia," only pointing out her second daughter's limitations. Likewise, Mr. Darcy, who only later becomes intent on marrying Elizabeth, initially calls her "tolerable; but not handsome enough to tempt *me*." However, when readers hear these descriptions, they judge them based on their impressions of the characters making the statements.

Mrs. Bennet, for example, throughout the book is seen as foolish and shallow, so we are not surprised at her comment about Elizabeth. Later, though, when she calls Elizabeth headstrong and foolish, her statement has some substance and irony. Mrs. Bennet makes the statement because she believes Elizabeth should not turn down a suitor, not taking into account how thoroughly ill-suited he is for her daughter. Mrs. Bennet's statement is not merely indicative of her lack of understanding or sympathy for her own daughter. This statement, even though Mrs. Bennet is not conscious of it, foreshadows some great truth, for as the novel progresses we see Elizabeth as, in fact, suffering because of her headstrong nature and foolish judgments. Mrs. Bennet's comment is accurate; but for completely different reasons than she realizes.

Similarly, when Mr. Darcy makes his assessment of Elizabeth, it is very early in the book, when he has been acting rather haughty. Later, as his negative characteristics diminish and positive traits are revealed, and as he becomes enchanted with Elizabeth, his description of her is quite different. At that later point he describes her "rendered uncommonly intelligent by the beautiful expression of her dark eyes."

But aside from Darcy, Elizabeth's biggest devotee is her father, Mr. Bennet, who very early in the book talks of his daughters: "They are all silly and ignorant like other girls; but Lizzy has something more of quickness than her sisters." Here and throughout the book we see that Elizabeth is his favorite and that she is most like him; he feeds her pride and offers an escape from her embarassing family. Mr. Bennet is intelligent, observant of people's foibles and continually witty. But Austen takes Elizabeth's character far beyond his, for while Elizabeth has most of her father's traits, unlike her father she is not almost always the outside observer. She also has great feeling for and involvement with a few people she cares about, and she even states, "I hope I never ridicule what is wise or good."

This devotion and care of Elizabeth's are shown when she cautions her good friend Charlotte on marrying for the wrong reasons. Additionally, Elizabeth demonstrates her love for her sister Jane when she immediately goes to Jane at Mr. Bingley's estate when she becomes ill. Not only does the act show Elizabeth's concern, but it clearly shows her disregarding convention, for she walks the three miles to the neighbor's on foot and unaccompanied, something unheard of at the time, because she could not wait for the availability of a horse at Longbourn (the Bennet home).

Other examples of Elizabeth's strong-willed personality occur when she is not only unintimidated by people of great wealth and/or social standing but actually confronts them, as demonstrated by Mr. Darcy's first proposal. Additionally, she does not play the piano so wonderfully well, as women are expected to do, but far outdoes her male partner in the usually male-dominated sport of shooting with a bow and arrow.

Ironically, the very things that Elizabeth prides herself on, her natural intuition and practical judgment, turn out to also be failings with serious consequences when she lets them guide her perception of others. Elizabeth misreads other characters in the novel by letting false information impede her judgment, and when she finally realizes her mistakes, she is crushed, recognizing that what she thought were her strengths have caused so much harm. "'How despicably have I acted!' she cried.—'I, who have prided myself on my discernment!—I, who have valued myself on my abilities! who have often disdained the generous candour of my sister, and gratified my vanity, in useless or blameable distrust.—How humiliating is this discovery!'"

But, being a resilient heroine, Elizabeth works to redeem herself, still appearing human by recognizing her faults and rectifying them as best she can. Indeed, she changes her behavior toward Mr. Darcy when she realizes that she has terribly misjudged him. In fact she is grateful to him, for he has proved himself to be unfailingly generous in arranging Lydia's marriage to Wickham after their shameful elopement, saving the Bennets from disgrace. Realizing he has no "improper pride," Elizabeth falls in love with Mr. Darcy, and agrees to marry him. Elizabeth is finally happy, and we see her unclouded liveliness as she jubilantly declares, "I am happier even than Jane; she only smiles, I laugh."

Contributors

HAROLD BLOOM is Sterling Professor of the Humanities at Yale University and Henry W. and Albert A. Berg Professor of English at the New York University Graduate School. He is the author of over 20 books, including *Shelley's Mythmaking* (1959), *The Visionary Company* (1961), *Blake's Apocalypse* (1963), *Yeats* (1970), *A Map of Misreading* (1975), *Kabbalah and Criticism* (1975), *Agon: Toward a Theory of Revisionism* (1982), *The American Religion* (1992), *The Western Canon* (1994), and *Omens of Millennium: The Gnosis of Angels, Dreams, and Resurrection* (1996). *The Anxiety of Influence* (1973) sets forth Professor Bloom's provocative theory of the literary relationships between the great writers and their predecessors. His most recent books include *Shakespeare: The Invention of the Human* (1998), a 1998 National Book Award finalist, *How to Read and Why* (2000), *Genius: A Mosaic of One Hundred Exemplary Creative Minds* (2002), and *Hamlet: Poem Unlimited* (2003). In 1999, Professor Bloom received the prestigious American Academy of Arts and Letters Gold Medal for Criticism, and in 2002 he received the Catalonia International Prize.

MARVIN MUDRICK was Professor of English and Provost of the College of Creative Studies at the University of California at Santa Barbara. Some of his work is collected in *Mudrick Transcribed: Classes and Talks*, ed. Lance Kaplan. He also published *On Culture and Literature* and *The Man in the Machine*.

ANDREW H. WRIGHT is the author of *Anthony Trollope: Dream & Art*, *Henry Fielding: Mask & Feast*, and *A Reader's Guide to English and American*

Literature. He has also written numerous books on education and/or spirituality.

C.S. LEWIS was Professor of Medieval and Renaissance English at Cambridge University. A prolific author, his most famous titles are *The Screwtape Letters*, *The Chronicles of Narnia*, and *Mere Christianity*.

HENRIETTA TEN HARMSEL is Professor Emeritus of English at Calvin College in Grand Rapids, Michigan. She has translated books of poetry, including the anthology of Dutch Christian poetry, *So Much Sky*.

HOWARD S. BABB was Chair of the Department of English and Comparative Literature at the University of California. He is the author of *The Novels of William Golding: Essays in Stylistic Analysis*.

STUART M. TAVE was Chairman of the Department of English at the University of Chicago. His publications include *Lovers, Clowns & Fairies: An Essay on Comedies*; and *The Amiable Humorist: A Study in the Comic Theory and Criticism of the Eighteenth and Early Nineteenth Centuries*.

SUSAN MORGAN is Professor of English at Miami University. She has published *In the Meantime: Character and Perception in Jane Austen's Fiction* and *Sisters in Time: Imagining Gender in Nineteenth-Century British Fiction*.

BERNARD J. PARIS is Professor Emeritus of English at the University of Florida. He is the author of several books, including *Character as a Subversive Force in Shakespeare: The History & Roman Plays*, and *A Psychological Approach to Fiction: Studies in Thackeray, Stendhal, George Eliot, Dostoevsky, and Conrad*.

SUSAN FRAIMAN teaches English and women's studies at the University of Virginia. Her publications include *Unbecoming Women: British Women Writing & the Novel of Development*.

DONALD A. BLOOM is an Instructor of English at the Alabama School of Mathematics and Science. He has written on a variety of topics that trace the use of literary ideas over time.

GLORIA SYBIL GROSS is Professor of English at California State University at Northridge. She has written *The Invisible Riot of the Mind: Samuel Johnson's Psychological Theory* as well as a book on Austen and Johnson.

Bibliography

Beer, Patricia. *Reader, I Married Him: A Study of the Women Characters of Jane Austen, Charlotte Brontë, Elizabeth Gaskell, and George Eliot.* London: Macmillan Press, 1974.

Bloom, Harold, ed. *Modern Critical Interpretations: Jane Austen's* Pride and Prejudice. New York: Chelsea House Publishers, 1987.

Bonnell, Henry Houston. *Charlotte Brontë, George Eliot, Jane Austen: Studies in their Works.* N.Y.: Longmans, Green, & Co., 1902.

Bowen, Elizabeth. "Jane Austen." Verschoyl, Derek, ed. *The English Novelists:* 101–13. New York: Harcourt, Brace & Co., 1936.

———."What Jane Austen Means to Me." *Everybody's* 15 (May 1954): pp. 19 and 39.

Brown, Carole O. "'Dwindling into a Wife: A Jane Austen Heroine Grows Up." *International Journal of Women's Studies* 5, no. 5 (1982): pp. 460–69.

Burgan, Mary H. "Mr. Bennet and the Failures of Fatherhood in Jane Austen's Novels." *Journal of English and Germanic Philology* 74 (1975): pp. 536–52.

Carr, Jean Ferguson. "The Polemics of Incomprehension: Mother and Daughter in *Pride and Prejudice*." Howe, Florence, ed. *Tradition and Talents of Women.* Urbana: University of Illinois Press, 1991.

Clifford-Amos, Terence. "Some Observations on the Language of *Pride and Prejudice*." *Language and Literature* 20 (1995): pp. 1–10.

Copeland, Edward. "Virgin Sacrifice: Elizabeth Bennet after Jane Austen." *Persuasions* 22 (2000): pp. 156–94.

Cowley, Malcolm and Howard E. Hugo. *The Lesson of the Masters: An Anthology of the Novel from Cervantes to Hemingway.* N.Y.: C. Scribner's Sons, 1971.

Craik, W. A. *Jane Austen: the Six Novels.* London: Methuen, 1965.

Curry, Mary Jane. "'Not a Day Went By Without a Solitary Walk': Elizabeth's Pastoral World." *Persuasions* 22 (2000): pp. 175–86.

Dabundo, Laura. "The Devil and Jane Austen: Elizabeth Bennet's Temptations in the Wilderness." *Persuasions* 21 (1999): pp. 53–58.

Dooley, D. J. "Pride, Prejudice, and Vanity in Elizabeth Bennet." *Nineteenth-Century Fiction* 20 (1965–66): 185–88.

Emsley, Sarah. "Practising the Virtues of Amiability and Civility in *Pride and Prejudice.*" *Persuasions* 22 (2000): pp. 187–98.

Erwin, R. E. "Pride, Prejudice and Shyness." *Philosophy* 65 (April 1990): pp. 137–54.

Fox, Robert C. "Elizabeth Bennet: Prejudice or Vanity?" *Nineteenth-Century Fiction* 17 (1962–63): pp. 185–87.

Giles, Paul. "The Gothic Dialogue in *Pride and Prejudice.*" *Text and Context* 2, no. 1 (Spring 1988): pp. 68–75.

Gilman, Priscilla, "'Disarming Reproof': *Pride and Prejudice* and the Power of Criticism." *Persuasions* 22 (2000): pp. 218–29.

Gray, Donald J., ed. *Jane Austen*: Pride and Prejudice, *An Authoritative Text, Backgrounds, Reviews and Essays in Criticism.* New York: W. W. Norton & Co., 1966.

Halperin, John, ed. "Inside *Pride and Prejudice*" *Persuasions* 11 (December 16, 1989): pp. 37–45.

———. *Jane Austen: Bicentenary Essays.* Cambridge: Cambridge University Press, 1975.

Heath, William, ed. *Discussions of Jane Austen.* Boston: D. C. Heath & Co., 1961.

Howells, William Dean. "Jane Austen's Elizabeth Bennet." *Harper's Bazaar* 33 (1900): pp. 323–28.

Jack, Adolphus Alfred. *Essays on the Novel as Illustrated by Scott and Miss Austen.* London: Macmillan and Co., Ltd., 1897.

Marcus, Mordecai. "A Major Thematic Pattern in *Pride and Prejudice*." *Nineteenth-Century Fiction* 16 (1961–62): pp. 274–79.

Mercer, Edumund. "Jane Austen and the Novel." *Manchester Quarterly* 21 (1902): pp. 16–33.

Moler, Kenneth L. "*Pride and Prejudice*: Jane Austen's 'Patrician Hero.'" *SEL* 7 (1967): pp. 491–508.

Morris, Ivor. *Jane Austen and the Interplay of Character*. London: Athlone Press; Somerset, NJ: Transaction Publishers, 1999.

Mount, G. "Three Representative Heroines in Fiction." *Atalanta* 8 (1894–95): pp. 774–78.

Newman, Karen. "Can This Marriage Be Saved?: Jane Austen Makes Sense of an Ending." *ELH* 50 (Winter 1983): pp. 693–70.

Nineteenth-Century Fiction, Jane Austen, 1775–1975, 30, no. 3 (December 1975).

Olsen, Stein Haugom. "Appreciating *Pride and Prejudice*." Hawthorn, Jeremy, ed. *The Nineteenth-Century British Novel*. Stratford-Upon-Avon Studies. Baltimore: Arnold, 1986.

Ortells, Elena. "Bridging the Gap Between Linguistics and Literary Criticism: The Role of the Narrator in the Presentation of Characters in Jane Austen's *Pride and Prejudice* and Henry James's *The American*." *SEL* 2 (2000): pp. 161–70.

Siefert, Susan Elizabeth. *The Dilemma of the Talented Heroine: A Study in Nineteenth-Century Literature*. Montreal: Eden Press, 1978.

Southam, Brian Charles, ed. *Jane Austen: The Critical Heritage*. London: Routledge & Kegan Paul Ltd.; NY: Barnes & Noble, Inc., 1968.

———. *Jane Austen:* Sense and Sensibility, Pride and Prejudice *and* Mansfield Park. London: Macmillan Press Ltd., 1976.

Swisher, Clarice. *Readings on* Pride and Prejudice. San Diego, CA: Greenhaven, 1999.

Tempest, Richard. "The Girl on the Hill: Parallel Structures in *Pride and Prejudice* and *Eugene Onegin*." *Elementa* 1, no. 2 (1993): pp. 197–213.

Trilling, Lionel. "Why We Read Jane Austen." *Times Literary Supplement* (March 5, 1976): pp. 250–52.

Walcott, Charles Child. *Man's Changing Mask: Modes and Methods of Characterization in Fiction*. Minneapolis: University of Minnesota Press, 1966.

Watt, Ian. *Jane Austen: A Collection of Critical Essays*. Englewood Cliffs, NJ: Prentice Hall, 1963.

Welty, Eudora. "A Note on Jane Austen." *Shenandoah* 20, no. 3 (1969): pp. 3–7.

Wiltshire, John. "Mrs. Bennet's Least Favorite Daughter." *Persuasions* 23 (2001): pp. 179–87.

Wisenforth, Joseph. "The Revolution of Civility in *Pride and Prejudice*." *Persuasions* (December 1994): pp. 107–14.

Acknowledgments

"Irony as Discrimination: *Pride and Prejudice*" by Marvin Mudrick. From *Jane Austen: Irony as Defense and Discovery*: 94–126. © 1952 by Princeton University Press. Reprinted by permission of Princeton University Press.

"Elizabeth Bennet" by Andrew H. Wright. From *Jane Austen's Novels: A Study in Structure*: 105–117. © 1953 by Chatto & Windus. Used by permission of The Random House Group Limited.

"A Note on Jane Austen" by C. S. Lewis. From *Essays in Criticism* 4, no. 4 (October 1954): 359–71. © 1954 by Oxford University Press. Reprinted with permission of Oxford University Press.

"*Pride and Prejudice*" by Henrietta Ten Harmsel: 69–79. From *Jane Austen: A Study in Fictional Conventions*: 69–79. © 1964 by Mouton & Co. Reprinted by permission.

"*Pride and Prejudice*: Vitality and a Dramatic Mode" by Howard S. Babb. From *Jane Austen's Novels: The Fabric of Dialogue*: 113–44. © 1967 by Ohio State University Press. Reprinted by permission.

"Affection and the Mortification of Elizabeth Bennet" by Stuart M. Tave. From *Some Words of Jane Austen*: 116–157. © 1973 by The University of Chicago. Reprinted by permission.

"Intelligence in *Pride and Prejudice*," by Susan Morgan. From *Modern Philology* 73, no. 1 (August 1975): 54–68. © 1975 by The University of Chicago. Reprinted by permission.

"*Pride and Prejudice*" (section 5 of chapter 4) by Bernard J. Paris. From *Character and Conflict in Jane Austen's Novels: A Psychological Approach*: 118–139. © 1978 by Bernard J. Paris. Reprinted by permission.

"The Humiliation of Elizabeth Bennet," by Susan Fraiman. From *Refiguring the Father: New Feminist Readings of Patriarchy*, edited by Patricia Yaeger and Beth Kowaleski-Wallace: 168–87. © 1989 by the Board of Trustees, Southern Illinois University, reprinted by permission of the publisher.

"Dwindling into Wifehood: the Romantic Power of the Witty Heroine in Shakespeare, Dryden, Congreve, and Austen," by Donald A. Bloom. From *Look Who's Laughing: Gender and Comedy*, edited by Gail Finney: 53–80. © 1994 by OPA (Amsterdam) B.V. Published under license by Gordon and Breach Science Publishers S.A. Reprinted by permission.

"Wit With a Vengeance: *Pride and Prejudice*," by Gloria Sybil Gross. From *In a Fast Coach with a Pretty Woman: Jane Austen and Samuel Johnson*: 78–103. © 2002 by AMS Press. Reprinted by permission.

Index

devotion and care for others, 244
disguising emotions through use
  of metaphor, 106–10
distorted view of Darcy through,
  88–91
elevated self–concept, 163
on her family's defects, 161–2,
  169–70
free spirit of, 143–4
freedom and intelligence in, 147
gradual change in, 70–1
growth of intelligence, 154–5,
  157–8, 159–60
humiliation of, 193–4, 239
impertinence of, 143
interplay between aggression and
  sexuality with Darcy in,
  229–30, 232
interpretation of Darcy, 27, 32–3
irony in, 31–2, 69–70
Jane Austen on, 30–1
on Jane Bennet, 17, 18
Jane/Bingley relationship and,
  18–9
judgment of Wickham, 46
as lacking pretensions to
  smugness and perfection, 84–5
lack of ideal beauty and
  accomplishment in, 68
Lady Catherine and, 16, 83–4,
  232–3
in latter part of the book, 158–9
loss of authority, 181–2, 184, 185,
  190–1
on Lydia, 13–4, 23–4
on Lydia/Wickham relationship,
  175–6
male identification of, 184
mortification in, 131, 135–42

motive for love of Darcy, 146
Mr. Bennet handing of to Darcy,
  186
Mr. Bennet on Darcy's
  relationship with, 80–1, 235–6
Mrs. Bennet's assessment of,
  243–4
on Mr. Collins, 15
as not sacrificing motives of,
  87–8, 110–1
as not taking life seriously, 152
observation by, 151–2
outrage vs. desire in, 234
outshining other 18th century
  heroines, 73
on her parents, 26–7, 237–8
on Pemberley, 171–2
physical description of, 243
power of choice and, 33–4
pride in, 3–5, 176
rage in, 230–1
realizing self–deception in
  herself, 55, 56
reasoning in, 100–1
reasons for attraction to Darcy,
  173–5
reasons for Darcy's attraction to,
  177, 222
reflecting on marriage with
  Darcy, 29–30
relationship with her father,
  183–4, 244
representing individualism, 145
resemblance to Johnson
  character, 227
similarities with Lydia, 190
struggle for narrative control
  with Darcy, 187–9
suffering from her family, 161–2

transformation into a complex
  character, 66
as a truly great heroine, 68
trust and confidence of her own
  perceptions, 91–2, 93–4, 96
unconventional behavior, 229
underestimating economic
  pressures of Charlotte Lucas,
  20–1
as unifying the novel artistically,
  72
warm feeling rather than cool
  sense informing decisions of,
  92–3
on Wickham's looks and charm,
  148–50
Wickham's persuasiveness with,
  22
will of, 5–6
wit with a vengeance in, 228
as witty heroine, 197
See also Prejudice
Ellis, Annie Raine, 83–4
Emerson, Ralph Waldo, 5–6
Emma (Austen)
  amiable characters in, 118–20
  undeception in, 55, 56
Emma (*Emma*), 55, 56

Fanny Price (*Mansfield Park*)
  deception and, 61
  insipidity in, 59, 60
  marriage without affection and,
  126
  mortification in, 132–3
  as solitary heroine, 58, 59–60
Fielding, Henry, 1–2, 233
Fitzwilliam Darcy. *See* Darcy
Fliegelman, Jay, 182

Florimell (*Secret Love*), 197, 206–7,
  208–9
"The Fountains: A Fairy Tale"
  (Johnson), 226
Fraiman, Susan, 181
Freedom and intelligence, 146–7,
  153–4, 157–8

George Wickham. *See* Wickham
Georgiana Darcy (*Pride and
  Prejudice*)
  powerlessness in, 16–7
  Wickham's seduction of, 22
Goldsmith, Oliver, 228
Gross, Gloria Sybil, 225

Harmsel, Henrietta Ten, 65
Henry Tilney (*Pride and Prejudice*),
  20, 88
Horney, Karen, 184
Humiliation, 193–4, 238, 239

Intelligence, 154–60
  Elizabeth believing story of
    Wickham and, 151, 152–3
  Elizabeth's growth and, 154–5,
    159–60
  freedom and, 146–7
  Jane Bennet and, 155–7
  prejudice and, 157–8
Irony, 1
  dangers of intellectual
    complexity, 38
  development of Darcy–Elizabeth
    relationship, 47
  in Elizabeth Bennet, 31–2, 68
  Elizabeth discovering faults she
    sees in others and herself,
    70–1